STUDIES IN ENGLISH LITERATURES

Edited by Koray Melikoğlu

Gianluca Delfino

Time, History, and Philosophy in the Works of Wilson Harris

STUDIES IN ENGLISH LITERATURES

Edited by Koray Melikoğlu

ISSN 1614-4651

9   *Shafquat Towheed (ed.)*
       New Readings in the Literature of British India, c.1780-1947
       ISBN 978-3-89821-673-9

10   *Paola Baseotto*
       "Disdeining life, desiring leaue to die"
       Spenser and the Psychology of Despair
       ISBN 978-3-89821-567-1

11   *Annie Gagiano*
       Dealing with Evils
       Essays on Writing from Africa
       ISBN 978-3-89821-867-2

12   *Thomas F. Halloran*
       James Joyce: Developing Irish Identity
       A Study of the Development of Postcolonial Irish Identity in the Novels of James Joyce
       ISBN 978-3-89821-571-8

13   *Pablo Armellino*
       Ob-scene Spaces in Australian Narrative
       An Account of the Socio-topographic Construction of Space in Australian Literature
       ISBN 978-3-89821-873-3

14   *Lance Weldy*
       Seeking a Felicitous Space on the Frontier
       The Progression of the Modern American Woman in O. E. Rölvaag, Laura Ingalls Wilder, and Willa Cather
       ISBN 978-3-89821-535-0

15   *Rana Tekcan*
       The Biographer and the Subject
       A Study on Biographical Distance
       ISBN 978-3-89821-995-2

16   *Paola Brusasco*
       Writing Within/Without/About Sri Lanka
       Discourses of Cartography, History and Translation in Selected Works by Michael Ondaatje and Carl Muller
       ISBN 978-3-8382-0075-0

17   *Zeynep Z. Atayurt*
       Excess and Embodiment in Contemporary Women's Writing
       ISBN 978-3-89821-978-5

18   *Gianluca Delfino*
       Time, History, and Philosophy in the Works of Wilson Harris
       ISBN 978-3-8382-0265-5

Gianluca Delfino

TIME, HISTORY, AND PHILOSOPHY IN THE WORKS OF WILSON HARRIS

ibidem-Verlag
Stuttgart

Bibliografische Information der Deutschen Nationalbibliothek
Die Deutsche Nationalbibliothek verzeichnet diese Publikation in der Deutschen Nationalbibliografie; detaillierte bibliografische Daten sind im Internet über http://dnb.d-nb.de abrufbar.

Bibliographic information published by the Deutsche Nationalbibliothek
Die Deutsche Nationalbibliothek lists this publication in the Deutsche Nationalbibliografie; detailed bibliographic data are available in the Internet at http://dnb.d-nb.de.

Cover art: L'Avvoltoio; copyright © 2011 by Francesca Corbelletto

∞

Gedruckt auf alterungsbeständigem, säurefreien Papier
Printed on acid-free paper

ISSN: 1614-4651

ISBN-13: 978-3-8382-0265-5

© *ibidem*-Verlag
Stuttgart 2012

Alle Rechte vorbehalten

Das Werk einschließlich aller seiner Teile ist urheberrechtlich geschützt. Jede Verwertung außerhalb der engen Grenzen des Urheberrechtsgesetzes ist ohne Zustimmung des Verlages unzulässig und strafbar. Dies gilt insbesondere für Vervielfältigungen, Übersetzungen, Mikroverfilmungen und elektronische Speicherformen sowie die Einspeicherung und Verarbeitung in elektronischen Systemen.

All rights reserved. No part of this publication may be reproduced, stored in or introduced into a retrieval system, or transmitted, in any form, or by any means (electronic, mechanical, photocopying, recording or otherwise) without the prior written permission of the publisher. Any person who does any unauthorized act in relation to this publication may be liable to criminal prosecution and civil claims for damages.

Printed in Germany

Table of Contents

Acknowledgements	ix
Preface	xi
1 – A Coherent Design: An Introduction	1
1.1 C.L.R. James's Heideggerian Interpretation	3
1.2 Hegelian Dialectics and Wilson Harris's Novels	6
1.3 Imaginative Poeticism: A Caribbean Perspective	9
1.3.1 Consciousness and Ego Dynamics	11
1.3.2 Poetics of Consciousness	18
1.4 Gnostic Tradition and Faustian Themes	22
2 – Time and History	31
2.1 Historiography and Contemporary Philosophies of History	32
2.1.1 Western Historiography and Authoritarian Narratives	32
2.1.2 Non-Western Traditions of History	56
3 – Jungian and Pre-Modern Influences	75
3.1 Jungian Influences	75
3.2 Archetypal Images	76
3.2.1 Archetypal Images in Earlier Novels	82
3.2.2 Doctor Faustus and The Infinite Rehearsal	84
3.2.3 *Jonestown* and the Shape of Evil	89
3.2.4 The Mask of the Beggar and Ulyssean Images	93
3.3 Archetypes, the Collective Unconscious, the World's Unconscious and the Quest for Unity	98
4 – Pre-Columbian Legacies	109
4.1 Amerindians	111
4.1.1 Guyanese Society	111
4.1.2 Amerindians: Historical and Anthropological information	113
4.1.3 Harris's Main Anthropological Sources	123
4.1.4 The Amerindian Legacy: An Imaginative Reading	135
4.2. Meso-American and South-American Main Civilisations	147
4.2.1 The Maya	147
4.2.2 The Inca and Atahualpan Void	162

5 – Conclusions: The Perspective of Living Landscapes	171
Bibliography	189
Wilson Harris: Fiction and Poetry	189
Wilson Harris: Non-Fiction	190
Other Sources	194

Acknowledgements

I would like to thank for their competent and kind support: Prof. Carmen Concilio, Prof. Pietro Deandrea, Prof. Ruth Anne Henderson, and Prof. Renato Oliva.

This study is indebted to the late Prof. Hena Maes-Jelinek's fundamental work on Wilson Harris.

Finally, my thanks go to Andreana, Oreste, Alice, and particularly Matteo; all my family; Carlo, Ele, Simone, Mara, Sirio, Pauch, Alan, Slash, Ale, Sescia, Guido, Gio, Alessandro and everyone who supported me during hard times.

Preface

The analysis of Wilson Harris's works presented in this study is based on the fundamental assumption that the whole body of his work can be seen as an essential contribution to the making of an autonomous Caribbean philosophical canon. To this end, the first chapter has been structured on the analysis of three important critical approaches which have recognised the philosophical value of Harris's literary achievements: C.L.R. James's *Wilson Harris: A Philosophical Approach,* a lecture published in 1965, Gregory Shaw's essay "The Novelist as a Shaman: Art and Dialectic in the Work of Wilson Harris," published in 1989, and Paget Henry's extensive analysis in his *Caliban's Reason: Introducing Afro-Caribbean Philosophy* (2002). These critical works widely support the basic assumption, but, especially Paget's, testify to the heterogeneous influences that inform Harris's thought and partly exemplify their multiple fictional manifestations. To overcome the problem of coping with such a wide variety of issues, the discussion of Harris's philosophy has been centred around a specific theme, with the belief that a reduction in scope would benefit its efficacy.

History, as a theme including the conceptualisation of time and the narration of past events, has been chosen for the particular importance it assumed in the Caribbean intellectual panorama and for its evident centrality in the better part of Harris's novels and critical works. Therefore, a second chapter has been structured around two overviews of the evolution of the concept of history and historiography both in Western academic worlds and in various post-colonial realities, with particular care not to relegate Harris's figure to a specific critical field, but to inscribe it in the widest possible debate. The inclusion of a writer of fiction in a traditionally scientific field is justified by the contemporary issues in the Western historiographical debate concerning the interrelationship of fiction and historiography, as well as by the usual strategy adopted by post-colonial writers to address history outside the ground from which, as subalterns included in an imperial authoritarian History, they have been traditionally excluded.

The third and the fourth chapters deal with two apparently distant themes which basically inform Harris's approach to history: psychoanalysis and pre-Columbian traditions. A Jungian reading of some of Harris's texts has been carried out in chapter 3, partly because of the direct links the Guyanese writer has recognised with Jung's work (although he suggests parallel development rather than simple influence), and partly for the evident archetypal nature of several Harrisian images and characters, which reveal the fundamental role of the "universal unconscious" in his philosophy, which is deeply related to Jung's "collective unconscious."

In chapter 4, the legacies of pre-Columbian cultures, Amazonian, South-American and Meso-American, have been extensively discussed with the aim of demonstrating that Harris's conception of time is not only based on speculative intellectualisations or on psychoanalytic studies, but principally derives from his actual experience of a cultural heritage which, despite systematic marginalisation, is alive and operating, not only for cultures of mixed ancestries, such as the Guyanese, but also for the Western culture as a legacy of the colonial encounter. In the concluding chapter, the issue of the "universal unconscious," as emerged in Jungian terms and surfaced in the discussion of pre-Columbian legacies, has been re-addressed with respect to environmentalism and Harris's peculiar interpretation of a living world, as this conception has characterised his literary production since the early beginnings, and has significantly intensified in his critical work since the 1990s. Finally, the framing of the concept of "historylessness," often attached to the Caribbean reality, has been shifted towards a more encompassing view which does not deny history as such, but redefines it in a different perspective which may appear "timeless" to the human intellect yet becomes historical, even though at an unconscious level, if referred to the entire cosmos: including humanity and the world of animals, rocks, trees and waters. Harris's view, which at times may appear unbalanced towards a sort of mysticism, should prove of profound importance for its ability to confront, at their own level, Western self-appointed scientific disciplines, demonstrating the possibility and effectiveness of the integration of seemingly contrasting cognitive methods, such as the Western one, linear and logical, and the one exemplified by Harris's mythical imagination: a living testimony of archetypal realities and pre-Columbian legacies.

1 – A Coherent Design: An Introduction

Wilson Harris has been writing novels since the early sixties at a phenomenal rate, producing a body of work that consists today of twenty-five novels. Each one has a particular plot and setting which may vary from the interior of 1950s Guyana to 1970s Edinburgh; they touch upon many different themes and reveal a stylistic evolution through the years, but seen as a whole they all seem to belong to a consistent project. This commonality is perceived partly through the direct references of the author to his own previous works, partly through the reappearance of some characters, even decades after their first appearance. Harris's specific approach to literature and to writing and his unique style, whose subtle variation is no less perceivable than its consistency, contribute to the strong feeling of commonality, but what strikes more than anything is the consistent and articulate thought that informs Harris's production, whether in the shape of poetry, fiction or literary essays. To clarify this point, it may be useful to quote a comment which curiously appears on the back covers of both his last two novels, as if popular and specialist press did not bother to review Harris's publications individually any more. To be honest, probably the reason for the repetition of this comment is not to be found in any other editorial choice than the one which recognises its poignancy and its effectiveness in identifying many key features of Harris's writing in a few lines. This is exactly the reason why Maya Jaggi's comment, originally included in a longer review of *The Dark Jester* (2001), functions as a perfect starting point for introducing a deeper analysis of some of these key features:

> Undoubtedly one of the great originals [...] Harris has lived in England since 1959 writing complex, philosophical, visionary novels that can be bewilderingly arcane yet also dazzlingly illuminating [...] Often he recalls Blake, with a prophetic vision that challenges and renews the senses and contorts the syntax. (Jaggi)

Harris's choice to live in England and the fact that he has now been living there for sixty-eight years is crucial if one considers the fact that his connection with Guyana and with the Caribbean Basin has always been evident and many of his novels are set in his own motherland of Guyana. However, to consider him a Caribbean writer would be as reductive as it would be to define him as an essentially British one. The figure of a "universal" writer might fit him better, even though this definition cannot be inscribed in any typical categorisation in literary studies, particularly in the post-colonial field. The difficulty critics and scholars have often found in defining him is a direct consequence of Harris's deep originality, which strongly emerges at first reading, for his novels are strikingly non-conventional in style and in mode of narration. "Comfortable realism" leaves the ground to complex, visionary, imaginative writing whose style "contorts the syntax" in such a way that reading can easily be puzzling and the contrasting and visionary images and metaphors may at times appear "arcane." Language is for Harris a constantly renewed "medium"; and it is crucial in his art as a means of expression, as a means of knowledge, but most of all as an instrument of creation. One has to get into this language, and the process is not easy: one has to leave aside that passive reading required by a novel written in the tradition of nineteenth-century realism and assume the role of an active reader to participate in this creation, a necessary participation rewarded with "renewed senses." The reader's senses, renewed by this act of participation, allow him/her to see through the apparent opacity of Harris's imagery and illuminate a whole world in restless becoming, a world much closer to reality (however partial) unveiled rather than a mere world of fiction. This unveiled reality is intuitive in nature, it cannot be explained through the linearity of logic. The perception of it and the speculation about it are both the object and the subject of the whole of Harris's fiction, whose philosophical quality begins at this point to emerge. It is his thought that makes all his production stand as a whole corpus, in which one can perceive evolution and change but cannot deny a stunning consistency and depth. This kind of philosophy cannot be considered the work of a philosopher, in proper terms: Harris is an imaginative writer, his tools are literary devices, not technical jargon nor extensive knowledge of philosophy, but he writes in a context, the Caribbean, which claims a perspective of its own and sees "philosophy [as] an intertextually embedded discursive practice, and not an isolated or absolutely autonomous one" (Henry 2).

Nevertheless it is undeniable that the vision of reality he has been constantly revising and refining through the whole of his career has the quality of a consistent philosophical vision. Those critics and scholars interested in Wilson Harris are all fully aware of the strong connection between his writing and philosophy, and since A.J. Seymour's clairvoyant comments on the first edition of Harris's early work of poetry, *Eternity to Season* (1954), many have tried to analyse this connection from different standpoints. In the following chapter some of these attempts will be discussed with the aim of presenting an overview of Harris's philosophy, which according to Henry is "difficult, if not impossible to present systematically" (94), and of grounding the subsequent detailed analysis of particular aspects, such as time and history in chapter 2 and pre-Columbian elements and cross-culturality in chapter 4.

1.1 C.L.R. James's Heideggerian Interpretation

In a lecture given at the College of Arts and Science and at the Department of Extra-Mural Studies of the University of the West Indies in St. Augustine, Trinidad, in April 1965, the great Caribbean writer and scholar C.L.R. James presented an interpretation of Harris's work in relation to some of Heidegger's concepts.[1] In this lecture James relates Wilson Harris's philosophical vision, as it appears in his first work of fiction *The Palace of the Peacock* (1960), to Heidegger's *Being and Time* (1927), or at least to the concept of *Dasein*. As James himself notices with irony, the works of Heidegger were not diffused in the West Indies, neither was a technical knowledge of philosophy which can be "as difficult and technical a business as Marine Engineering, or Medicine" (C.L.R. James, *Philosophical* 4); nevertheless, the Caribbean was not excluded from philosophical debates: "whether he knows it or not everybody has a certain philosophical view" (4).

With such a low profile James starts the analysis of *The Palace of the Peacock* to highlight its intrinsic correlation to philosophy. After a brief introduction, he makes his position clear by asserting that "Harris is to be seen as a writer of the post war period who is in the full philosophical tradition and has carried to an extraordinary pitch the work of two German philosophers: [...] Heidegger and Jaspers" (*Philosophical* 6). Despite its authority, James's position sounds a bit odd today, even though Harris himself has associated his work with some post-war writers such as Samuel Beckett, especially with his short story "Imagination Dead Imagine" (*Jonestown* 46): the direct connection between Jaspers and Heidegger appears more tortuous than he assumes. Anyway, he offers a personal view that may be interesting to explore. Heidegger's concern about everyday life and the life of *everydayness* and the concept of *inauthentic existence* as opposed to *Dasein*, or authentic existence, are the key points to James's discussion. He tries to relate the search for truth through the practice of *Dasein* to Harris and he finds a connection in language, which he both interprets as the means to live an authentic existence and, less controversially, as the main feature of Harris's originality. Unfortunately, in doing so he conflicts with later theorizations by Harris himself about living landscapes and non-human existence by saying "mountains are, horses are, books are, but only man exists" (James, *Phi-*

---

[1] St. Augustine University published a revised version later in the same year.

losophical 8). On other occasions, however, he builds fertile connections such as the importance he gives to Heidegger's idea of history and temporality. The subjectivity of time is in fact a key concept for Harris and it seems to partially coincide with what James says of Heidegger. In his interpretation of the concept of *the now* he sees its nature in the past, "as the result of all that has happened before" (James, *Philosophical* 8), but he also recognises another element which Heidegger calls *the futural*: Heidegger "says you are aware that you are going to be dead. He says that is the only thing nobody can do for you, you have to die for yourself" (*Philosophical* 8). In fact, this first notion of the intermingling of past and future can be connected to a feature of *The Palace of the Peacock:* the visionary experience of each member of the expedition at the time of their death. James highlights this in his analysis: "[he] has a vision of where he is reaching and what he expects is going to happen to him" (*Philosophical* 5).

Coming to Jaspers, James sees a strong connection with Harris in the idea of the limit situation, an extreme boundary situation, in which man can find what he is, a theme he felt pressing in those years of early post-independence. As for Harris, James notices how the everydayness of the life in Georgetown (British Guiana at that time) is broken by extreme situations experienced in the interior where "the realities of human life are stark and clear" (*Philosophical* 10). In that way, he sees Harris linked to both Jasper and Heidegger and to *the transcendendal*:

> Harris gives you a big slab of actual everyday existence, the inauthentic life we all lead, and then, within the same novel, he takes you to an extreme situation, [...] within the covers of the same volume he proceeds to give you pages of philosophical exploration. (*Philosophical* 11-12)

James also presents a possible connection with Jean-Paul Sartre's idea of choice between inauthentic life and the authentic, which bears a stronger political meaning, to stress Harris's commitment to some sort of anti-colonial cause. This is in fact an often neglected, but important aspect, especially regarding his first theoretical writings,[2] although it must be considered under the complex and various shades Harris's thought has revealed in the course of the years.

James's straightforwardness let him notice the exceptionality of Harris's philosophical work in relation to the Caribbean in a way that appears less problematic than Harris himself would have put it: "I think that it is most remarkable

---

2 See, in particular, *Tradition, the Writer and Society* (1967).

that this West Indian, uneducated in German, uneducated in European universities, should have found out those things practically for himself and should be writing the kind of books that he does" (James, *Philosophical* 8). It will be discussed later how Harris's knowledge of the German philosophers was not so narrow and, even more importantly, how Harris's philosophy can be seen as inscribed in different traditions with a validity of their own. Anyway, James is right in highlighting Harris's independence of academic thought and he finds pregnant examples about the strategy of recovering the history of African slaves through intuitive and mythic devices rather than Western academic anthropology.

Another piercing intuition of James's is the importance of the connection with fifteenth-sixteenth century Europe, often mentioned by Harris himself:

> The special point I want to make in regard to the West Indies is that the pursuit of a strange and subtle goal, melting pot, call it what you like, is the mainstream (though unacknowledged) tradition in the Americas. And the significance of this is akin to the European preoccupation with Alchemy, with the growth of experimental science, the poetry of science as well as of explosive nature which is informed by a solution of images, agnostic humility and essential beauty rather than vested interests in a fixed assumption and classification of things (*Philosophical* 14).

Such instances and Harris's belonging to a certain tradition of gnosticism-hermetism will be discussed in depth in the last part of this section. What remains to be mentioned about James's essay is the awareness about the issue of independence that Harris has often raised when referring to Caribbean literary and philosophical tradition: the complete absence in the West Indies of those kinds of fixed assumptions he sees as intrinsic in European-Western thought. This awareness, however, does not prevent James from unintentionally assuming some sort of hierarchical relationship in validating Harris's position through its connection with Western philosophers, even though they represent, to James's eyes, the internal awareness that "the European preoccupation or acceptance of the material basis of life, a fixed assumption[...] has broken down" (*Philosophical* 15). What emerges at the end of James's analysis, despite his effort to link Harris's concepts to the *Dasein*, the "being there," is a profound difference which comes from a very different background, a cultural situation in which "there has never been that fixed assumption of things, that belief in something that is many centuries old and solid" (*Philosophical* 15).

1.2 Hegelian Dialectics and Wilson Harris's Novels

The connections between Harris's writing and the Western philosophical tradition have been discussed by Gregory Shaw in a subsequent essay which appeared in *The Literate Imagination* ("Novelist"). Curiously, the same quotation about the lack of fixed assumptions reproduced above reappears in the first two pages of the essay and Shaw notices its tendency to "slip away in a strange flux of language and categories" ("Novelist" 143). Despite its impalpability, the fact that "eclecticism is *constitutive* of the Caribbean experience" ("Novelist" 143) seems to be central once again. Moreover, the presence of different philosophical traditions, often neglected, which characterise Harris's thought is acknowledged once again by quoting the same passage about the similarity of the West Indies and sixteenth-century Europe. Shaw further expands this concept by revealing non-Western elements that refer to shamanic figures and Amerindian myths. This new background, however, must be seen in close relation to the "mythic substratum" (Shaw, "Novelist" 143) of his early novels, which is mainly classical (in European terms); Shaw, with a touch of irony, notices how "the extensive use of Amerindian myth develops fairly late and may have derived from later researches in the libraries of Europe and America" ("Novelist" 143), while Harris himself has always stressed the importance of his direct experience in the interior of British Guiana.

With respect to this early episode of the writer's life, Shaw abandons the controversy to introduce his main argument. In those times, Harris's interests were not limited to classical mythology and land surveying, but, according to Shaw, rumours said that "he carried his books wherever he went on his expeditions into the interior; he was just as likely to be found poring over a volume of philosophy as standing over a theodolite" ("Novelist"145). On the basis of such folkloric elements, not to mention strict textual analysis, Shaw praises James's "intuitive flash" for grasping Harris's close relationship with philosophy, but reproaches him as "one so familiar with the dialectic" for having wandered "off-tract [sic] in speaking of Heidegger and Jaspers, [sending] quite a few scholars on a wildgoose chase trying to connect Harris to the phenomenological school" ("Novelist"145). This sarcastic statement introduces Shaw's interpretation of Harris's eclectic style on the uncompromisingly Western basis of a Hegelian reading, supported again by "rumours," this time attributed to Professor Gordon

Rohlehr (UWI St.Augustine) who affirms that a Guyanese historian, Dr. Robert Moore, "remarked that Harris never went into the bush unless he was armed with several volumes of Hegel" ("Novelist" 145).

Although this evidence does not seem to found Shaw's interpretation on any better basis than James's "intuitive flash," it at least gives a suggestive explanation for Harris's undoubtedly "dialectic" fiction and it creates the occasion for a fruitful discussion. According to Shaw, who recalls the importance of the Hegelian dialectic of master and slave (*The Phenomenology of Mind*) for the debate among colonial intellectuals such as Fanon, Harris's use of language – "[a] word [...] liberated" ("Novelist" 146) – is characterised by "the yoking together of contradictory or antithetical images" ("Novelist" 146). This dialectic "results in a voiding of the word or concept that negates its given or conventional meaning" ("Novelist" 146), giving way to a dissolution of images which continually reassemble themselves in "'paradoxical juxtapositions' reflecting a universe in the process of becoming" ("Novelist" 146). Therefore, Harris's novels actually represent "boundary situations" not only, as stated by James, on the ground of experience, but mainly on that of meaning, where they create a "void pregnant of possibilities, without committing [themselves] to the specific" (Shaw, "Novelist" 147). The continuous reciprocity and reflection of partialities of meaning create an idea of totality, a kind of consciousness which Shaw connects with Hegel's absolute consciousness of the philosopher:

> [Harris's] narratives represent the unfolding of mind itself, an all-embracing entity whose manifestation is the realm of phenomena – history, landscape and society. Just as in Hegel, the quest of spirit culminates in the absolute consciousness of the philosopher, so in the typical Harris novel the hero's quest ends in the apotheosis of the artist who is the embodiment of that self-same spirit. (The symphonic conclusion of *Palace of the Peacock*, for instance, appears to be modelled on the triumphant climax of the *phenomenology*, even in such details as the major images of "light" and the "artificer") ("Novelist" 148).

Although the unity of Wilson Harris's work is an assumption that informs my thesis, the identification of a "typical Harris novel" is not easily performed especially regarding his latest publications; nevertheless, Shaw's is an interesting reading of *Palace of the Peacock* and it could work for other novels. What appears as a step further, on the road to a deeper comprehension of the complexities of Harris's thought, is the inclusion of history, society and landscape as fundamental elements in his writings. Particularly the latter, considering the exclusions operated by James on the claim of the exclusive "existence" of man, reads as an illuminating insight into the recent evolution of Harris's philosophy and it anticipates a theme that will be extensively discussed in the final chapters.

Unfortunately, the urgency of validating Harris's theories by an excessive adherence to the authoritative Hegelian dialectic leads Shaw to attribute to the mind and the imagination the shape of an "imperialist [...] hero" ("Novelist" 151) embodied in the artist. It may be worth recalling the stress on the lack of fixity and the continuous reformulation which characterises Harris's imagination, whose "empire" could only be a non-hierarchical wholeness. However, on the path to this controversial conclusion, Shaw touches upon several points worth mentioning, paradoxically affirming the same concept of "unity of being," which appears to undermine his conclusion. The image with which he describes Harris's fictional constructs is particularly vivid: in his word they derive "from [...] an inner vision of the shapes, contours, topography of the mind and that shimmering frontier where mind meets world" (Shaw, "Novelist" 149). The "inner dialectic" that characterises Harris's fiction, according to Shaw, translates the world into "categories of mind [...] explod[ing] the object and translat[ing] it into inner formal categories" ("Novelist" 150). What he sees, a "brilliant and cunning assault on the object" ("Novelist" 150) appears as a process of recognition of a reality Shaw himself does not fail to perceive: "the totality of human experience, the universal, the infinite, rendered in a metaphysical form or outline freed of specific content because embracing all content" ("Novelist" 150).

But this reality is not only a "flood of subjectivity that dissolves the "facts" of history and environment" (Shaw, "Novelist" 150) and the apparently free associations Shaw identifies are not completely free. Reality is not a simple product of the mind; the imagination, in Harrisian terms, works in the recognition of linkages and connections that are only partially created by the mind. As Harris himself has often remarked, those linkages are really there, especially when compared with the post-modernist assumption that "there is no depth to reality[...] [it] is false. There *is* depth" ("Judgement" 22). Harris has always supported the truth of fiction: "[f]iction is not irrelevant, it is profoundly relevant" ("Judgement" 29), for him "art is not a game" (interview by Riach 58) and the "living absences" or "living fossils" which characterise his vision of the past are not products of the mind but re-discoveries, such as that the environment and "the objects" contain parts of ourselves in a sort of "Quantum immediacy":

"parts of ourselves are embedded everywhere – in the rock, in the tree, in the star, in the river, in the earth, everywhere" ("Absent Presence" 81) and therefore are not translatable to mere "categories of mind" to explode. In the words of Hena Maes-Jelinek: "[he] posits the existence of intuitively accessible metaphysical essences [...] differ[ent] from the absolute entities that used to underline Western systems of thought" (Maes-Jelinek, "Latent Cross-Culturalities" 41). In Harris's own words:

> The mystery of the subjective imagination lies, I believe, in an intuitive, indeed revolutionary grasp of a play of values as the flux of authentic change through and beyond what is given to us and what we accept, without further thought, as objective appearances. It is not a question of rootlessness but of the miracle of roots, the miracle of a dialogue with eclipsed selves which appearance may deny us or into which they may lead us. ("Subjective Imagination" 65-66)

As will be extensively discussed later, this kind of insight reveals meaningful interconnections of these "metaphysical entities," which appear as a path of universalism/humanism: "We see connections. We see that there is an unbroken thread which runs through humanity" (Harris, "Judgement" 26).

1.3 Imaginative Poeticism: A Caribbean Perspective

The two essays analysed above, though groundbreaking and variously stimulating, are the work of two scholars who have no specialisation in philosophy, and this is reflected in their approximations and superficiality on some diverging issues, not least the shared lack of a broader definition for Harris's thought other than its relationship with Western philosophers. As stated before, it is not the purpose of this study to enter into deep philosophical discussion; nevertheless, at this point, the need emerges for a more comprehensive and articulate view.

The occasion for defining Wilson Harris's philosophy in its own context comes with the inclusion of a monographic chapter in Paget Henry's essential publication *Caliban's Reason. Introducing Afro-Caribbean Philosophy* (2000). It must be acknowledged that the years that divide James's essay and Henry's book have seen the birth of an academic philosophical tradition in the Caribbean, of which James himself regretted the absence, but the fact is that Henry, associate professor at Brown University and leading scholar in the field of Africana thought[3], recognises the priority of the issue. He starts by immediately compensating the lack of context which was perceivable in the preceding essays: "[we] move to the center of the region's [the Caribbean] poeticist tradition of thought. Harris's work is rooted in the creative space of this tradition" (Henry 90). In this space, Harris is not alone: with due differentiation, the Caribbean poeticist tradition includes other writers, such as Sylvia Winter, Edouard Glissant or Derek Walcott, and it divides the ground with Caribbean Historicism, of which C.L.R. James can be considered a precursor.

Subsequently, Henry introduces another important aspect of Harris's philosophy: "a dialogue with traditional African philosophy" (90), a connection that will be useful to explain certain fundamental points about the consciousness/ego relationship in Harris's thought. On the other side, Henry is perfectly aware of the contributions by Seymour, James and Shaw, therefore he indulges in a witty critique of the misreadings that emerge from their essays. First he acknowledges the vast quantity of influences that converge in Harris, as a "quintessential creole thinker" (92), then he identifies the key to his philosophy in "his own encounters with the depths beyond the everyday ego" (92) and he explicitly rejects any correlation with the German philosophers mentioned by either James or Shaw: "[t]o get to these depths, Harris needs neither Hegel or Heidegger" (92). For Henry, Harris's universal consciousness does not take the form of Hegel's absolute spirit or Heidegger's being-towards-death; he sees instead the possibility for a sort of "*archetypal life*" (92). Moreover his philosophical approach to consciousness does differ from the two Germans' even though it is "indeed phenomenological"; it belongs to a different kind of phenomenology: it is "imagistic, mythopoetic" rather than "conceptual" (92).

Proceeding by degrees, the first assumption about the identification of a broader and somehow academically recognised context must be clarified. Henry stresses the eclectic nature of the Caribbean intellectual tradition which sees many different cultures, grouped by tragic events, emerging and trying to delegitimise European colonial rule. Subsequently, in a post-colonial situation, the main theme, according to Henry, is the "role of the self" and its recovery, its reconstruction as "an important precondition for institutional recovery" in line with Fanon's theorisations "as he transitioned from the poeticist to the historicist

---

3 The term Africana refers, according to L. Outlaw, to the universal concept of "the experiences and situated practices of dispersed *geographic race*" (29), therefore including the Diaspora into African philosophy, which is itself "still in its embryonic stage" (Kaphagawani 86).

school" (93). This consideration about Fanon is useful for a definition of the two main schools of thought Henry identifies in the Caribbean basin: historicism and poeticism. The first, which he claims to belong to, is a sort of "onto-historic response to the colonial thrust into history" (120), rooted in the conception that the historical event of colonialism has severed Caribbean society from its "mythopoetical order" and compelled it to a process of liberation through the medium of history, "in which Caribbean identities would experience redefinition and reconstellation" (120). The second approach contrasts with the first especially at a methodological level:

> [It] seeks to replace the special constituting given to history by the historicists with the task of reassembling the mythopoetic fragments of our shattered premodern world. History as the medium and place of postcolonial recovery is replaced by the creative powers of mythopoetic self-determination. (Henry 120)

1.3.1 Consciousness and Ego Dynamics

For Harris the recovery of the self is achieved "through the creative affirmation of the colonial trauma and its existential deviation" (Henry 94) with the help of the creative imagination, a "mythopoetic action," which operates in "a vertical 'drama of consciousness' [that] competes with or displaces the horizontal historical dramas of nationalism, proletarian liberation, or societal reorganisation" (Henry 121). This is a position he shares with other poeticists, particularly Walcott, although his formulation may be slightly different, and it represents, in Henry's opinion, "the most important discursive influence in Harris's work" (94).

The "mythopoetic action" of the creative imagination works on different levels: on the historical level it recognises the necessity for a de-centring agent in all ego-centered historical projects: "In Harris's view historical action is often the product of the surface layers of an ego-centered mind" (Henry 121). On the psychological level it is realised in the opposition of the centralising role of the ego and the adversarial role of consciousness (or soul) in the regeneration of the self. In both cases it is consciousness that plays the main role: "centralizing tendencies can only be balanced or compensated by the actions of a de-centered agent such as consciousness" (Henry 121). The case of history and Harris's original interpretation of time and the past will be analysed extensively in the following chapters: here, the attention will be put on the "ontology of consciousness" *strictu sensu*, which Henry sees as the basis of Harris's philosophy and "one of the most original philosopical developments in the poeticist tradition" (94).

The often recalled difficulty of Harris's philosophy is ascribed by Henry to "his very complex and expansive view of consciousness" and to "the unpredictable ways in which it penetrates and interacts with the worlds of self, society, and nature" (95). The definition of consciousness as formulated by Henry has a particular quality of inner contradiction that perfectly fits Harris's rhetoric: "consciousness is a universal living medium whose activities are necessary for the emergence and sustenance of all life forms" (95). It is a consciousness "that can be the unconscious of material life forms" (94). This apparent contradiction is explainable if we consider Harris's own words:

> When I speak of the unconscious I am not only speaking of the human unconscious, but of the unconscious that resides in objects, in trees and in rivers, I am suggesting that there is a psyche, a mysterious entity that links us to the unconscious in nature. ("Composition" 20)

It is this same entity, whether defined positively as "mysterious psyche" or as unconscious, that closely recalls Jung's "collective unconscious," although Harris expresses some doubt: "I don't know if it is the best term. I would rather call it the world's unconscious" ("Judgment" 25). Henry interprets this concept as "the unconscious existence of consciousness" (95) whose behaviour he associates to Hegel's spirit, but much more interestingly to traditional African religion, as will be discussed later. Other core aspects of consciousness are identified by Henry in the "founding capability," "unending creativity" which is so strongly supported by Harris, against any attempt at intellectual grasping and fixity of theory: "[a]t their best such attempts will produce only revealing traces or fragmentary revelations of its vastness" (Henry 95). The images used by Harris to represent these traces are many and varied, including "living fossils" and "absent presence" in a sort of "quantum representation" of the mentioned "world's unconscious." Despite the elusiveness, its traces, according to Harris, are enough for us to recognise the creative impact it imposes on the social world as an "objective process." Therefore, the tradition and culture of a people enter a new dimension in which, according to Henry, they are "not just human creations but also manifestations and meditations of a unique relationship with universal consciousness" (96).

Consciousness, as theorised by Harris (Imagination),[4] does not play its creative role exclusively in the universal dimension of the "world's unconscious," it is a structural element in the formation of the self. It has been discussed above how this dimension is inscribed in Caribbean poeticism. However, the struggle between ego and consciousness, as it appears in Harris's work (conscious/unconscious), can be connected to and explained in relation with African philosophy. In traditional African philosophy, particularly among the Akan, there are three main divisions of the human person: "the *Okra*, or soul, the *sunsum*, or ego, and the *honan*, or body" (Henry 27). A complete individual is "the ontic unity" (28) of these three parts, and the fulfilment of the *sunsum* is strictly dependent on "the guidelines encoded with the *Okra*" (28). This interdependency, however, is not easily realised, but it generates several contradictions leading to a sort of conflict between the *Okra* and *sunsum* in the process of self-formation, a "cosmogonic challenge" which is "[a]t the core of African existentialism" (Henry 31). This parallels Harris's conscious/unconscious, or, in Henry's terms, the ego/consciousness relationship. Regarding this struggle, Henry goes into more specific ground, which will be here reported with necessary simplification: nevertheless, the main concepts are not extremely difficult to grasp and they can help a deeper understanding of the basis, often taken for granted, of Harris's thought which will support subsequent discussion of particular aspects.

According to Henry, "the ego is [in] a relation of self-concealment in which consciousness transforms itself into an absent presence" (97). As an intentional structure, he continues, "the ego has self-creative powers" (97) and this self-institution tends to absoluteness and complicates the dialectic with consciousness: "the more absolutely it believes in the reality it has created, the less it is able to experience consciousness" (97). These constitutive tendencies of the ego are pre-reflective and justify the intentional structure which allows the ego "to define, recognize and respond to internal and external threats" (Henry 97). However, this tendency is extremely prone to error and can be paralleled with the "cosmogonic difficulties of the ego in African existentialism" (7) in which the subversive tendency of the *sunsum* "toward the everyday world" leads to "misguided attempts to usurp or replace" the *Okra*'s "creative authority" (32). Harris's "ontological dynamic between the ego and consciousness" is similar to

---

4 The terminologies used by Harris and Henry do not coincide, however one can correlate Harris's imagination to the active part of consciousness, Henry's consciousness (as a state) is related to Harris's "the unconscious," while the ego recalls Harris's definition of "the conscious."

this process and identifies as a precondition the role of the ego in distinguishing analytically "binary opposites that exist side by side in consciousness" (Henry 97). This state of closure is referred to by Harris in "clearly Heideggerian terms [...] as 'ontic tautology'" and in imagistic terms as "straitjacket" or "embalmed facts" and it parallels "hardening tendencies in the institutions and social practices that maintain the reality of the social world" (Henry 98).

The idea of "mechanical institutions" is what informs Harris's rejection of an "ontological paramountcy of the world of everyday life" (Henry 98). In relation to the analytic tendency of the ego it is important to quote Harris: "we live in a world where we fasten on the word clarity, where everything has to be clear. But how often do we deceive ourselves? In our blindness we mistake our clarity for sight, and we have to judge that clarity as partial" (Harris, "Judgment" 20). This dynamic relationship between analytic ego and intuitive consciousness in the interpretation of the phenomena of reality reveals fundamental differences from the intellectualistic "explosion of the object" theorised by Shaw and discussed above: it does not deny the role of the ego, it prevents it from excessive closure. Harris says: "I feel that one may fall into the trap of intellectualising issues which lie so much deeper" (interview by Riach 34).

According to Henry, Harris's "ontology of the everyday ego" parallels Western existentialism, particularly "Sartre's ontology of the human self" and reflects "the regulatory negations by which the ego is shaken out of its spiritual ignorance in African existentialism" (98). The function of Harris's consciousness is performed, in Henry's philosophical translation, in the disturbing role it plays in "voiding or de-intentionalizing an area of the self-activity" (Henry 98-99) and fulfilled in the positioning of the ego in what Harris calls "void" or "abyss." The new dimension of the "void" forces the ego to face realities other than its own. It is in the "eruption of the concealed consciousness into the life of the ego" that Harris mainly finds the material for his fiction and for his philosophy: "The unconscious can erupt through the conscious and address one in a startling way that strikes at one's prepossessions. So one finds that one's prepossessions, which are so dear to one, are dislodged" ("Composition" 16).[5] The unwanted intrusion of universal consciousness "illuminates a key concept in African magical discourse" (Henry 99) especially "the theft of an individual's vital force by an intrusive deity, ancestor, or human being" (99) which, according to Henry, is

---

5 Henry quotes this passage with the inclusion of a parenthetical comment linking "conscious" with the ego and with the minor mistake of changing "prepossesions" into "presuppositions."

characterised by the same "experience of loss or negat[ion] of intentionality" of the Harrisian "void," revealing "the oppositional relationship between ego and spiritual ground" (99). There are many examples in Harris's fiction of this intrusive role of consciousness, whether it be through dreams or visions or particular moments, both in fiction and in the creative process. In this context, the frequent literary device by which Harris introduces his own fictional characters into different novels has already been mentioned, but after Henry's reading it is possible to give this practice a deeper philosophical meaning. The intrusion of fictional characters is even more startling when it comes to the confession he makes about aspects of the creative process in real life:

> A couple of weeks ago I was sitting in my study. I had typed out very carefully the address I was to give this evening. I had placed it at the side of my typewriter. It looked neat – everything seemed satisfactory and happy – and then Aunt Alicia, one of the characters from *The Four Banks of the River of Space,* entered the room. I saw that she had something in mind which I would not relish, and indeed before I could blink she had seized my typescript and torn it into scraps and flung it on the floor. Then she said to me: 'That's no good. No sort of formal essay for you. No over-simplifications. Speak out of your vulnerability. Speak from within the resources of your creative experience.' (Harris, "Fabric" A 69)

Actually he has often followed this advice and he has stressed several times the fact that his creative process has much to do with visionary intuition:

> In other words, the narrative seems to "revise" itself of its own accord. One concentrates on it as closely as one can. One does all that he can. But there are clues that come into the narrative as if they are planted by another hand, as if they come out of the unconscious. One looks at those and, instead of cutting them out as irrelevant, one works with them. (Harris, "Fabric" A 71)

On another level, those intrusions of consciousness contribute to clarify certain issues such as the one that has been raised in the analysis of James's essay about man's presumed position of primacy in terms of true existence while animals, trees and all inanimate entities would be relegated to an incomplete existence. It should be clear, by now, that the idea of "world's consciousness" comprises diverse manifestations of reality, and the intrusion of consciousness into the reality of the ego can be effected not only through human beings. This is particularly the case of Guyanese landscapes:

> I sensed that I was being tested very deeply about the nature of reality, how I viewed reality, and not just by the people but by the landscape, which for a long time people had accepted as passive. I mean there are formidable writers who declared that landscape is a passive creature. But landscape is not a passive creature because it has rhythms, it has complexities, it has dimensions, that address one in terms of all sorts of faculties that one eclipsed in oneself. The landscape, the life of the landscape, would seem therefore to have to do with some mystery of psyche which one shares with non-being. There is a link between being and what one calls non-being. (Harris, "Composition" 17)

Even more radically, it is often by means of the intervention of such "living fossils" that the mind of the artist, of the dreamer or of other archetypal characters of Harris's is illuminated by the vision of "*realms beyond bland convention*" (*Beggar* 149), "realms of opposites" (*Beggar* 97) or other forms of "universal consciousness." James's statement about the importance of language in Harris's work is not incorrect, but it must be included in a broader vision in which the borders of language expand revealing "the inadequacies of using the language as a tool" (Harris, interview by Riach 35) and reaching a sort of archetypal language of consciousness:

> For example, you go into the interior of Guyana [...] if you come upon a man who appears to have nothing to say, it is as if his tongue exists in the rock, or it exists in the bark of a tree which is very old and which has all sorts of peculiar markings on it. The tide has risen, so you can see that on an ancient tree, that at one stage the floodwaters rose and left a mark there, and so on and so forth. His eloquence comes out of a whole body of resources which need to be translated. This, to some extent, has been translated, that body has been translated, but you can never completely translate that body of resources. The dumb creature, then, pushes one into the cavern of oneself in which some other tongue exists in addition to the tongue that one has, the tongue that has

been conditioned to speak in a certain way and is locked into a certain kind of tautology. (Harris, "Composition" 17)

Coming back to the strictly philosophical theme of the archetypal life of the ego and consciousness, Henry identifies the main point of divergence with James's and Shaw's theories. It is precisely the acknowledgement of the ego of all the realities addressed by the "universal consciousness," including those concerning the life of landscapes and their language, that differentiates Harris's thought from Hegel's and Heidegger's. The voidings and vulnerabilities brought up by consciousness have to be confronted by the ego to grasp a "profound, universal understanding" (Harris, *Beggar* 9), and this confrontation might bring the ego to limit its hubris and to recognise the possibilities that "an ability to digest certain traumas" (Henry 101) may suggest, whether it sprouts from the overcoming of divisions between nature and humanity or from the reconciliation between the "diverse racial figures [...] we have imprisoned in our minds *as though they were separate, absolutely separate identities*" (Harris, *Beggar* 68). It is precisely in this unifying quality of the ego/consciousness dialectic that Harris's "answer to the problems of closure and inauthenticity" differentiates itself from "Heidegger's being-towards death, or Hegel's philosophical intuiting of absolute truth" (Henry 101). Moreover, the intrinsic character of the archetypal life is different from those Western theorisations in its continuous redefinition or "infinite rehearsal," for "Harris's fulfillment is the opposite of consolidation" (Henry 101). According to Henry, the main similarities are once again with African philosophy: "these ego-fulfilling aspects [...] parallel in important ways the reconciliatory aspects of the destinal life of African existentialism" (102). This consideration may throw new light on the connections Harris has drawn with Afro-Caribbean traditions such as Haitian Voudun[6] and Limbo: "a limbo gateway between Africa and the Caribbean" (Harris, "History, Fable and Myth," in Bundy, ed. 157).

Henry concludes his analysis of the archetypal life of the ego/consciousness by stressing once again the importance of the dynamic process: "Although Harris clearly privileges the level of consciousness, what is important is the relativity, the mutuality and interpenetrability of quantum-based ontological activities. Thus the ego can mold consciousness and vice versa" (Henry 104).

---

6   See "The Writer and Society" (Harris, *Tradition* 48-64).

1.3.2 Poetics of Consciousness

All the philosophical issues discussed above are derived from Wilson Harris's poetics, which is the main site for their application and development. The poetic discourse often referred as "the arts of the imagination" is the place in which all the connections denied by the everyday ego are recognised and discussed through the use of a medium of language which reflects the opacity of consciousness. A perceptive character, usually an artist of some sort, is the preferred actor for revealing those philosophical concepts with the detachment that derives from the de-intentionalisations mentioned with respect to the intrusions of consciousness: "I am an unkempt sculpture with a tormenting way of expressing what is *apparently* beyond the norms of language" (Harris, *Beggar* 56). However, Harris's poetic field of action expands from the restricted area of "the strategies by which meanings are produced in a text" to the broader "ordering of meanings that is capable of shaping human behaviour" (Henry 104). It is in this expanded field that poetics and mere philosophy encounter and contribute to the definition of "a grammar of human self formation and motivation" (104) which, according to Henry, is the most distinguishing feature of Harris's poetics. Henry divides this grammar into two aspects defined as "the explicit way it incorporates consciousness into the system of meanings by which it orders human behavior" and "the imagistic phenomenology through which it approaches consciousness" (105).

The first assumption can be clarified if one thinks of it as the independence of consciousness of the rules that determine the reality of the ego: in other words, consciousness must be considered as having its own distinct textuality. It is because of this distinction that Harris feels the inadequacy of conventional language and realistic modes of narration. The textuality of consciousness must allow the perception of a deeper unity among the various quantum planes of possible existences that "the intentional codes and mechanical laws" (Henry 105) of conventional language can only portray as separate, as has emerged in the discussion of the confrontation of the ego with the void. On several occasions Harris has written about the role of language in this expanded textuality: it is particularly illuminating when he faces it in the text of the lecture given at the University of Cambridge in 1990, published as *The Fabric of the Imagination*:

> the table comes from a tree in the forest, the forest is the lungs of the globe, and the lungs of the globe breathe on the stars. There are all sorts of connections and those are quantum connections.

> Quantum mechanics and physics would embrace those connections. At that stage I had read nothing of quantum mechanics and I simply addressed my repudiation of absolute chains upon nature (my repudiation of a nature there to serve me, to prop up my structures) as an intuitive disturbing necessity. I needed to immerse myself in the living, disturbing, but immensely rich text of landscapes/riverscapes/skyscapes. Language began to break its contract with mere tools framed to enshrine a progressive deprivation. There was a more complex and intuitive approach to language in which one suffers and through which one perceives the peculiar ecstasies of dimensionality. (Harris, "Fabric" A 72)

Henry refers to this kind of textuality as "archetypal textuality" and he identifies in it the locus for the codification of "the unwritten book of life, the unstruck music of the universe, and the unargued philosophy of our world" (105). Harris effectively describes it as "the fabric of the imagination" ("Fabric" A 69) curiously entitling two different publications with this same label.[7] This fabric works as a realisation of the universal reality of consciousness with which the imaginative textuality of the ego can interact, freeing itself from the "ontic closure" defined above.

The second feature of Harris's poetics identified by Henry refers to "the method of how to approach consciousness from the plane of the ego" (Henry 106), that is to say the way in which the imaginative textuality of the ego intermingles with the fabric of the imagination. Henry concisely situates this "imagistic phenomenology" among the Western and non-Western traditions that came into discussion with particular effectiveness:

> In African religions there is the method of spiritual possession. In the religions of Asia, it is yoga and meditation. In Western phenomenological philosophy, the method of the phenomenological and eidetic reductions were used to disclose a transcendental consciousness that was not visible to the everyday or 'natural attitude.' Harris's method differs from all of these, but in their

---

7 Henry refers to "The Fabric of the Imagination," *Commonwealth to Post-Colonial*, ed. A. Rutherford, Mundelstrup/Sydney: Dangaroo Press, 1992, 18-29, print, while quotations here are from "The Fabric of the Imagination," *The Radical Imagination: Lectures and Talks*, ed. Alan Riach and Mark Williams, Liège: L3 - Liège Language and Literature, English Department, University of Liège, 1992.

terms could be best described as a combination of the African religious and the Western phenomenological approaches. (Henry 106)

Subsequently, Henry justifies the connection of Harris and Western phenomenology by clarifying the particular meaning he attributes to this philosophical approach: "a reflective description of the activities of consciousness following the bracketing of the natural attitude by some ego-displacing technique." (Henry 106) Moreover, he identifies two main "bracketing techniques" used by Harris: "*a de-intentionalised reduction*" and "quantum reading" (106).

The first technique identifies the way in which "voids, traumas, or de-intentionalized states" (Henry 106) are transformed by Harris into gateways, "It built a hole in myself – a hole or a Wound I understood more deeply than ever before" (Harris, *Jester* 35),[8] through which we can glimpse what is beyond ego awareness. This technique, Henry affirms, is in fact very different from the "eidetic and phenomenological reductions" of Europe-based transcendental phenomenology (Husserl); despite the bracketing process they share, the function of the ego and intentionality are true points of divergence.

The second technique is related to the quantum reading of creative images, which is performed by re-establishing connections between different planes of existence conventionally suppressed by everyday experience, such as in the quotation above where the table becomes a tree and the tree the lungs of the globe reaching the stars, or the rose becoming particle and wave: "a rose is a noose is a particle is a wave" (Harris, "Comedy" 129). According to Henry, creative images are "the carriers of codes and meanings" (107) shared by ego and consciousness and operate the mentioned interconnection at the level of the fabric of the imagination. Quantum reading tries to fix the ego's broken perception by identifying those connections between creative images, "quantum immediacy" (Harris, "Absent Presence" 81), and by creating new ones:

> If we are to understand the life of the imagination, the very foetus of the imagination, then we must also understand how endangered it is when those links are broken. Progressive realism has consistently broken those links by making passive creatures of

---

8 Harris's general idea of wound can be found in the brief definition he gives in *The Mask of the Beggar*: "*The Wound is a curious, creative possibility of bringing together cultures that are separate into an unseizable wholeness*" (77; emphasis in the original).

the very earth on which we move, by making the animals subject to our rages and our lusts and our greeds. We broke all of that. How can we repair it, unless there is some kind of thrust in the imaginative arts that begins to take up such complexities? [...] How can we really come to grips with what is crying out from within ourselves for an expression that challenges us, that makes us read, that makes us look at the revisionary capacity that comes out of the intuitive potential in images? (Harris "Fabric" A 79)

As often happens in the application of the quantum reading of creative images to Harris's own work, the tendency of narrative emerges "to 'revise' itself of its own accord" (Harris "Fabric" A 71). This is the case of the vessel image in *The Carnival Trilogy,* or Yorukon's bone flute, or the architecture of the tides in *The Four Banks of the River of Space,* all discussed in the Cambridge lectures (Harris, interview by Riach 81). The ability of narrative to reinterpret itself, the presence of clues "that come into the narrative as if they are planted by another hand, as if they come out of the unconscious" (Harris "Fabric" A 71) all sustain an intrinsic "intuitive component in an image, in the imageries of fiction" (70)[9] that can be considered, as by Henry, an objective process. In addition, Harris stresses the importance of not falling "into the trap of intellectualising issues which lie so much deeper" (interview by Riach 58), and Henry's awareness of this leads him to insert the cross-cultural connections brought up by quantum reading in a logic that is not the ego's, intentional and intellectual, but a "different mythopoetic logic" (Henry 107).

For Harris, the artist is the primary agent of the revolutionary project of creating a "new architecture between the Caribbean ego and consciousness, [...] a whole new set of 'subconscious alliances'" by addressing not to "overt political and economic structures, but rather at the inauthentic onto-existential connections between ego and consciousness" (Henry 106). This is essentially true, but Harris is not always so detached from politics, especially in recent years when he has often addressed more worldly problems such as environmental issues; this is functional to Henry's discussion of the differences between a poeticist attitude and a historicist one like his own. He aims to build bridges between the two, but in order to do so he must draw a division, disregarding some minor aspects of Harris's political involvement.

---

9 There is an apparent incongruence between Henry's and Harris's texts which troubles the checking of the quotation.

This division is realised in the historicists' difficulty in recognising three major points in Harris's thought. The first, closely linked to the political issue, is the priority of the ego/consciousness relationship in relation to the ego/society relationship. The second, a criticism usually levelled at Harris, regards the divergence in interpreting the colonial past as traumas, voids whose digestion leads to positive achievements (such as in ego/void confrontations). The third, more technical, is about the precondition of the transformation of the ego for post-colonial reconstruction. However, the contribution to the building of Caribbean philosophy cannot be underestimated, and Henry himself is conscious of this, as he demonstrated in his extensive analysis of "the originality and distinctiveness of the philosophy that exists implicitly in Harris's fiction and essays" (Henry 113) and in the suggestion, despite Aunt Alicia's warning about overtheorisations, that "Harris's imagistic connections constitute an inexhaustible source of Caribbean philosophical ideas" and "should not be overlooked by philosophers" (Henry 114).

1.4 Gnostic Tradition and Faustian Themes

Besides Henry's massive philosophical work about Caribbean philosophy, there have been interpretations of Harris's work in completely different lights, linking it to apparently distant traditions such as Gnosticism and Faustian figures. This is the case of Michael Mitchell's essays "The Magus at Angel Inn" and "The Seigniory of Faust" whose major issues are summarised and expanded in "Gift of the Magus," a chapter from his book *Hidden Mutualities*. The connections between Harris and sixteenth-century European themes, such as alchemy or Hermeticism, have been raised by Harris himself as he often refers to Frances Yates's *The Art of Memory:* a reference which deserves a separate analysis. Here, it may be useful to start from an assumption about Gnosticism that can be gathered from an interview published in *The Radical Imagination*:

> I've always been interested in the origins of confession. I am not a member of any church, though I would claim to be a kind of Christian Gnostic, if you like. Not Gnostic in the extreme sense in which the Cathars were Gnostics. They said that the creation was the work of a demiurge. I can't accept that. I believe we live a field of the creation, which we have to see as linked up with other fields of the Creation [...] as if we are placed here to do something essentially creative. (Harris, interview by Riach 57)

In addition to this, the connection with Faust is evident in Harris's *The Infinite Rehearsal* (1987), where Doctor Faustus appears as a character on the top of the Mountain of Folly. Since Gnostic and Hermetic elements are to be found on many other occasions throughout Harris's fiction and critical work, it is interesting to follow Mitchell's analysis for it draws on a variety of texts and highlights the strong relationship that exists with a philosophical tradition often neglected but deeply embedded in Western culture and fundamental in Harris's cross-cultural imagination.

In "The Seigniory of Faust," Mitchell rightly identifies Gnostic and Hermetic influences as part of a tradition which "*returns, which nourishes us even though it appears to have vanished*" (Harris, "Literacy" 27) and informs Harris's philosophy. In particular, some of the concepts expressed in the *Corpus Hermeticus* and in the writings concerning Simon Magus are extremely important in relation to Harris's thought, such as the image of totality and wholeness defined by the "Nous," which is "simultaneously the image of the human psyche and infinitely beyond it, microcosm and macrocosm" (Mitchell, "Seigniory" 171). The importance of this assumption will emerge in the course of this study, revealing itself as a fundamental feature of Harris's concept of time and space.

The creative power assigned to Humanity by Gnostic doctrines is another element of convergence with Harris's thought, a position which postulates a "fundamental identity between Humanity and God" (Mitchell, "Seigniory" 171). According to Mitchell this might be a common feature that could justify the frequently mentioned similarities between Harris, Blake, Yeats and Joyce. In this light, the Faustian figure can be seen as "the Gnostic seer who seeks to perfect his knowledge to become a 'mighty god' through magical operation" (Mitchell, "Seigniory" 171). However, this kind of "hubris" has to confront reality and to acknowledge a fundamental impossibility: "impossible dream, impossible quest for wholeness" (Harris, *Infinite* 173); otherwise it might be "sidetracked into a one-sided relationship with the material world" (Mitchell, "Seigniory" 171), and lose its "soul" as Marlowe's Doctor Faustus did. This "one-sided relationship" is the breaking point which sees Gnosticism, microcosm and macrocosm relationships, analogy and magic on one side and analytical, causal, measuring proto-science on the other. According to Mitchell this contrast is typically embodied in Fludd's poetic attitude and Kepler's scientific method. By presenting the Kepler/Fludd dispute, Mitchell brings to attention the subsequent direction taken by European culture towards exclusively scientific knowledge which determined a period of denial for Gnostic/Hermetic traditions: "Gnostic/Hermetic initiative was quickly marginalized and eclipsed. Partly, I have suggested, because it rejected divine and mundane authority, placing the human being at the centre of creative power and responsibility" (Mitchell, *Mutualities* 273). Therefore, according to Mitchell, it is significant that in 1952 a volume containing both Jung's "Synchronicity, an Acausal Connecting Principle" and Pauli's "The Influence of Archetypal Ideas on the Formation of Scientific Theories in Kepler" was published. Following his considerations, this represents the birth of "a new context for the ancient Gnostic conception of the place of humanity in the cosmos" (Mitchell, "Seigniory" 173) which sees Jung and Pauli's agreement on "a speculative model of a quaternio of principles: Space-Time Continuum, Indestructible Energy, Causality and Synchronicity. 'The result in that case,' says Jung, 'would be a unity of being which would have to be expressed in terms of a new conceptual language'" (Jung, *Collected Works* Vol. 8, 960; qtd. in "Seigniory" 173). The pregnancy of the issues raised by Mitchell is evident if we consider a series of elements: Harris's theorisation of "world's consciousness" and Jung's "collective unconscious"; Harris's interest in quantum physics and in the "interdependence of observer and object (Pauli)" ("Seigniory" 173); the direct reference to Gnostic tradition and Renaissance culture mentioned above; and Harris's urgent concern for "a new conceptual language" other than that of realism. These elements will be touched upon in due place, with particular attention to convergences with and divergences from Jung.

Regarding the Gnostic tradition, Mitchell goes deeper in his essay "The Magus at Angel Inn" where he relates W.B.Yeats (especially his experiments in automatic writing), Blake and Fludd to Harris in their common effort to build "a system founded on the interplay of contraries" ("Magus" 155) with which to participate "in the divine nature of the created universe" ("Magus" 156) in a somehow Faustian way. Moreover, he parallels Harris's concern with language to Yeats's vision of multiple personalities as opposed to a "sovereign ego consciousness," which is realised, for Harris, "in rejecting mimetic linear narrative in favour of a dynamic density" ("Magus" 157). In Harris's words: "We need today, it seems to me, an openness to the language of the Imagination simultaneous with a grasp of the sacred, which requires self-confessional and profound, self-judgmental art rooted in a spectrum of variable identity" (Harris, "Imagination" 191). This is applied in the fragmentation of Harris's typical characters whose elusiveness is often realised in their lack of corporeal dimensions, the Dreamer in *The Dark Jester* or Ghost in *The Infinite Rehearsal*, and even more often in multiple, contrasting, or complementary figures such as *Jonestown*'s triad (Jones-Bone-Deacon) or the twinship between the dreamer narrator and Donne in *Palace of the Peacock*.

In "Gift of the Magus," Mitchell returns to the Faust myth, which represents the major example of the survival of the Gnostic/Hermetic tradition, and he finds a way to summarise the concepts expressed in the previous essays, applying them to various of Harris's novels. Mitchell identifies an attitude among post-colonial writers, parallel to the "implacable opposition between the monolithic former oppressor and the newly liberated," which seems "to be laying claim to an intimate dialogue with a central position in traditions rejected by early postcolonial theorists as alien and [E]urocentric" (*Mutualities* 275). Wilson Harris is certainly to be included, with a privileged position, in this last category and he fits perfectly among Mitchell's selection of writers who "had recognized a tradition within Europe that European culture had itself marginalized" (Mitchell, *Mutualities* 275). It is this Gnostic-Hermetic tradition that has always included those "hidden mutualities" which give the title to Mitchell's book and serve to effectively define "the resurgent margins of mutual concerns, the empowerment of the human being" (*Mutualities* 275), peculiar to Harris's fiction. To support his view, Mitchell significantly quotes Harris, and it is useful to quote this reference:

> 'Is space itself a giant shell, a giant surrogate ear of a multidimensional God?' A surrogate ear? And this is where I must confess my allegiance to the gnostic heresy. I believe that the creation in which we live is, that it will be continuously, tormented. But yet it can evolve, it can evolve and in evolving it moves towards some Spirit which possesses absolute knowledge. But that absolute knowledge is not available to us. We evolve towards that absolute knowledge. (Harris, "Ways to Enjoy" 207)

This dense passage is fundamental to Mitchell's reading of Harris, but it will also be extremely useful in this study in relating Harris's mystical theorisation of "living landscape" and his complex interpretation of pre-Columbian cultures. The consequent view of reality determines Harris's rejection of mimetic language and of the realist mode, in favour of a new language mirroring that open and imperfect system. As will be extensively discussed, this is reflected in his concept of time and history, seen in a restless creative process centred in the imagination. In Mitchell's words, as quantum mechanics destabilised the Newtonian conception of of the cosmos by introducing indeterminacy into the description of phenomena, Harris creates a new conceptual language of the imagination to describe a world where things simultaneously are and are not both within and beyond time. (Mitchell, *Mutualities* 279)

The imagination which functions as a creative element and as a means of intuitive knowledge is not something apart from material reality; it is often referred to by Harris as generated from actual experience in the very different world of the interior of Guyana and this is confirmed by T.J. Cribb in his essay "T.W. Harris – Sworn surveyor" (1993), where several clues for interpreting Harris's early fiction are extracted from the official documents of British Guiana's Commission of Land and Surveys. As Mitchell puts it,

Imagination here is not a solipsistic function of the conscious ego, but plays the same soteriological role implicit throughout the Gnostic/Hermetic writings. It is not the result of theoretical considerations, but of sensual engagement with the material world. (Mitchell, *Mutualities* 279)

In the analysis of Harris's earlier fiction, Mitchell highlights Jungian elements in a more detailed way, such as the function of Donne and the Dreamer in *Palace of the Peacock* (1960) and Poseidon and Fenwick in *The Secret Ladder* (1963), which exemplify the Jungian concept of "adversarial twins" and the image of the "cri de Merlin"; but these will be discussed separately. Here it is useful to report Mitchell's interpretation of other novels that will be used more extensively in later chapters, such as *The Infinite Rehearsal* (1987), *Jonestown* (1996) and to a lesser extent *Tumatumari* (1968). The last novel mentioned is important for the parallels that Mitchell draws between the characters and an image dear to Harris: Titian's painting "Allegory of Prudence." In this painting, a "male face or mask" (Harris, "Liberty" 218) is represented just above three animal heads: a wolf, a lion and a dog. Harris has often quoted Frances Yates's interpretation of the painting (Yates 165-166), which sees the three animals as the attributes of prudentia: memoria, intelligentia and providentia, and Mitchell reads the main characters of *Tumatumari* as personifications of these qualities. Prudence, the protagonist, is bound up with the fates of three other characters: Henry Tenby, the historian, as "memoria"; Roi Solman, the engineer, as "intelligentia"; and the child "she apparently loses at the start of the novel, but which in fact becomes the 'body of fiction' itself" (Mitchell, *Mutualities* 286), as "providentia." The "multi-dimensional imagery" that characterises *Tumatumari* allows Mitchell to link the mentioned connections with Renaissance imagery and the dense layers of meaning that the novel discloses, especially when it presents Roi Solman's Faustian "'hubris' of electric technology" as opposed to the Amerindian "suppressed qualities of soul" (*Mutualities* 288), re-contextualising the Kepler/Ludd controversy mentioned above. The infinite superposition of layers is perceived on other occasions, particularly when the "memoria" figure, Henry Tenby, is presented in relation to colonial history, bringing up images of "repression and remorse" (*Mutualities* 289) which create "generations of inbuilt prejudice, histories, volumes under which he suffocated" (Harris, *Tumatumari* 45). Technology and History appear again in these terms, but constantly evolving, in other novels such as *The Angel at the Gate* (1982) and *Black Marsden* (1972), mentioned by Mitchell, but a sort of turning point is possibly seen in *The Infinite Rehearsal* where "Faust appears as a character and is a presence underlying the whole work" (*Mutualities* 297). Here, in a particularly effective way, "Harris's characters, though discrete, are multiple, like the same archetype taking different paths" (*Mutualities* 298), and one of them is even named Ghost, simultaneously a real character and a spirit rising from the wreck of the ship on which Emma, Peter/Robin, Alice and Miriam sink and drown (also a slave-ship). The protagonist (if it is possible to consider him as such, for he acts in conjunction with Peter, an alter-ego), known as Robin Redbreast Glass, a pork-knocker, addresses the narrator in a note at the beginning claiming that: "W.H. has stolen a march on me and put his name to my fictional autobiography" (Harris, *Infinite*). Here, the narrator is once again identified by the two initials of Harris's full name: W.H. Ambiguities of this kind and adversarial relationships are immediately presented as the main features of the fictional population of the city of "Skull," in the country of "Old New Forest." The opposition between Ghost and the immigration officer, Ulysses Frog, is the first of a series that finds its peak in the relationship between Robin and Doctor Faustus. Faust himself bears some characteristic of his literary alter-ego, Mephistopheles, for his sinister relationship with technology: "Faust here has a dangerous aspect as a projection of hollow technologies" (Mitchell, *Mutualities* 299). It is in fact his addiction to "the drug of material progress" (*Mutualities* 300) that marks the Faustian figure in *The Infinite Rehearsal;* a strongly negative kind of "hubris," which, among the other layers, has a great importance, as "the novel remains consistently aware of the political and economic realities of the postcolonial world" (*Mutualities* 301).

At a more "mystical" level, other interpretations are presented by Mitchell, but here it will suffice to report his reading of "unmistakeable indications [...] of the Gnostic quest to unite the spark of divinity carried within each human being with the true, absent God" (*Mutualities* 304). These must be confronted with the difficulty "to find a true balance between such carrying vessels of nature and such seeking from vessels of spirit" (Harris, *Infinite* 259) and the fascinating dangerousness of the rush for hollow technology.

Harris's Gnostic quest continues and develops into the alchemical exploration of *Jonestown*, where, according to Mitchell, he "conforms to the axiom of Maria Prophetissa: 'One becomes two, two becomes three, and out of the third comes the one as the fourth'" (Mitchell, *Mutualities* 304-305). This interpretation is readily explained: "'One becomes two,' because each person and thing carries its adversarial complementary or compensatory twin" (*Mutualities* 306), and this is especially true for *Jonestown*, where Bone and Deacon are the quintessence of the doubled Harrisian character, symbolising the concept that it is "only through one's twin and the apparently contradictory point of view shared with the twin that true sight becomes possible" (*Mutualities* 306). This true sight is what allows the perception of the simultaneity of a microcosm and a macrocosm ("what is above is the same as what is below"): a fractal representation of the characters being "simultaneously within parallel universes" (*Mutualities* 306). This concept is fundamental to the analysis of time in the following chapters and it will be discussed again in depth; however, to support this assumption here, it is important to notice that Mr Mageye, "the Magus, the Gnostic seeker" (*Mutualities* 307). has a camera which can see into the future and the past, parallel universes whose unity can be experienced through creative imagination.

"Two becomes three," according to Mitchell, is applicable to Jonestown when we consider the triad formed by the two elements of the axis, Deacon and Bone and the new element of Jonah Jones, the founder of Jonestown, partially modelled on the real Reverend Jim Jones, founder of the People's Agricultural Temple, infamous for the mass suicide of 1979 in Guyana. Mitchell affirms that they form together the figure of a triadic identity which sees Jones at the head, "Deacon (right-hand man) and Bone (left-hand man)" (*Mutualities* 308). Bone's task is to recognise the archetypal relatedness between him and each one of the other two, in spite of their reticence. Yet, to completely perform his allegorical role, he must preserve their distinguishing differences: "[i]n other words, the synthetic powers of the unconscious must be combined with the analytic tools of the consciousness" (*Mutualities* 308). The male triad is counterbalanced by the female triad of the three virgins, The Virgin of Albuoystown, Bone's mother, Marie Antoinette, the bride of Jones and Marie de port Mourant, Deacon's bride.

The function of all those triads in *Jonestown*'s fiction is mainly that of a kind of historical revision through multiple lenses, performed with ethereal allegories, such as the case of the three Marys, who respectively evoke Christian, European and Creole elements. The choice of such intangible references is both linguistic and functional, as Mr Mageye clarifies: "[w]hen music and unspoken prayer animate language, all proportionalities of being and non-being, genesis and history, are subject to a revisionary focus" (Harris, *Jonestown* 97). According to Mitchell, the fourth stage, regression to one, is to be seen allegorically in the death the triad experiences, when Jones is killed by the hand of Deacon, and Bone recognises his identity with the latter and voluntarily accepts his mask for judgement.

Mitchell's analysis has been presented with due adaptation. It is actually much more fully articulated, but it has been useful to trace some of the existing connections with Gnostic/Hermetic tradition, especially non-linearity and multifaceted allegorical images. Furthermore, it has brought to light elements that will be discussed further on, taking care not to fall into a too misty mysticism such as sometimes, albeit rarely, Mitchell seems to indulge in.

2 – Time and History

I have discussed some general aspects of Harris's philosophy in connection with different traditions, such as the Western canon, Africana thought and Gnosticism/Hermeticism, which contribute significantly to Harris's thought. It must be said that these do not exhaust all influences which indeed come from a much wider range of traditions, but it is a necessary, even if partial, background for analysing some aspects of Harris's work that will lead to the consideration of another constitutive element of his philosophy: pre-Columbian and Amerindian views of the world. In this process it is again very useful to limit and define the analysis to a specific field, in such a way as to better clarify the connections that exist amongst some of the extremely numerous influences which constitute Harris's thought.

The theme of history and the narration of history will be used here as a leitmotif to contextualise the historical view that Harris has built around his particular concept of time, in the course of his literary career. This theme is particularly important for a writer who comes from the Caribbean region, which among the various post-colonial realities has produced a significant and original philosophy of history. The importance of history in the Caribbean basin has already been mentioned in the previous chapter, particularly within the analysis of Henry's work, but it will be presented in greater detail during the discussion of non-Western traditions.

On a broader scale, history has been a significant discipline for the post-colonial discourse, for its "emergence [...] in European thought is coterminous with the rise of modern colonialism" (Ashcroft et al., *Reader* 355). The political meaning of this lies in the role of "prominent [...] instrument for the control of subject people" (Ashcroft et al., *Reader* 355) that "History" has assumed in the relationship between Europe and the colonies, which continues in the ongoing struggle for cultural independence of the new liberated nations. While the recognition of other histories by the West has been difficult and their relegation to the margins is still common practice, in recent years, a new attitude towards the writing of history has gained relative centrality. The problem of history and the philosophy of history, even though it has been systematically formulated only in relatively recent times, has often been an important ground for thinkers to apply and verify the principles of their metaphysics, frequently exposing cultural biases and preconceptions such as the case of Hegel's emblematic exclusion of Africa from the possibility of history. However, recently, Western historians and philosophers of history have showed a new, more conscious attitude, thanks to seminal works such as Hayden White's *Metahistory* (1973), which seems to parallel some of the issues brought up, not only in the Caribbean context, by many post-colonial writers, such as Harris and Walcott. The function of fiction in the writing of history has gained more and more attention, as will be analysed in the course of this chapter, and it has revealed many features in common with post-colonial theory, in the problematisation of historical production.

In the field of history, philosophy and psychoanalysis have often come to interact in defining concepts of time and memory. The discussion, which has been limited, almost exclusively, to philosophical and literary issues, will incorporate a brief analysis of some psychoanalytical contributions, mainly centred around Jung and the many connections that can be found with Harris. For the sake of space and time, all the profound interrelationships that can be found between Harris's work and recent theories of physics, such as chaos theory and quantum mechanics, especially regarding time and the object/observer interrelationship, will be treated in lesser detail, while all the implications which emerge from the pre-Columbian background deserve a separate discussion, in the fourth chapter.

2.1 Historiography and Contemporary Philosophies of History

It would be a hard task to produce a detailed analysis of the evolution of the concept of history through the works of Western philosophers, even if limited to specific periods. Therefore, the focus will be put on the development that historiography and the philosophy of history have recently witnessed in contemporary European and in Western academies. Subsequently, an equally reductive overview of non-Western traditions of historiography will be presented, drawing mainly on literary sources. The general picture presented aims to reveal some of the important connections that exist between the recent achievements in the academic West and the applications of Harris's philosophy to history and historical fiction. On the other hand, non-Western traditions will contribute to identify the background to which Harris often refers, demonstrating how his theories tend, in an unusual way, towards a possibility of synthesis and re-elaboration of both Western and non-Western elements in a cross-cultural perspective.

2.1.1 Western Historiography and Authoritarian Narratives

As already mentioned above, the role of history has been of great interest in the West since the first historical accounts, but still in the early twentieth century Collingwood expressed the necessity of a deeper insight: "An inquiry into the nature of historical thinking is among the tasks which philosophy may legitimately undertake; and at the present time [1935] there are reasons, as it seems to me, for thinking such an inquiry not only legitimate but necessary" (Collingwood 231). Since Collingwood's call, many Western intellectuals seemed to have been busying themselves to provide an answer, and their involvement has resulted in a systematisation of the knowledge and practice of history, not without frequent disagreements. As will be discussed later, in even more recent times, this interest has led to the questioning of the authority of history on the basis of its not completely scientific nature and of its controversial overlapping with fiction. It is not the aim of this discussion to produce an exhaustive analysis; however, it is necessary to present an overview of the evolution of historiography and the philosophy of history to better understand the issues brought up by academics and scholars in the last decades. The line followed by Lionel Gossman in his article "History and Literature. Reproduction or Signification" (1978) offers an excellent reference for this overview. His arguments will be expanded with a selection of other works, privileging the post-colonial field; therefore, strictly philosophical questions or technical issues about historiography will not be taken into consideration, as a mainly literary critical perspective will be adopted.

It is commonly held that the practice of history as such can be traced back to the Greek world; already in the "Histoire" entry of his Encyclopaedia, Voltaire, "one of the founding fathers of modern historiography" (Gossman 12), finds in Herodotus the starting point of historical tradition, despite the persistence of some fabulous elements:

> Il faut avouer que l'histoire ne commence pour nous qu'aux entreprises des Perses contre les Grecs. On ne trouve avant ces grands événemens que quelques récits vagues, enveloppés de contes puériles. [...] Hérodote eut le même mérite qu'Homère; il fut le premier historien comme Homère le premier poëte épique. (Voltaire 223)

Curiously, Voltaire avoids the threats of Eurocentrism by identifying in the Chinese chronicles an equally authoritative example:

> Celle que nous nommons ancienne, & qui est en effet récente [histoire], ne remonte guère qu'à trois mille ans: nous n'avons avant ce tems que quelques probabilités: deux seuls livres profa-

nes ont conservé ces probabilités; la chronique chinoise, & l'histoire d'Hérodote. (Voltaire 223)

In his article, Gossman, partially overlooking the early beginnings, starts from Rome and readily presents the often neglected interrelationship between history and literature by pointing out that "Quintilian treats history as a form of epic [...] [b]ecause his object is not to demonstrate or argue or persuade, but to narrate and to memorialize" (3). Cicero, according to Gossman, distinguished between the chronicles of events *sine ullis ornamentis,* typical of the Roman annalists and the productions of the Greek historians, confirming the existence of a different rapport between literature and history in the Greek world. Cicero's idea of the historian as "the impersonal mirror of reality" (Gossman 4) is inscribed by Gossman into traditional philosophy and aesthetics, shared by "other writers who concerned themselves with history: Tacitus, Polybius, Plutarch, Lucian" (4). Therefore, with the exception of Quintilian, it seems that the Greeks' literary approach to history was softened by the Roman concept of a historian who "may say nothing false,[...] must dare to say all that is true,[...] must avoid partiality" (3-4). The attitude, however, remained that of considering history as a literary genre and the ancients' theory of history "was limited largely to questions of technique and presentation" (Gossman 4).

Later, during the Renaissance, historiography conformed to the precepts of the ancients and "the sense of a practice, a technique" (Gossman 4) also characterised the seventeenth and eighteenth centuries although, on a more strictly philosophical ground, the eighteenth century saw the return of history as an important subject. After the partial rejection of history by Descartes and other rationalists on the basis of its not completely scientific character, Leibniz, Bayle and above all Vico recognised the importance of a discussion of the philosophy of history: the historical method proposed by Vico in opposition to the earlier mistakes which he attributed to both philosophers and historians prepares the ground for the consideration of history as a science by limiting its field to events that can be experienced by man, therefore excluding cosmology.

This can be considered an important stage of the process of methodological and epistemological division between literature and history, which Gossman tries to dismantle by demonstrating how they have always been linked despite the intellectual trends. This process saw the progressive breakdown of the long association of rhetoric and literature, because of the gradual association of the term "literature" with poetry, culminating in the romantic idea of "a corpus of privileged or sacred texts [...] which could be opposed to the empirical world of historical reality and even, to some extent, to historiography as the faithful record of that reality" (Gossman 5). The writer, who could formerly approach writing much more easily – "every reader was himself, in a lesser way a writer" (4) – was then "not so much a revealer of truths, a speaker of divine language, as a maker of meanings and a restorer of human languages" (6). This new status acquired by literature was paralleled by the divergent direction history took. Gossman sees in the work of Chladenius the development of the mentioned process of history's becoming a science which conflated in "a more comprehensive theory of historical objectivity" (7). Later on, Hegel worked in this direction building the foundations, with his *Lectures on the Philosophy of History* (1837), of a conception of history, linked to the nation states, which promoted the grand nineteenth-century narratives whose influence on the creation of the colonial self will be discussed in the following sub-sections.

Going back to the eighteenth century, the consolidation of the division between history and fictional story-telling is promoted by Voltaire, who distinguishes the materials out of which history and epic poetry are composed: "historical material and legendary material were now distinct" (Gossman 12). At the same time, for the historian, the precepts of Aristotle about the primacy of "action" over "facts" remained alive, and already by the eighteenth century "the first [...] requisite in an historian [was] to give as much unity as possible" (Gossman 12). Moreover, with Vico's *Scienza Nuova*, "the idea of Universal History [...] was introduced to modern thought" (Gossman 4). In this light it is clear how "in neoclassical historiography the part is thus subordinated to the whole [and] once the general principles have been grasped, everything that can possibly come out of them can be embraced in a universal view, and the details are only an entertaining diversion" (Gossman 17). At the end of the century, Schiller theorised the construction of the order of history: "the historian thus draws that harmony forth from himself, and transplants it, outside himself, in the order of external things, that is to say, he brings to the course of the world a rational end, and a teleological principle to world history" (Gossman 20). Conversely, this sort of rational direction for history is derived by Kant inverting the elements, thus considering the rationality of nature as the driving principle: "A philosophical attempt to work out a universal history according to a natural plan directed to achieving the civic union of the human race must be regarded as possible and, indeed, as contributing to this end of Nature" (Kant, "Idea"). As Louis O. Mink states, regarding Kant, "Universal History was the work of divine Providence, but, as the idea became secularized by the eighteenth century, God the Author retreated, leaving the idea of a story which is simply there" (Mink 137). These unproblematic attitudes fit into Gossman's account and exemplify how the Enlightenment historian had the attitude of an ironic spectator and showed, as Voltaire did, "a healthy respect for truth" (Gossman 23), without questioning the assumed identity of truth-reality-representation, not dissimilarly from his contemporary novelists.

Despite Schiller's attempt to foreground the imposing subjectivity of the historian in the making of history, the nineteenth century saw the success of a historiographical attitude which resulted in the unconditional support to the growing nation-state histories and their colonial enterprises on the basis of their supposed "naturality" in the evolution of humanity. Nineteenth-century historiography was characterised by the pretension of scientific objectivity despite its "want of conceptual rigor and failure to produce the kinds of universal laws that the sciences characteristically seek to produce" (White, "Historical Text" 42), and the reconstruction was not perceived as an act of imagination:

> The nineteenth century narrator appears as a privileged reporter reconstructing what happened. The historical text is thus not presented as a model to be discussed, criticized, accepted, or repudiated by the free and inquiring intellect, but as the inmost form of the real, binding, and inescapable. In the struggle to establish *philosophie*, in other words, the eighteenth-century historian accepted his ideological function proudly; in the nineteenth century, the historian's ideological function and the rhetoric he deployed in its service were denied, in the deepest sense, since the historian himself did not recognize them. (Gossman 24)

In this context, the work of Hegel, as already mentioned, has enormously influenced traditional historiography (and it played a fundamental role in the construction of Marxism, which was to characterize many twentieth-century approaches to the philosophy of history). For Hegel, the mentioned rationality of the world, which for Kant was mirrored in the emanation of history from nature and for Schiller reflected the historian's own rationality, was realised in the teleological scheme of the "coming to consciousness" of the Spirit. The complexity of all the implications of Hegel's philosophy of history will not be discussed here; some brief considerations will suffice. First, the geographic realisation of the stages of the evolution of the Spirit must be introduced. This division informs the quoted assumption about Africa's lack of history, the relegation of

Asia to infancy and, not surprisingly, it sees Europe as the apex in a hierarchical representation, while Africa appears as the limit of historical development, Asia as the start of historical development, and Europe as the continuation of it. Secondly, it is useful to report the association of the Spirit to the idea of the nation-state: "The State is the Idea of Spirit in the external manifestation of human Will and its Freedom. It is to the State, therefore, that change in the aspect of History indissolubly attaches itself" (Hegel, *History* § 49). It is clear how such a philosophy perfectly supports and justifies the mentioned idea of imperialism as the natural development of European nations. British histories of the time such as Seeley's *Expansion of England* (1883) and *The Growth of British Policy* (1895) or Macaulay's *History of England* (1849) "profited largely from the ideas of the (Protestant) imperial state" (Stutchey, "World Power" 222), and "*liberty* by *Empire*" was considered "the new pattern of English history [...] echoed by Carlyle, Stephen, and other English historians who believed that the imperial philosophy, political authoritarianism, and national consistency embodied by some of its representatives was the most suitable remedy for the decline of the Western world-system as reflected in capitalism and democracy" (226).

This kind of self-appointed predominance over the representation of the real, from a biased, subjective, and ideologically determined standpoint, characterised the histories of the second wave of Western colonialism. It is, therefore, clear how the critique of the self-assumed objectivity of history as presented by Gossman and White can parallel the concepts of different and resisting histories which sprouted within the processes of de-colonisation. Gossman, in fact, presents his overview in such a way as to highlight the persistence of the interrelationship between history and literature on the basis of their common nature of fiction: he presents the situation of the nineteenth century, which in his own opinion still earns credit today, to undermine its lack of foundation with the arguments he gets from another, minor tradition. According to Gossman, the repudiation of realism in some modern fiction, the new concept of time "no longer [...] a uniform medium in which historical events occur" (26). discontinuity, all support the attack on realism which has gradually grown since the nineteenth century: "nineteenth-century philosophers challenged the naïve realism of the classical historians and emphasized the place of subjectivity in historical knowledge" (Gossman 26). In a certain way, despite the main trend, the awareness was beginning to emerge that in the process of historical knowledge "the knower is himself involved in the historical process as a maker of history and is thus unable to achieve the 'objective' view aspired to by the natural scientist" (Gossman

26). On this side, Nietzsche's critique of Hegelianism, and his interest in mythic thinking can be seen as an original step on the path to the problematisation of the writing of history.[10] Curiously, the concept of "eternal return" can be put in relation to Wilson Harris's "infinite rehearsal," with which it shares some common features, despite fundamental differences, and it will be briefly discussed in the second part of this chapter. What is important to report here is Nietzsche's stress on Metaphor as the trope that characterises historical language, a position that can be paralleled to Harris's in "Metaphor and Myth" (1982), but, for instance, represents, according to Hayden White, one of the few exceptions in Western traditional philosophies of history to the predominance of Metonymy and Synedoche. White's theory will be discussed further on, while some other aspects of Nietzsche's philosophy will be mentioned here because of their originality and put in relation with Harris's ideas. The importance of art in the progress of knowledge can be considered as one of these aspects, for Nietzsche held that "only art, not philosophy or science, can offer a metaphysical justification for the life of man" (White, *Metahistory* 343). What differentiates the two is the belief Nietzsche expressed about "the whole history of Western man [...] [as] one great progressive movement from mere existence, through alienation, to reconciliation [...] with the self" (*Metahistory* 345), whereas Harris expressed a much feebler belief in a kind of "positive direction." Nietzsche's Critical history as opposed to Monumental and Antiquarian histories, represented a way to "bring the past to the bar of judgement, interrogate it remorselessly, and finally condemn it," (Nietzsche, *Genealogy* 42; qtd. in *Metahistory* 349) in a process of problematic interpretation of "the language of the past" seen as "always *oracular*" (*Metahistory* 353).

The common trend of historiography, on the other side, reflected a cultural assumption which T. Niranjana sees as constitutive of Western thought: "the Western philosophical notions of reality, representation, and knowledge" which support the vision of a "Reality [...] as something unproblematic, 'out there'," where "knowledge involves a representation of this reality; and representation provides direct, unmediated access to a transparent reality" (Niranjana 2). And Gossman himself recognises the persistent influence of this assumption: "despite decades of demonstrations by philosophers and by historians themselves that history is a construct, the belief that it is an immediate representation of reality

---

[10] All references to Nietzsche's ideas about history are drawn from *The Birth of Tragedy* (1872-1886) and 'The use and Abuse of History' (1874) and from their discussion in H. White's *Metahistory* (1973).

[...] [has] remained remarkably vigorous" (32). However, in his opinion, the twentieth-century critical attempts at disrupting it can be traced back already to the late nineteenth century. This may be reflected in the birth of Marx's philosophy and of historical materialism, which represents a source for many twentieth-century historical discussions, and which will be considered here mostly for its critical attitude towards the writing of history. In this sense, Marxism represents a sort of "coming to consciousness" of history writing, even though it does not avoid some controversial issues of Hegel's biased philosophy, such as Eurocentrism: "Marx's philosophy was fundamentally Eurocentric, hence he developed his model of the evolution of distinct stages in history based on the experience of Europe" (Stuchtey and Fuchs, "Introduction" 43). Another controversial point is the functional justification of imperialism:

> Marxism's universalising narrative of the unfolding of a rational system of world history is simply a negative form of the history of European imperialism: it was Hegel after all, who declared that 'Africa has no history,' it was Marx who, though critical of British imperialism, concluded that the British colonization of India was ultimately for the best because it brought India into the evolutionary narrative of Western history, thus creating the conditions for future class struggle there. (Young 2)

However, the new methodology of historical inquiry proposed by Marx gained great consideration among twentieth-century thinkers. Historical materialism has greatly contributed to the scientific evolution of historical method: "This conception of history depends on our ability to expound the real process of production, starting out from the material production of life itself, and to comprehend the form of intercourse connected with this and created by this mode of production (i.e. civil society in its various stages), as the basis of all history" (Marx, *German Ideology* 2.7). Such an important role has been attributed to Marxism as an approach to history that P.K. O'Brien identifies in Marx's "towering intellect," alongside with Max Weber's, the source for the "modern paradigms of investigation" (O'Brien 67) in the historical tradition which begun with Herodotus. Its founding role for many twentieth-century historical approaches is, in the line of this discussion, the most interesting aspect of Marxism because it promoted a discussion which is still, in some way, active, producing a variety of theories which allowed Western historiography to challenge its own role in a wider context, despite the mentioned Eurocentrism of the origins. This development has involved the work of authoritative philosophers, among whom Sartre, who extensively investigated the problems of history. He was still conditioned by a strong Eurocentrism, "for Sartre 'human history' was identified with the history of the West" (Young 42), but he was conscious of the particular circumstance of his theories: "Marxism is rigorously true if History is totalization; it is not so any more if human history decomposes into a plurality of particular histories" (Sartre, II 25; qtd. in Young 34). This is in fact true, and Lévi-Strauss's critique of Sartre's claim "to have established the human foundation of a 'structural, historical anthropology' for Marxism" (Young 42) exposed the biased concept of history as a totalisation, foregrounding the problems of ethnocentrism and Eurocentrism which recent post-colonial approaches have coped with. Lévi-Strauss raised another question important for post-colonial theories and particularly central to the discussion of Harris's concept of time: the code by which history, as a model of knowledge, analyses its object (the past), "this code consists in chronology" (Young 45). According to Young's interpretation of Lévi-Strauss's thought,

> The use of chronology in historical writing, or in literary history, gives the illusion that the whole operates by a uniform, continuous progression, a linear series in which each event takes its place. But in fact, Lévi-Strauss argues, the progress model of history is an illusion. (Young 45-46)

The assumption that "historical continuity is [...] often fraudulently constructed out of discontinuous sets which each have different temporalities" (Young 46), is particularly important if compared to the time-travelling narrative of Wilson Harris, as will be discussed later, and the discrediting of "a progressive totalization of totalizations [...] dependent on a notion of chronology which assumes a synchronic homogeneous notion of time" (Young 46) partially reflects Harris's vision of quantum parallel universes.

Successive critiques of Marxism include post-structuralist positions such as Althusser's, who "more than anyone else, appears to have attempted to eliminate history" (Young 53) in a process of rejection of history as a system of progression and evolution. In the formulation of his view, "Althusser found it difficult to maintain a Marxist theory of history while avoiding its customary Hegelian form" (Young 54), and exposed the interrelationship of the two philosophical views. On a deeper level, Althusser's concept of history and time, in a further expansion of Lévi-Strauss's seems to parallel Harris's even more:

unlike the Hegelian essential section, where each event can be shown to be in an essential articulation with the whole in a continuous and homogeneous spatio-temporality, a cross-section at any particular moment will show a heterogeneous array of presences and absences. (Young 56)

A further common feature between Althusser's philosophy and Wilson Harris's is shared also by another important figure for the problematisation of historical thought: Michel Foucault. In fact, according to Young, In his early works we can see that Foucault's position involves a remarkable development of Althusser's hints that art can function as a privileged category that provides an 'internal distance' from ideology by relating histories, writing reports" (72). The special role assumed by art in such a context is important for Hayden White's theories about the fictionality of history, confirming Gossman's view of the continuous relationship between history and literature. However, on a specific ground, Foucalut's contribution has a much wider range than this, and it focuses on other issues such as the division of history to serve the mentioned different temporalities in relation to specific disciplines. This is the case of, among others, *Histoire de la folie à l'âge classique – Folie et déraison* (1961) or *Histoire de la sexualité* (1976-1984) which exemplify "the notion of discrete temporalities, with a recognition of a historicity proper to each discipline or area of knowledge. Instead of a great historical narrative common to all, everything now ha[s] its own chronology and its own history" (Young 73). In Foucault's words:

> Ainsi sont apparues, à la place de cette chronologie continue de la raison, qu'on faisait invariablement remonter à l'inaccessible origine, à son ouverture fondatrice, des échelles parfois brèves, distinctes les unes des autres, rebelle à une loi unique, porteuses souvent d'un type d'histoire qui est propre à chacune, et irréductibles au modèle général d'une conscience qui acquiert, progresse et se souvient. (Foucault, *Archéologie* 16)

The already questioned unity and teleological quality of traditional history are here definitely negated by Foucault; in Paola Brusasco's words: "human history does not progress toward emancipation, but goes from domination to domination in a cyclical process" (45). The question of power also informs Foucault's critique of the subject:

> according to Foucault [...] the philosophy of the subject [...] was specifically introduced in order to provide a 'shelter for the sovereignty of consciousness' against the intrusion of heterogeneity. Foucault demonstrates how the individual is constituted through specific technologies of power. (Young 79)

As will be analysed further on, power, and even more technology are, for Wilson Harris, important elements in the definition of the historical subject. His rejection of single, individual subjects/characters, particularly in *The Infinite Rehearsal* (1987), functions, in my opinion, as a representation of the intrusion of heterogeneity which challenges the pretension, in Foucaldian terms, of "the sovereignty of consciousness."

The analysis of the relationship between knowledge and power, foregrounded by Michel Foucault, has revealed the mechanisms by which dominant ideologies have shaped the past to justify themselves in the present, with particular evidence in the case of the linear, cause-effect narratives that characterised traditional Western historiography. As will emerge further on, this critical attitude has generated a new awareness among historians, as is the case with Hayden White, who tend to acknowledge the ineffectiveness, at least, of such universalising grand narratives. Moreover, the concept of history as archaeology and the consequent integration of discontinuity into historical research have permanently broken the assumptions of "homogeneous relations and rational causality" (Brusasco 48) which characterised the unproblematic, traditional approaches. The function of ideology, identified by Foucault in the biased reconstruction of such a fragmentation, as proposed by totalising histories, has ultimately undermined the eighteenth/nineteenth-century theorisation of a "natural" teleological development of history, whether in terms of Hegelian Spirit or of Marxist class struggle.

Successively, the themes of fragmentation and problematisation have been central to the postmodernist discourse about history. Frederick Jameson refers to traditional historiography as "that first, now unavailable option of nineteenth-century realism, of history in its immediacy" (Young 106), rejecting the unproblematic assumption about the transparency of representation mentioned above, but he opposes Foucault's ideas in proposing a step backwards to Marxist totalisations:

> Only Marxism can give us an adequate account for the essential *mystery* of the cultural past... This mystery can be re-enacted

> only if the human adventure is one... These matters can recover their original urgency for us only if they are retold within the unity of a single great collective story... only if they are grasped as vital episodes in a single vast unfinished plot. (Jameson 19-20)

Such a "retreat" from Foucault's positions is comparable, despite the explicit differences he always highlights, to Wilson Harris's vision of the globality of history, which in a way manifests "a positive direction" (Harris, interview by Riach 20). Therefore, the seemingly overtaken teleological aspect of history is still an object of discussion: it will be analysed that Harris's vision presents elements of unity but avoids any dogmatism, as it is open to all possibilities, and reflects a completely different background.

Postmodernism has often been put in relation to post-colonialism, but as in Harris's case, this relationship has been quite controversial. Among other examples, Jameson's statements about "Third-World" literatures have been criticised by post-colonial intellectuals, Aijaz Ahmad in particular. Jameson stated that "all third-world texts are necessarily... to be read as... national allegories" (Ahmad 78) provoking Ahmad's reaction which maintains, quite convincingly, that such an assumption is tainted by the ideology of nationalism, not very dissimilarly from Hegel's vision of Africa.[11] In fact, Ahmad criticises the definition of 'Third World' "exclusively in terms of 'the experience of colonialism and imperialism'" (78) on the basis that it renews colonial dependency and denies legitimation, promoting the division of the world "between those who make history and those who are mere objects of it" (78). The kind of unity Ahmad suggests, which ironically counterparts Jameson's mentioned concept of "single great collective story," shows radically different premises, partially meeting Harris's own position: "we live not in three worlds but in one; [...] this world includes the experience of colonialism and imperialism on both sides of Jameson's global divide" (80). These episodes show how general assumptions about postmodernism, such as "postmodernism can best be defined as European culture's awareness that it is no longer the unquestioned and dominant centre of the world" (Young 19), or "postmodernism [...] involves the loss of the sense of an absoluteness of any Western account of History" (Young 19), have to be problematised, in the same way as more overtly Eurocentric schools of thought.

---

11 Young highlights how "Jameson may deride the argument that links Hegelian forms of thought to nineteenth- and twentieth-century European history, but his own use of Hegel is striking in this context" (114).

However, postmodernism is part of a growing trend towards a sort of de-centring of historical thought with the recognition of different, non-Western systems and through the inner analysis and de-construction of Western historical discourse. External contributions will be analysed in the following section, while other inner critical approaches, such as deconstruction, will be here briefly mentioned, leaving space to the work of Hayden White which has been identified, among its contemporaries, as the most relevant for this study.

According to Tejaswini Niranjana,

> [an] aspect of post-structuralism that is significant[...] is its critique of historicism, which shows the genetic (searching for an origin) and teleological (posing a certain end) nature of traditional historiography. 'Historicism' really represents as *natural* that which is *historical* (and therefore neither inevitable nor unchangeable). (10)

The exposition of unproblematic approaches seems to be an important point in post-structuralist critiques of historical writing and this is even more true for deconstruction. De Man's critique of traditional historicism was supported by the provocative assumption that "we are all 'orthodox Hegelians'" (Niranjana 25, quoting De Man, 1982), which resets the centrality of the teleological scheme of Hegelian or Marxist history. Lyotard, as Young reports, has often been sceptical towards historicist universal narratives, "advocating instead the possibility of a multiplicity of heterogeneous, conflicting and incommensurable histories" (Young 63). This has also been Derrida's main concern about history, in his insistence on speaking about "the need to *reinscribe* the notion of history by revealing its discontinuous and heterogeneous nature" (Niranjana 161), therefore negating the aforementioned unity: "origin is always heterogeneous" (Lawlor).

Thus, it can be said that the fragmentation of history first observed in Foucault's theories is here brought to the very nature of historical writing, therefore denying any kind of total or progressive history.

Similar issues can be traced in the writings of Louis O. Mink, Lionel Gossman, Hayden White, which come to the rejection of traditional history-writing through a different path, less linked to pure philosophy and closer to historiography, showing a deep concern with narration and fiction/facts relationships, thus building a bridge, as has already been mentioned, towards literature.

As analysed above, within Western academies, particularly in the context of the discussions concerning postmodernism and post-structuralism, the meaning of history and the practice of historiography have been investigated under a new light, revealing the flaws in the totalising attitude that had characterised the evolution of this discipline since the Enlightenment, culminating in the grand narratives of the late nineteenth century. Foucault's abovementioned discussion of the relationship between knowledge and power reveals the mechanisms by which dominant ideologies have shaped the past to justify themselves in the present. The relevance of such an assumption for Hayden White's analysis of Western historiography is made evident when he writes: "in short, it is possible to view historical consciousness as a specifically Western prejudice by which the presumed superiority of modern, industrial society can be retroactively substantiated" (*Metahistory* 2). However, to uncover the arbitrary assumption of objectivity claimed by Western totalising histories, White does not limit his discussion to the agency of power over history, but he addresses the very process by which this is made possible. History is made to serve a particular ideology thanks to its intrinsic narrative quality, which reveals its inner fictional nature:

> historical situations do not have built into them intrinsic meanings [...]. How a given historical situation is to be configured depends on the historian's subtlety in matching up a specific plot-structure with the set of historical events that he wishes to endow with a meaning of a particular kind. This is a literary, that is to say fiction-making, operation. (White, "Historical Text" 48)

On these premises, White builds a convincing analysis of historical writing, based on the concept that "a given historian is forced to emplot the whole set of stories making up his narrative in one comprehensive or *archetypal* story form" (*Metahistory* 8). He begins by distinguishing five "levels of conceptualization," namely: "(1) chronicle; (2) story; (3) mode of emplotment; (4) mode of argument; and (5) mode of ideological implication" (*Metahistory* 5). By distinguishing chronicles, which are "strictly speaking, open-ended" and "have no inaugurations," as they "simply 'begin' when the chronicler starts recording events. And they have no culminations or resolutions" (*Metahistory* 6), he specifies the concept of "stories" which have "a discernible form which marks off the events contained in them from the other events that might appear in a comprehensive chronicle" (*Metahistory* 6). That is to say, as White himself eventually clarifies in a footnote, the level on which 'invention' intervenes is that of "story," being also the level on which historical and fictional writing overlap. Therefore, histories, as a selection of events in the chronicles, are at a certain point considered as "the *entire set of events*" (*Metahistory* 7) from which questions emerge such as "what does it all add up to?" or "what is the point of it all?" (*Metahistory* 6). The possible answers to these questions are analysed and categorised by White in the three modes mentioned above.

The first, the mode of "explanation by emplotment," borrows some concepts from Northrop Frye's *Anatomy of Criticism* (1965) in identifying "four different modes: Romance, Tragedy, Comedy, and Satire" in which historians emplot their narrative account of "what happened."

Without excluding others, such as the Epic – which, however, "would appear to be the implicit form of chronicle itself" (*Metahistory* 8) – and allowing particular stories to switch between these modes, White discusses the four modes with actual examples of classical works of history, demonstrating the validity, in the field of historiography, of these traditionally literary critical tools.

Secondly, "explanation by formal argument," which is the more relevant conceptualisation for this discussion, is presented by White as the level on which the historian "may seek to explicate 'the point of it all' or 'what it all adds up to'" (*Metahistory* 11). This is the level on which causal relationships are assumed as leading principles in historical evolution, in other words, this is the place where the traditional teleological views of history are grounded:

> On this level of conceptualization, the historian explains the events in the story (or the form of the events which he has imposed upon them through his emplotment of them in a particular mode) by construction of a nomological-deductive argument. This argument can be analyzed into a syllogism, the major premise of which consists of some putatively universal law of causal relationships, the minor premise of the boundary conditions within which the law is applied, and a conclusion in which the events that actually occurred are deduced from the premises by logical necessity. (*Metahistory* 11)

White differentiates "four paradigms," "Formist, Organicist, Mechanistic, and Contextualist" (*Metahistory* 13), which will not be discussed here in depth. It will suffice to characterise each of them with a brief explanation: the 'Formist' paradigm is to be found "in any historiography in which the depiction of variety, color, and vividness of the historical field is taken as the central aim of the historian's work" (*Metahistory* 14); the Organicist one depicts "the particulars discerned in the historical field as components of synthetic processes [obeying] a metaphysical commitment to the paradigm of the microcosmic-macrocosmic relationship" (*Metahistory* 15); Mechanists conceive the objects in the historical field "as existing in the modality of part-part relationships, the specific configurations of which are determined by the laws that are presumed to govern their interactions" (*Metahistory* 17); as regards Contextualism, it is informed by the presupposition that "events can be explained by being set within the 'context' of their occurrence" the explanation of their occurrence is revealed by "the specific relationships they bore to other events occurring in their circumambient historical space" (*Metahistory* 17-18). According to White, all of these four models may be used with equal authority, but this has not been the case of traditional historiography, where "Formism and Contextualism have represented the limits of choice among the possible forms" (*Metahistory* 20). As will emerge again later, Organicist and Mechanistic views have characterised the relegation to "the nefarious 'philosophy of history'" (*Metahistory* 20) of their practitioners, on the basis of their presumed less scientific quality. According to White, who opposes this attitude, "there does, in fact, appear to be an irreducible ideological component in every historical account of reality [...] simply because history is not a science" (*Metahistory* 21).

This last assumption will be discussed shortly, while here it is useful to confront the pervasiveness of ideology to Foucault's ideas, and contextually point out the quite dissimilar conception of ideology White makes use of, i.e. "a set of prescriptions for taking a position in the present world of social praxis and acting upon it (either to change the world or to maintain it in its current state)" (*Metahistory* 22). Referring directly to Karl Mannheim, White starts by exposing the last level of conceptualisation, explanation by ideological implication, by borrowing a simplified version of Mannheim's classification of ideologies, with four basic positions: Anarchism, Conservatism, Radicalism, and Liberalism.[12] For the sake of fluency, a discussion of each term will be left aside, given the relative correspondence of their contingent signification and their current meaning, but a general consideration must be reported: these terms "are meant to

---

12 The criteria for this selection are extensively discussed by White in a footnote on page 22. However it is useful to report the main reason: "In short, the nineteenth-century forms of Anarchism, Conservatism, Radicalism, and Liberalism are 'cognitively responsible' in a way that their 'authoritarian' counterparts are not" (*Metahistory* 22).

serve as designators of general ideological preference, rather than as emblems of specific political parties" (*Metahistory* 24).

The three modes of explanation discussed earlier contribute in White's view to the construction of a specific historiographical style. Their combination, however, is not indiscriminate: "there are, as it were, elective affinities among the various modes that might be used" (*Metahistory* 29). Therefore, there appear to be privileged combinations, which depend, according to White, on a "prefigurative act," a "*poetic* act" which is "indistinguishable from the linguistic act" (*Metahistory* 30). This is a central point in White's theory, because "in the poetic act which precedes the formal analysis of the field, the historian both creates his object of analysis and predetermines the modalities of conceptual strategies he will use to explain it" (*Metahistory* 31). If the historiographical explanation is comparable to poetic language, it is possible to analyse it with the same four principal tropes: Metaphor, Metonymy, Synecdoche, Irony. To better follow White's argument it is necessary to report his definition of these tropes:

> Irony, Metonymy, and Synecdoche are kinds of Metaphor, but they differ from one another in the kinds of *reductions* or *integrations* they effect on the literal level of their meanings and by the kinds of illuminations they aim at on a figurative level. Metaphor is essentially *representational*, Metonymy is *reductionist*, Synecdoche is *integrative*, and Irony is *negational*. (*Metahistory* 34)

According to White's formalist analysis, there can be seen a close connection between particular tropes and three of the four modes of explanation by formal argument, where "Metaphor is representational in the way that Formism can be seen to be. Metonymy is reductive in a Mechanistic manner, while Synecdoche is integrative in the way that Organicism is" (*Metahistory* 36). The fourth trope, Irony, is White's favourite and he characterises it by its "metatropological" quality, "for it is deployed in the self-conscious awareness of the possible misuse of figurative language" (*Metahistory* 37). Irony is also presented in relation to the other conceptualisations by contrasting it with "the 'naïve' formulations of the Formist, Mechanistic, and Organicist strategies of explanation" (*Metahistory* 38), and the antagonism of Satire, its fictional form, is remarked in relation to Romance, Comedy, and Tragedy.

With its consistently fictional nature, the Ironic attitude towards history has not enjoyed particular success, especially after the Enlightenment, when history's claim to objectivity and scientificity was still unquestioned. It is with the "crisis of historicism," as identified by White in the consequences of Nietzsche's and Marx's theories, that it emerged again, thanks to Benedetto Croce's response to this crisis, which according to White, in spite of its intended aim, "succeeded [...] in historicizing philosophy, thereby rendering it as Ironically self-conscious of its limitations as historiography itself had become" (*Metahistory* 38).

Despite White's conclusion, which tends to the historicisation of art and philosophy, what is relevant to this discussion is the effective treatment of the subject of history through mainly literary devices, which, apart from demonstrating how "the same basic modalities of conceptualisation appear in both philosophy of history and historiography" (*Metahistory* 42), reveal a much more articulated nature for history than that of a scientific discipline. In fact, the conceptualizations of the modes of explanation reveal the process of selection and invention which characterises historical writing, and the structural function of the linguistic tropes allows the insertion of different ways of approaching the past, which, for the sake of scientificity, have long been despised, such as memory, art and myth. In this context it is possible to see Wilson Harris's works regarding time, myth, and memory as a sort of historical accounts, concerning forgotten cultures and native traditions: this will be extensively analysed in chapter 4. Here, a further support to this view can be found in the briefly mentioned critique of the presumed and often claimed scientific nature of history. Earlier in time, in the field of history the presumed objectivity of narration had already been challenged on various grounds, since R.G. Collingwood identified the main issue in the differentiation of historical writing from fiction writing on the basis of the need of the former for "evidence" and consistency of time and place: "there is only one historical world" (Collingwood 246), while fictional realities need not agree and cannot clash, because of their dependence on a completely free imagination. This is still the main argument for those who tend to promote the scientific side of the discipline of history, but it also offers the clues for White's specific critique of the same aspect, which reveals, at best, a proto-scientific methodology for history writing. Gossman's assumption on this topic similarly sets fiction writing and historical narration on common ground, echoing Lévi-Strauss's considerations about time: "space and time are not absolute but are themselves defined by the historian [...]." They "do not appear to be objective realities that found the historian's work and differentiate it from the imaginary writings of the novelists" (Gossman 30). As emerged from the analysis of White's introduction to *Metahistory* (1973), this appears to be supported by the fact that the very act of writing "always implies selection, organisation, signification and the making of meaning" (Gossman 18). Therefore, no writing process, historical as much as fictional, can claim authority on the basis of a "found" meaning, pre-existent in a presumed objective reality, despite the diehard unproblematic attitude of the majority of historical thinking before Marx. The critique of traditional historiography promoted by Gossman, White, etc. works on two different levels: on a deeper level, as discussed above, the very nature of history writing is presented as closely interconnected with narrativity and therefore compared to fiction-writing, but at a higher level these scholars expose the lack of foundation of the claims for a preeminently scientific quality of the discipline of history through a relatively simple comparison. Collingwood's assumptions are discussed and scientifically confuted by simply comparing them with "really" scientific disciplines, thus bringing up the fundamental points of the unity of the "historical world" and of the agreement of historians over it:

> the physical sciences appear to progress by virtue of the agreements, reached from time to time among members of the established communities of scientists [...]. But history differs from the sciences precisely because historians disagree, not only over what are the laws of social causation that they might invoke to explain a given sequence of events, but also over the question of the form that a 'scientific' explanation ought to take. [...] Among historians no such agreement exists. (White, *Metahistory* 12)

> This may merely reflect the protoscientific nature of the historiographical enterprise, but it is important to bear in mind this congenital disagreement (or lack of agreement) over what counts as a specifically historical explanation of any given set of historical phenomena. [...] History remains in the state of conceptual anarchy in which the natural sciences existed during the sixteenth century, when there were as many different conceptions of 'the scientific enterprise' as there were metaphysical positions. (*Metahistory* 13)

The equal status of history and fiction is thus demonstrated by the inadequacy of history as a purely scientific discipline and by the belonging of the two to a common "critical world" in which categories, tropes and modes serve with equal efficiency to explain the processes of history writing and fiction writing, for they make use of a common "poetic language."

It must be acknowledged, at this point, that apart from Nietzsche, in the Western philosophical tradition of history there can be found some examples of historical poetic language used with profound awareness: such is the case, among others, of Walter Benjamin. The Jewish writer, whose particular vision of historical materialism distinguishes his work from other more orthodox Marxist philosophies of history, presents, through a language characterised by mysticism and allusions, a series of short meditations on history, commonly known as *On the Concept of History* or *Theses on the Philosophy of History*, which are held to be his last completed piece of writing, dating around 1940. A messianic language and specifically Jewish themes, linked with Marxist revolutionary politics, characterise the eighteen "theses," in which Benjamin draws a bleak picture of the role of man in history and overtly criticizes progress, especially in the renowned ninth thesis. This is where Benjamin takes inspiration from a painting, as Wilson Harris often does,[13] to build a visionary interpretation:

> A Klee painting named 'Angelus Novus' shows an angel looking as though he is about to move away from something he is fixedly contemplating. His eyes are staring, his mouth is open, his wings are spread. This is how one pictures the angel of history. His face is turned towards the past. Where we receive a chain of events, he sees one single catastrophe which keeps piling wreckage upon wreckage and hurls it in front of his feet. The angel would like to stay, awaken the dead, and make whole what has been smashed. But a storm is blowing from Paradise; it has got caught in his wings with such violence that the angel can no longer close them. This storm irresistibly propels him into the future to which his back is turned, while the pile of debris before him grows skyward. This storm is what we call progress. (Benjamin, "Angelus Novus"; qtd. in Walder 364)[14]

---

13 It is useful to remember the above mentioned discussion of Titian's "Allegory of Prudence" and the frequent inclusion of painters and paintings in the works of fiction, as in *Da Silva da Silva's Cultivated Wilderness* (1977) or more recently in *The Mask of the Beggar* (2003), among others.

14 Es gibt ein Bild von Klee, das Angelus Novus heißt. Ein Engel ist darauf dargestellt, der aussieht, als wäre er im Begriff, sich von etwas zu entfernen, worauf er starrt. Seine Augen sind aufgerissen, sein Mund steht offen und seine Flügel sind ausgespannt. Der Engel der Geschichte muß so aussehen. Er hat das Antlitz der Vergangenheit zugewendet. Wo eine Kette von

As a conclusion, coming back to Hayden White's discussion of the fictional nature of history, it is possible to acknowledge a new trend in historiography based on the rejection of the concept of neutral, scientific objectivity:

> narrative is not merely a neutral discursive form that may or may not be used to represent real events in their aspect as developmental processes but rather entails ontological and epistemic choices with distinct ideological and even specifically political implications. Many modern historians hold that narrative discourse, far from being a neutral medium for the representation of historical events and processes, is the very stuff of a mythical view of reality, a conceptual or pseudoconceptual "content" which, when used to represent real events, endows them with an illusory coherence and charges them with the kinds of meanings more characteristic of oneiric than of waking thought. (White, *Content* ix)

Among the "many modern historians," it is possible to identify two figures, Michel de Certau and Paul Ricoeur, who fit into White's scenery, as they oppose, more or less directly, the other modern trend of historiography, which sees the French group of the *Annales* (LeGoff, Braudel, etc.) being "most critical of narrative history" and "social-scientifically oriented" (White, *Content* ix). Especially Ricoeur, in the philosophical effort of building a "metaphysics of narrativity," identifies a few key points which reflect, as will be analysed, some aspects of Wilson Harris's approach, such as the importance of temporality, especially regarding "the plural unity of future, past, and present" (Ricoeur 171), and its strict relationship with language. According to White, Ricoeur worked on the "reconceptualization of the possible relations existing between the three principal kinds of narrative discourse – mythic, historical, and fictional – and the 'real world' to which they undeniably referred" (*Content* 170), granting a "cognitive

---

> Begebenheiten vor uns erscheint, da sieht er eine einzige Katastrophe, die unablässig Trümmer auf Trümmer häuft und sie ihm vor die Füße schleudert. Er möchte wohl verweilen, die Toten wecken und das Zerschlagene zusammenfügen. Aber ein Sturm weht vom Paradiese her, der sich in seinen Flügeln verfangen hat und so stark ist, daß der Engel sie nicht mehr schließen kann. Dieser Sturm treibt ihn unaufhaltsam in die Zukunft, der er den Rücken kehrt, während der Trümmerhaufen vor ihm zum Himmel wächst. Das, was wir den Fortschritt nennen, ist dieser Sturm. (Benjamin, "Über den Begriff der Geschichte" 697)

authority" (170) to both mythical and fictional narratives, and insisting on the common "ultimate referent" that history and literature share: in White's words, "a considerable advancement over previous discussions of the relations between history and literature" (*Content* 175). This is not the place for a thorough discussion of Ricoeur's complex philosophy; however, in the discussion of Harris's concept of time and of his mythical views, particular aspects may be usefully considered.

Regarding de Certeau, it is important to report the definition of heterology, under which his philosophy of history can be described: "heterology is a term that has come to designate a philosophical countertradition that, in short hand, could be described as being deeply suspicious of the Parmenidean principle of the identity of thought and being" (de Certeau vii). As will be clarified later, the connection is evident with Harris's literary strategy of dividing the characters into alter-egos, thus realising in many of his novels this kind of disgregation, which nevertheless finds a new unity, not exclusively human. Moreover, his study of the interconnection of historiography and psychoanalysis partly reflects what will be said further on about the possible connections of some points of Jung's theories and Harris's view of the past; and the importance given by de Certeau to language, with large recourse to Lacanian theories, can be paralleled to the role of language in Harris's philosophy. De Certeau's relevance is not limited to these particular connections, but, on a broader scale, it addresses the post-colonial world in general with direct considerations about the process of decolonisation, especially regarding the other/same relationship.

The political implications alluded to by White and the philosophical achievements stating the equal status of fiction writing and history as recently theorised within Western academies assume a powerful importance if considered in relation to the post-colonial condition in which realities that were denied official history have often claimed their own histories with the use of fictional devices. The non-Western situation and some specific cases of historical thinking rooted in other areas than the West, such as the Caribbean, will be the object of the following section, while here, a final consideration may bring together the issues discussed above. As a reply to White's popular theories, David Carr has formulated a convincing interpretation of the relationship between history and fiction. From Carr's point of view White's assumptions can generate a controversy which may not actually reflect the interdependency of history and fiction in the representation of the past; he states that following White's ideas "might lead to the conclusion that the distinction between history and fiction must be abandoned. I think this would be a mistake" (Carr). This might seem to conflict with the main issues discussed above, but Carr's reframing of the problem will prove particularly useful to support the historical role of Harris's fictional writing. By quoting R. Barthes, L.O. Mink, and H. White, he presents the contemporary controversy which, as discussed above, limits the scientific value of historical narration by recognising the structural role of fiction in its production. Carr argues that this may be true, but its implications should be reconsidered. There is no doubt that contemporary scholars tend to agree that "From the time it was firmly established in the academy, history has striven to maintain its respectability as a 'scientific' discipline [...]. But this attempt to make history into a science has never been very convincing" (Carr, ch. 1), as has clearly emerged in this discussion. However, according to Carr, even for White or Ricoeur there is still a view of history as "asserting its capacity to 'represent' the past 'as it really was,' i.e. as claiming 'scientific' status for its results" (Carr, ch. 1). As a solution for this ambiguity, Carr proposes an interesting interpretation at a cognitive level, which gives this whole analysis a clearer direction. First, the mentioned ambiguity should be expressed in Carr's terms: "Barthes, Mink et al., emphasize those features of historical discourse which differentiate it from scientific explanation, but instead of defending history as a legitimate cognitive enterprise in its own right, they challenge its cognitive pretensions" (Carr, ch. 2). Carr formulates a response on three different grounds, but here only the role of imagination will be considered, being the most relevant to this study. According to Carr,

> The second tacit assumption of this view [White's] [...] involves a strong opposition between knowledge and imagination. Knowledge is a passive mirroring of reality. Imagination, by contrast, is active and creative, and if imagination gets involved in the process of knowing, and actively creates something in the process, the result can no longer qualify as knowledge. (ch. 2)

From another perspective a different approach could be taken towards the cognitive role of imagination, which can be supportive rather than impedimental to "knowledge":

> The capacity to imagine is opposed to knowledge as if they were mutually exclusive. Knowledge as "representation" is thought to be the passive reflection of the real, simply registering or reporting what is there. But this is a naïve and simplistic conception of

knowledge which ignores some of the best insights in modern philosophy. Since Kant we have recognized that knowledge is anything but passive, its result not merely a copy of external reality. Rather, it is an activity which calls into play many "faculties" including sense, judgement, reason, and, very importantly, the capacity to conceive of things being other than they actually are. It may be thought that anything that is the object of the imagination must be imaginary in the sense of non-existent. But this is only part of what we mean by imagination. In the broadest sense, imagination is best described as the capacity to envision what is not directly present to the senses. In this sense we can imagine things that were, or will be, or exist elsewhere, as well as things that don't exist at all. (Carr, ch. 2b)

This leads to an important extension of the concept of history, in which facts and time assume a different hierarchy in relation with subjectivity:

Indeed, in this realm time itself is human, narratively shaped by beings who live their lives, not from moment to moment, but by remembering what was and projecting what will be. Although it is assuredly embedded in the physical world and is datable, human time is not that of the numbered sequence [...] or even the time of the before and after, earlier and later, but the time of past and future as experienced from the vantage point of the present by conscious, intentional agents. (Carr, ch. 2c)

This vision, which derives from a long tradition of investigation into history and historiography in the West, up to H. White, P. Ricoeur, D. Carr et al., and comes into a new relationship with non-Western views, is the point of contact with Harris's concept of history and time, as it emerges from his works. It bridges, in a truly cross-cultural way, the pre-Columbian elements of Harris's tradition, which, as will be argued in chapter 4, extend the "human time" up to a more inclusive "time of the world," and the unconscious elements which will emerge in the chapter about Jungian interpretations of Harris's works, under the spell of the "creative imagination."

2.1.2 Non-Western Traditions of History

Outside the West, the discussion concerning history has not been less profound. Because of the role of historical objects, in Hegelian terms, attributed to the colonised by an Imperial power which proclaimed itself as the sole agent of history, the relationship of colonial and prominently post-colonial societies with history has been discussed with particular emphasis during the peak of the decolonisation process, when many former colonies gained their independence. For this reason, the theme of history has been felt in the post-colonial world urgently and on a more specifically political ground. This urgency is grounded in the fact that history has been used, as mentioned above, as "a prominent, if not *the* prominent, instrument for the control of subject people" (Ashcroft et al., *Reader* 355) and the struggle for independence and identity has seen the appropriation of a denied history as a fundamental achievement for the affirmation of a legitimate existence. The negation of histories other than a totalising and exclusive "History" has been, as discussed above, a frequent attitude in the West particularly during the colonial period. This exclusion, which has progressively revealed its persistence in the consideration of the liberated colonies, has often been regarded as a key issue in the determining of post-colonial identities. The problem posed by Foucault about what it means to have a history assumes a new significance if considered in a broader context than the West: if "to have a history is the same as what it means to have a legitimate existence" (Ashcroft et al., *Reader* 355), by negating the right to history the very existence of post-colonial realities is questioned.

Each particular reality has developed a different strategy to claim back its own history, and in the course of this chapter some of the most important will be mentioned; however, the unifying function of the common colonial experience will be kept in mind. In practice, one first unitary quality of post-colonial historical discourses is the vehement questioning, promoted by non-Western writers and historians, of "the myth of the story of history as a simple representation of the continuity of events, [...] a single narrative truth which was 'simply' the closest possible representation of events" (Ashcroft et al., *Reader* 355) which supports the exclusive representation of Western identity. On the other side, considering the many differences, the necessary revision of history applied to such heterogeneous realities as those included within the term "post-colonial" leads inevitably to a split into particular histories. This fragmentation may reflect some aspects and critical attitudes of postmodernism, but the urgency for the recognition of an active role in the histories of their own countries and in the history of the world, as felt by post-colonial subjects, has a profoundly political nature that comes not from recent critical speculation but from prolonged political oppression. As already mentioned above, the oppressive nature of Western historical discourse has recently been recognised also within the West and it has been clearly expressed by Hayden White in the definition of historical consciousness as Western prejudice, serving the present ideology.

Since the first literary works by non-European writers in English were published and gained a substantial readership, the centrality of the theme of history has been evident, but the great number of realities that emerge from the former British colonies suggests a less consistent and single-sided critique of the subject of history than the theories generated in a relatively consistent West. For instance, literatures from the Caribbean and from the Indian subcontinent have contributed, with different issues, to particularly effective re-readings of history, delineating respectively an original "poeticist"[15] approach, as emerged in the previous discussion of Henry's *Caliban's Reason*, and a revolutionary strategy for provincialising the self-assumed centrality of Europe. This last strategy, labelled after Gramsci's term "subaltern studies," has assumed the responsibility of a struggle on the very field of traditional Western historiography, while the other positions examined here share a generally literary nature. However, the group of the "subaltern studies," represented by Ranajit Guha, Dipesh Chakrabarty, Gayatri Chakravorty Spivak (to a certain extent), and others, makes use of non-traditional devices, "antihistorical devices of memory and antihistorical 'histories' of the subaltern classes" (Chakrabarty 384), and can be seen, in a way, as a parallel, theoretical development of the issues that influence the work of some contemporary Indian novelists, such as Amitav Ghosh or, in some aspects, even Salman Rushdie. Fragmentation, memory and partiality are recurring elements in this view of the narration of history. Among the mentioned members, Spivak is more grounded in philosophical and literary discussion, where she enjoys widespread international academic credit, despite her sometimes foggy style, which reflects the deconstructivist influences consistently contributing to her approach, since her translation of and preface to Derrida's *Of Grammatology* (1976). Nevertheless, she contributed to the work of the "subaltern studies" group on many occasions, the best known of which certainly is the arti-

---

15 Here the poeticist approach is favoured over the "historicist" for the arbitrary reason that it appears to be the more original and typical of the two, assuming that Caribbean "historicism" is indebted both to Western academic traditions and to Marxism while "poeticism," according to Henry, appears as more "endemic" to the region.

cle "Can the Subaltern Speak?," published in 1988, in which the actual impossibility of the subaltern to speak is theorised.

At this point a very brief overview of Spivak's positions will suffice. In the article mentioned above, Spivak sets up a controversy with part of postmodern and post-structuralist thought opposing, on a strictly philosophical ground, particular views about the experience of oppression, historically linked to the experience of colonialism. In simple words, she argues that the concepts of power, ideology, and desire, as proposed by Foucault and Deleuze, tend to reintroduce a totalising view which does not take into account "the micrological textures of power," (Spivak, "Subaltern" 279) re-proposing a generalised idea of "culture." Through a complex analysis of the rite of self-immolation of Indian women, a quintessential "subaltern" subject, and the British policy towards it, she theorises that the subaltern has no possibility of speaking because he/she, according to the Foucaldian critique of the subject, is always conditioned by the granting of speech from the outside which invariably encounters the main problems of a) a logocentric assumption of cultural solidarity among a heterogeneous people, and b) a dependence upon Western intellectuals to "speak for" the subaltern condition rather than allowing them to speak for themselves. In conclusion, "as Spivak argues, by speaking out and reclaiming a collective cultural identity, subalterns will in fact re-inscribe their subordinate position in society" (Graves).

Spivak's article, despite its pessimism, actually supports the work of Ranajit Guha and the "subaltern" group, who, in fact, explicitly declare the aim of giving word to the dispossessed. A more positive position is taken by Dipesh Chakrabarty, who has brought up, in a more historiographical context, an interesting project labelled "the provincialization of Europe." This project starts from the assumption that regarding history as a discourse produced at the institutional site of university, "'Europe' remains the sovereign theoretical subject of all histories, including the ones we call 'Indian,' 'Chinese,' 'Kenyan,' and so on" (Chakrabarty 383). This reflects, in a way, the informing principles of Spivak's article, which see a non-Western history in a position of "subalterneity," due to the place of its representation, Western academic discourse, which inevitably renders it a projection of "the history of Europe." Chakrabarty, however, agrees with Homi Bhabha, when he sees the only possibility for Indian self-representation in the strategy of "mimicry." Bhabha's theories will be touched upon later on, while the consequences of Chakrabarty's position need to be analysed here. The consideration of "antihistorical 'histories,'" where the "peasant/worker constructions of 'mythical' kingdoms and 'mythical' pasts/futures find a place" (Chakrabarty 383), reveals, in line with Spivak's article, their inevitable subordination: "The antihistorical, antimodern subject, therefore, cannot speak itself as 'theory' within the knowledge procedures of the university even when these knowledge procedures acknowledge and 'document' its existence" (Chakrabarty 384).

This is an important point to consider when, as will be theorised later on, fiction writing is used as a form of historical writing, taking advantage of the already reported flaws which emerged in totalising Western historical discourses. Here, however, the solution proposed by Chakrabarty works on a fairly different ground: if non-Western history is completely dependent, and it is understood that "'we' all do 'European' history" (384), it is possible, through a conscious use of the strategy of "mimicry," to promote a sort of "politics and project of alliance between the dominant metropolitan histories and the subaltern peripheral past" (384). This is what Chakrabarty calls "the provincialization of 'Europe.'" According to him, this is achieved by "writing into the history of modernity the ambivalences, contradictions, the use of force, and the ironies that attend it" (386). The first step is to reveal the connection of the importance of history, and its role in Western societies as "a compulsory part of education of the modern person," with the rise of the nation-state. As has emerged earlier, the second wave of colonialism and the spread of Hegelian totalising ideas of a teleological history of the world found their roots in the late eighteenth-century rise of the nation-state, whose model has been exported to and imposed on the colonies. Chakrabarty's awareness that "nation-states have the capacity to enforce their truth games, and universities [...] are part of the battery of institutions complicit in this process" (384-385) complicates the strategy of alliance mentioned before, but it explains very convincingly how the importance of history is neither natural nor innocent: "Why should children all over the world today have to come to terms with a subject called 'history' when we know that this compulsion is neither natural nor ancient?" (384).

This first step in the relativisation of European history by negating its universality reflects, partially, what has recently happened in the internal debate presented above, but it also gives voice to a widespread situation which sees the fundamental importance of history as a discipline, a privileged way of narrating the past, as a typically Western obsession. In a recent lecture given at the University of Turin, Amitav Ghosh, who has worked with the "subaltern" group publishing a famous article in *Subaltern Studies* (Ghosh, "Slave"), and very frequently includes historical issues in his novels, spoke exhaustively about history and fiction and clearly remarked how "the study of the past has not historically been an important concern in Indian society, [...] history has never been at the heart of our society" (Ghosh, "Talk" 81). Rather than confirming the tendency to sometimes overrate the role of the discipline of history in non-Western cultures, Ghosh represents the figure of an artist who effectively works on the border of fiction and traditional historiography, including several "facts" and documents in his novels. The case of *In an Antique Land* (1992) is typical, since it draws on Ghosh's own anthropological work, which informs the article mentioned above, and on his knowledge of Arabic, to re-build the reality of a village in Egypt and the travels from Tunis to India of Ben Yiju, a Jewish merchant. In a later novel, *The Calcutta Chromosome* (1996), real historical documents and facts are used again, to build a story that functions as a counterpart of the official version of the discovery of the cause of malaria. Ghosh's work is particularly relevant to this discussion because he represents an authoritative example of a writer who mixes fiction writing and historiography without the excessive reverence towards the scientificity of the subject of history which characterises European attitudes and often limits the post-colonial claims for legitimation.

This kind of involvement in the struggle for the recognition of a proper history, whose difference emerges as much in philosophical and cognitive bases as in different modes of narration, is widely shared among post-colonial writers, who, far from exclusively writing about "national allegories," often include the history of their country, of their particular characters, or the interconnection of both, in a project of re-writing Eurocentric or simply "official" versions of the past. In this light, the case of Wilson Harris will be extensively analysed, but the number of writers who adopt this strategy, with infinitely differentiated methods and results, is extremely large. Salman Rushdie's *Midnight's Children* (1981), despite its distance from the "subaltern" group's object of interest, can be considered, among others, for its alternative telling of India's history, including partition, the assassination of Mahatma Gandhi, and more recent political issues, such as the "Emergency period," where the discrepancies with the official version are more evident. The rethinking and the retelling of history can be considered as a feature common to post-colonial intellectuals and fiction writers because, despite the particular attitudes of their different cultures towards it, it has been culturally imposed by the experience of colonialism, and the issue vehemently emerged during the process of de-colonisation. Outside the English-speaking world, during 1960, Frantz Fanon, considered one of the major figures of the struggle against colonialism, wrote *The Wretched of the Earth*, a book in which the violence of colonialism is denounced, not only in relation to the ongoing Algerian War, but as a structural characteristic which manifested itself on many different levels. As a psychoanalyst, without denying the brutality of physical violence, Fanon was well aware that the violence of colonialism operated systematically on the psyche of the colonised, preventing the formation of a dignified subject and mining identities. The exclusivity of colonial history and the consequent negation of the colonised subject's past is one of the deeper levels on which colonial violence operates:

> The settler makes history and is conscious of making it. And because he constantly refers to the history of his mother country, he clearly indicates that he himself is the extension of that mother country. Thus the history which he writes is not the history of the country which he plunders but the history of his own nation in regard to all that she skims off, all that she violates and starves. The immobility to which the native is condemned can only be called in question if the native decides to put an end to the history of colonization – the history of pillage – and to bring into existence the history of the nation – the history of decolonization. (Fanon, *Wretched* 51)[16]

Fanon worked in a context of urgency due to the crumbling of colonial empires after World War II which came to a peak during the 1960's-1970's and this situation may have influenced the militant attitude of his writings. Moreover, his experience in Algerian psychiatric hospitals during the 1950's, and his subsequent personal involvement in the Algerian war, and, not least, the leukemia that constrained him to finish *The Wretched of the Earth* from his deathbed, can be seen as strong elements in determining his radical position as a supporter of violent uprising. This aspect of Fanon's theory is the most controversial, but, despite the mentioned circumstances, it belongs to a situation in which the necessity for actual and real opposition is undeniable, and it was widely shared among the colonised.

---

[16] Le colon fait l'histoire et il sait qu'il la fait, et parce qu'il se réfère constamment à l'histoire de sa métropole, il indique en clair qu'il est ici le prolongement de cette métropole. L'histoire qu'il écrit n'est donc pas l'histoire du pays qu'il dépouille mais l'histoire de sa nation en ce qu'elle écume, viole et affame. L'immobilité à la quelle est condamné le colonisé ne peut être remise en question que si le colonisé décide de mettre un terme à l'histoire de la colonisation, à l'histoire du pillage, pour faire exister l'histoire de la nation, l'histoire de la décolonisation. (Fanon, *Damnés* 53)

In this context, the rise of the Négritude movement, promoted by Léopold Senghor from Senegal and Fanon's teacher Aimé Césaire from Martinique, can be seen in strict relation to this strategy of decolonisation and of re-evaluation of black cultures. History has been one of the fields in which the Négritude and other 1960's decolonisation movements operated, generating strong critiques to the authority of European-based "History," whose implicit colonial prejudices were deeply challenged, such as in a lecture by Cheikh Anta Diop about the falsification of history. There, he brings Egypt as an example of the negation by Western official history of any form of civilisation to Africa (as, in other terms, Hegel did) through the negation of precise historical facts, such as the African elements ("Black Egypt") of Ancient Egypt in favour of an exclusively "oriental" representation (Diop). Despite its effectiveness and its historical necessity, the informing principle of direct opposition to colonial power resulted in a kind of mirroring of the Western biases against which the decolonisation process worked. As clearly appears from Fanon's quotation, the strategy of decolonisation saw the promotion of violent opposition and the recourse to nation-state rhetoric, which has been considered in the discussion about the "subaltern" group above, for its intrinsically European and colonial nature. However, I will analyse later how this direct opposition and the deriving Manichean view are seen by recent post-colonial theorists, such as Homi Bhabha, as outdated at best, but more often ineffective and incorrect. Without referring directly to this controversy, Wilson Harris frequently remarks how the complexity of the colonial experience cannot be resolved in direct oppositions and how violence can be overcome through the "digestion" of colonial wounds. Nevertheless, the analysis of colonial violence has been fruitful, especially for Césaire, in the understanding of the mutuality of the effects of colonialism on both the colonised and the colonisers, complicating the attitude of mimicry of the first, which as a consequence of "relations of domination and submission" is turned into "an instrument of production" and the "*decivilizing*, [...] *brutalizing*" of the second into "a classroom monitor, an army sergeant, a prison guard, a slave driver" (Césaire, "Discourse" 216).

Nevertheless, the process of decolonisation is still a difficult matter today, as emerges from later analyses such as Edouard Glissant's *Le Discours Antillais* (1981), in which the economic situation of the former French colonies and the "départements d'outre-mer" is closely related to France's economic policy, up to the point of mirroring a colonial dependence (economic neo-colonialsim). Glissant, more than others, turned his interest to the possibility of a Caribbean historiography, through the construction of a "collective consciousness" out of an inevitably fragmented inheritance:

> The French Caribbean is the site of a history characterized by ruptures and that began with a brutal dislocation, the slave trade. Our historical consciousness could not be deposited gradually and continuously like sediment, as it were, as happened with those peoples who have frequently produced a totalitarian philosophy of history, for instance European peoples, but came together in the context of shock, contraction, painful negation, and explosive forces. This dislocation of the continuum, and the inability of the collective consciousness to absorb it all, characterize what I call a nonhistory. (Glissant 62)

This fragmentation of experience and the consequent difficulty of building a "highly functional fantasy" such as the totalising history of the West lead Glissant to reconsider the role of historians in the Caribbean: "As far as we are concerned, history as a consciousness at work and history as lived experience are [...] not the business of historians exclusively" (Glissant 65). By saying this, he allows the creation of the historian-poet, such as Walcott or Brathwaite, or the historian-fiction writer, such as Harris, as a prominent role in the construction of a common Caribbean history, "a subterranean convergence of our histories" (Glissant 66), of which he proposes a periodicisation, ironically mimicking the usual Western methodology.

Among the other post-colonial writers/intellectuals directly involved in the rewriting of some kind of Western/authoritative history, the case of Chinua Achebe and the controversy about Conrad's racism in "An Image of Africa: Racism in Conrad's *Heart of Darkness*" (1977) is an example of an opposing attitude towards the canon of Literature derived form the former colonial power. As they present colonial history's unquestioned biases, his fictional works can be also interpreted as a re-telling of particular episodes of Nigerian colonial history, proposing alternative versions, such as *Things Fall Apart* (1958), where the traditional way of life of a Nigerian village is tragically subverted by the arrival of British missionaries, thus counterbalancing the unproblematic official version of the humanitarian role played by men of faith. Similar re-interpretation of Nigerian colonial history through fictional devices can be seen in the work of the Nobel-prize winning playwright Wole Soyinka, whose main effort of promoting African theatre is paralleled by novels-memoirs works, such as *Aké: The Years of Childhood* (1981) the account of the early years of a relatively privileged Nigerian boy, whose education reflects the divisions Nigerian society had to face during colonial domination. Many examples can be reported of works of fiction which re-visit the colonial past, but they do not exhaust their literary value in their political meaning, and Jameson's reading of "Third-World literature" (II.i.a) appears, in this context, limited and biased. On the other side, here, the intention is not to suggest that post-colonial realities have not produced "traditional" histories, which indeed exist as a direct colonial heritage or as indigenous traditions, but the contemporary crumbling of traditional, authoritative, scientific approaches to history in the West, allows a wider selection of sources, and the works of fiction have often revealed the more self-conscious strategies for the recovery of history (these strategies usually respond to national issues, which is the reason for the structure of this section). Moreover, some post-colonial intellectuals, who significantly work and teach in the USA, have addressed the issue with a more international scope, such as Homi Bhabha and Edward Said, and their contribution will be discussed, at the end of this chapter, in relation to Wilson Harris's trans-national cross-culturalism.

Continuing the overview of notable contributions from national literatures, the case of Australia and Patrick White's *Voss* (1957), must be mentioned because of its literary significance and also because the visibility that the Nobel Prize (awarded to its author in 1973) brought to the post-colonial phenomenon. Here, the journey of a German explorer into the "outback" of Australian territory is the occasion for a reflection on the history of the country and the oppressive social situation of the few populated coastal zones, while the main theme of the interconnection of history – human experience – landscape, including the "living creatures" which seem to be part of it (the aboriginals), parallels Wilson Harris's concerns, as Harris himself highlights in his work of literary criticism *The Womb of Space* (1983). Fairly dissimilar issues inform South African writers, who have to face a particularly tragic history, and the experience of Apartheid characterises many novels whose authors try to cope with history and the scars South African society bears. Two different examples can be mentioned: Andrè Brink's *A Dry White Season* (1979), which deals directly with the bloody facts of pre-1994 South Africa, and J.M. Coetzee's *Waiting for the Barbarians* (1980), a meditation on otherness, violence and torture. South African fiction writers express the moral legacy of what has often represented the symbol of colonial violence, whose terrible meaning has partially escaped mere historical accounts.

What has fairly often escaped official history, and sometimes even chronicles and authority control, because of the practical, down-to-earth problems of identity and its intrinsic trans-national nature, is the phenomenon of migrants. As an effect of both colonialism (indentured labour) and recent globalisation, not to consider the natural flux of migrations, the reality of non-Western people moving towards Europe and the USA brings to the forefront many of the contradictions of colonialism, not least history. In this context, the works of early migrant writers such as Samuel Selvon and V.S. Naipaul is integrated by more recent contributions, among which Michael Ondaatje's and Caryl Phillips's. As to Selvon, his *The Lonely Londoners* (1956) depicts with humour the life of the first Caribbean immigrants to London, offering a history to those people who were officially recognised only when their number was considered excessive and the right to British citizenship, formerly accorded to all Commonwealth subjects, suspended.[17] Today, the relevance of the Caribbean community in London and in the UK is evident if traditional black boroughs such as Brixton or major public events such as the Notting Hill Carnival are taken into consideration. Such a huge component of British society could have remained in a historical back-light if the fictional works of Selvon and the successive commitment of Caryl Phillips, among others, had not performed the function of social histories besides their mainly literary aim. The assigning in 2001 of the Nobel prize for literature to V.S. Naipaul has, in a way, recognised the contribution of Caribbean elements to British culture, which the Indo-Trinidadian writer has always, with deep controversy, wished to be assimilated to.

Similarly, the stories of heterogeneous immigrant workers, who played a fundamental role in the construction of the major Canadian cities, in this case Toronto, has been testified by Micheal Ondaatje's *In the Skin of a Lion* (1987). With a more conscious attitude, Ondaatje operated on a stricter historical level by researching documents and evidence on which he built his fragmentary narrative which explicitly counterparts the monolithic and exclusive official history of Canada. Curiously, among the many ethnic groups cited in the novel, there does not appear any Sinhalese character, the author being originally from Colombo. Ondaatje reserves another novel to the tormented history of his mother land, *Anil's Ghost* (2001), where a particular episode, the reconstruction of the

---

17 Restrictions started with the Commonwealth Immigrants Act (1962), sharpened in 1968, and successively even more restrictions were introduced mainly in 1971 and 1983, up to the last Immigration, Asylum and Nationality Act of 2006. See <http://www.ind.homeoffice.gov.uk/>.

skull of a murdered Sinhalese (buried in a communal grave, concealed by the government), brings into play several issues of the epistemological controversy about Western history. The Western educated protagonist, a forensic anthropologist, must recognise the ability and the effectiveness of the reconstruction operated in a traditional and seemingly un-scientific way by Ananda, a local painter-artisan. The deeper insight into the history of that particular culture, based on totally different epistemological assumptions, is represented on many layers by characters such as Ananda and other natives, with respect to the scientific "superficiality" of Anil which does not fully understand either the socio-historical situation, or the dangerousness of her "pure" Western-like commitment to "truth."

Outside the English-speaking world, as seen in the case of the Négritude movement, the involvement of historical questions in the process of decolonisation has not been less important. Framing the vast realities of postcolonial cultures towards the Caribbean basin, the Brazilian writer Mario deAndrade can be mentioned for his recovering of the mythical figure of Makunaima, which in the novel *Macunaíma, O Herói sem Nenhum Caráter* (1926) is made to represent the history of the main ethnic groups of modern Brazil by the reinterpretation of various folk legends, in particular, alongside with his brothers, in the myth of the origin of the three main skin colours of Brazilian people. In Spanish-speaking South America there can be found several examples of writers who re-interpret the history of their country, with different aims, often supporting the process of independence and the creation of national identities, or a more transnational identity based on the colonial experience of the whole continent, starting from the "discovery," ending with the recent history of totalitarianism and political turmoil. With due differentiation, the big names of the Argentinian Jorge Luìs Borges, the Peruvian Mario Vargas Llosa[18] and the Colombian

---

18 Mario Vargas Llosa's *El Hablador*, bears significant similarities to Harris's fiction, especially regarding the spiritual view of the rain forest:
   lo que le parecìa admirable en esas culturas. Era algo que, por más diferencias que hubiera entre ellas, tenían todas en común: la buena inteligencia con el mundo en el que vivían inmersas, esa sabiduría, nacida de una práctica antiquísima, que les había permitido, a través de un elaborado sistema de ritos, prohibiciones, temores, rutinas, repetidos y transmitidos de padres a hijos, preservar aquella Naturaleza aparentemente tan exuberante, y, en realidad, tan frágil y perecedera, de la que dependían para subsistir. Habían sobrevivido porque sus usos y costumbres se habían plegado dócilmente a los ritmos y exigencias del mundo natural, sin violentarlo ni trastocarlo profundamente, apenas lo indispensable para no

Gabriel García Marquez must be cited for their interest in historical fiction. However, despite the frequent grouping of Wilson Harris's style with Marquez's under the label of "magical realism," for the sake of this discussion it is more relevant to highlight the common elements with part of Cuban literature, in particular with Alejo Carpentier.

Carpentier, who spent a great part of his life divided between La Habana and Paris, showed a deep interest in Caribbean history, especially Haitian, and he set one of his most famous novels on that island. The fascination with Haiti is shared with Wilson Harris, although he focused more on cultural and social aspects, while Carpentier made of Haitian revolutionary history the central theme of *El Reino de Este Mundo* (1949). The Cuban writer continued his historical inquiry analysing the historical effect of the French Revolution and its libertarian ideas in the colonial reality of the Antilles (*El Siglo de Las Luces*, 1962), but he also wrote about another aspect of South-American/Caribbean reality which is extremely important for a discussion about Wilson Harris: the landscape. The journey up the Orinoco river and the relativisation of human culture in the context of the Amazonian forest are two of the main themes of *Los Pasos Perdidos* (1953), which, at times, bears some significant similarities[19] to Harris's imagery (e.g. the forest in *The Palace of the Peacock*). Regarding Caribbean history and culture, Carpentier's most important work is undoubtedly *El Reino de Este Mundo*, for two different reasons. First, the subject is a fundamental part in the history of decolonisation, since the Haitian revolution led to the formation of the first independent reality in a still solid colonial context. Historical figures, such as Toussaint L'Ouverture, regarded as a transnational hero throughout the Caribbean, or Henri Christophe, the first black governor of Haiti, all play a nearly mythical role in Carpentier's novel, alongside "subaltern" characters such as Mackandal, a black slave who led the maroons during the revolution, or the protagonist: Ti Noel, a black slave himself.

It must be acknowledged that the history of Haitian revolution has been extensively documented since its beginning, with chronicles and historical accounts dating back to 1794 (see Descourtilz). The interest in the history of Haiti has generated several colonial monographic account and the same Toussaint L'Ouverture himself wrote an autobiography/book of memoirs, which contributed to the cult of his heroic figure, which is still an object of discussion.[20] In the

---

    ser destruidas por él. (Vargas Llosa 29)
19 A further similarity is discussed in 4.1.3.
20 Substantial information can be found on the internet at <http://thelouvertureproject

Caribbean context, a major historical work must be mentioned: *The Black Jacobins* (1938) by C.L.R. James, whose figure has already been introduced. There he applies a Marxist approach to history in the narration of the relationship between the French and Haitian revolutions. What is particularly important of Carpentier's fictional version is the interest in humble characters and the effort to give them an official historical record, through a precise documentation:

> The reader must be warned that the story he is going to read is based on rigorous documentation which not only respects the historical truth of the events, the names of the characters (even the minor ones), of the places, and even of the streets, but which also conceals under its apparently non-chronological facade a minute collation of dates and chronologies. (Carpentier, *Kingdom*, prologue)[21]

In this way, Carpentier manages to recover the figures of slaves whose stories have been denied by official historiography, which focuses more on L'Ouverture, Henri Christophe, or Dessalines. Such a method can be paralleled with the discussed project of the Indian based "subaltern" group, although it is much more reminiscent of Ghosh's "fictionalisation" of the subject. Moreover, Carpentier supports the authority of his historical view with a fairly different argument, which situates his work in a deeply Caribbean context, which will come into play in the discussion about Wilson Harris. The mythical and supernatural aspects of Ti Noel's vision, the return to life of Mackandal or his transformations are not presented in a context of systematic "supernaturalization of the real"

.org/>.

Among the many historical works produced it is worth mentioning Stephen Alexis's monograph (*Black Liberator: The Story of Toussaint Louverture*, 1949) because of the eminence of the Haitian writer and the consequent authority of this internal point of view.

It may also be useful to report a few of the earlier texts which can be consulted on the Internet: John Brown, *The History and Present Condition of St. Domingo*, Vol. II; Marcus Rainsford, *An Historical Account of the Black Empire of Hayti*. For a general overview see José L. Franco, *Historia de la revolución de Haití*.

21 Porque es menester advertir que el relato que va a leerse ha sido establecido sobre una documentación extremadamente rigurosa que no solamente respeta la verdad histórica de los acontecimientos, los nombres de los personajes – incluso secundarios –, de lugares y hasta de calles, sino que oculta, bajo su aparente intemporalidad, una minuciosa cotejo de fechas y de cronologías. (Carpentier, *Reino* 11)

(Scarano 17) as is typical of Magical Realism, but, as Carpentier precisely points out in the famous prologue to the novel, they are the result of the intrinsic supernatural reality that characterises the Caribbean and the Amazon areas.

Therefore, his account is actually a realist one, not less documented than a traditional work of historiography; consequently, the "realism" of the Caribbean is not fundamentally different from a European realism except for the nature of the subject, a sort of "real maravilloso," in Carpentier's own words. Moreover, this consciousness is shared by the slaves who perceptively live this reality:

> They all knew that the green lizard, the night moth, the strange dog, the incredible gannet, were nothing but disguises. As he had the power to take the shape of hoofed animal, bird, fish, or insect. Mackandal continuously visited the plantations of the Plaine to watch over his faithful and find out if they still had faith in his return. (Carpentier, *Kingdom* 41)[22]

Despite his rejection of realism, Wilson Harris seems to share the conception about the particularity of Caribbean reality and he often stresses the actuality of the psychic experiences that derive from the rapport with the Caribbean-South-American landscape. Carpentier's introduction, on another side, represents one of the first attempts to theoretically approach South-American literature, planting the seeds for a founding critical work, such as Roberto Fernàndez Retamar's *Calibàn* (1971), which represents a fundamental essay also for non-Latin literatures of the continent. The essay testifies the existence of a Latin-American culture by means of a successful simile which links a Shakespearian character from *The Tempest* to the South-American subject. It is one of the best examples of the post-colonial reading of the role of Caliban:

> Our symbol then is not Ariel, as Rodó thought, but rather Caliban. This is something that we, the *mestizo* inhabitants of these same isles where Caliban lived, see with particular clarity: Prospero invaded the islands, killed our ancestors, enslaved Caliban,

---

22 Todos sabían que la iguana verde, la mariposa nocturna, el perro desconocido, el alcatraz inverosímil, no eran sino simples disfraces. Dotado del poder de transformarse en animal de pezuña, en ave, pez o insecto, Makandal visitaba contínuamente las haciendas de la Llanura para vigilar a sus fieles y saber si todavía confiaban en su regreso. (Carpentier, *Reino* 41)

and taught him his language to make himself understood. (Retamar, *Caliban* 14)[23]

Retamar theorises in his essay a sort of "hybridity" – the "mestizaje" – which, despite the general impossibility of the purity of culture, especially characterises South-American cultures: "existe en el mundo colonial, en el planeta, un caso especial: una vasta zona para la cual el mestizaje no es el accidente, sino la esencia, la linea central: nosotros, 'nuestra América *mestiza*' [Josè Martì]" (Retamar, "Calibán" 347). Saying this, Retamar mirrors Harris's position about the cross-cultural nature of human experience, but he stresses its South-American nature. In line with this view, the Martinican Edouard Glissant focuses on the Caribbean situation, clearly expressing the thesis about the particular creolisation of culture that takes place in the Caribbean archipelago in his book *Le Discours Antillais* (1981). Here, from a Marxist point of view, he proposes a strategy of resistance to the neo-colonial powers which economically oppress the former French colonies, which can be applied to the broader context of the Caribbean/South American realities. By considering the "créole" nature of the Caribbean culture, he proposes a sort of "antillanité" as a unifying quality for the construction of a real Caribbean identity. While Glissant's view does not match Harris's because of its particularity, in many ways opposing the Guyanese's tendency towards universality, it represents a valuable strategy because it overcomes some of the ambiguities of the post-colonial identity-building process, and recognises the common historical experience of a wider area, thus avoiding the mimicry of European-based nation-state rhetoric.

A larger perspective can contextualise the issues of "hybridity" and identity by quickly taking into account two of the most widely accepted post-colonial theories: Edward Said's views, as expressed in *Orientalism* (1978) and *Culture and Imperialism* (1991) and Homi Bhabha's analyses published in *Nation and Narration* (1990) and *The Location of Culture* (1994). While history is not the central subject of these "post-colonial classics," the wider discourse on culture includes many aspects relevant to this discussion. First, the problem of representation and of the construction of tradition emerges from Edward Said's analysis of the relationship between Europe and "the Orient," the main theme of his

---

23   Nuestro símbolo no es pues Ariel, como pensó Rodó, sino Calibán. Esto es algo que vemos con paricular nitidez los mestizos que habitamos estas mismas islas donde vivió Calibán: Próspero invadió las islas, mató a nuestros ancestros, esclavizó a Calibán y le enseñó su idioma para poder entenderse con él [...]. (Retamar, "Calibán" 363-364)

groundbreaking *Orientalism*. There he analysed the long tradition, mainly focusing on 19th century Europe, of stereotypical representation of the Eastern-Oriental culture by the Western-Occidental intellectuals, concluding that no real observation could justify the negative image of the oriental man purported by 19th century European orientalists which deeply affected popular imagery and still exerts its influence. Consequently, Said theorises the ideologically driven construction of "the other" as a counterpart to the process of building an identity, in this case an occidental one. The political will to forward a determined set of values was realised by arbitrarily attributing opposite values to an indiscriminate group of people (oriental may equally refer to a Maghreb man or to a Pakistani woman) in order to provide an "other" in relation to whom identity may be negatively defined. The question is deeper and would deserve a separate discussion, but considering the extensive literature and the constant attention *Orientalism* has enjoyed in the post-colonial field, it will not be performed here. Nevertheless, it can be useful to briefly cite the mutual relationship between the object and the subject which Said identifies in the ideological process of identity building, which recalls Harris's theorisation of their mutual roles in the cognitive process, as repeatedly staged in his fiction and discussed in his essays,[24] particularly those concerning the parallels with quantum physics' consequences, such as the indeterminacy principle. On the other side, Hena Maes Jelinek notices that despite Harris "anticipates by some twenty five years some of the analytical statements and recommendations in *Culture and Imperialism*" (Jelinek, "Future" 3), he is altogether ignored by Said in this late application to literary criticism of the concepts developed in his early work.

Conversely, the convergence of Bhabha's and Harris's theories has been often suggested by scholars, particularly when addressing a way out of the closure emerging from the early Manichean approaches to post-colonial psychology (by Fanon and Césaire, as well as Négritude) emerged in the sixties. These convergences, however, tended to overshadow some basic differences between "hybridity" and "cross-culturalism." Bhabha's main arguments in favour of a new approach to post-colonial criticism, as expressed especially in *The Location of Culture*, may seem an extension of Hispano-Caribbean "mestizaje" or Glissant's "métissage" to the wider context of all former colonies, but they are actually pointed towards a general intellectualisation of the phenomenon. To my understanding, Bhabha's "hybridity" is a strategical approach[25] available to the colo-

---

24 See, in particular, Henry's examples discussed in 1.2.
25 In the same way as mimicry could be strategically used by the colonised.

nised (as well as to the coloniser, although this is not always clearly stated) to come to terms with the colonial experience and to claim back an original identity which is not based on a nostalgic recuperation of ancient roots (Brathwaite, Garvey) but on the theorisation of a "hybrid third space" in communication, where colonial and pre-colonial legacies melt in the formation of a new, legitimate, complex subject. The "liquid" nature of this "third space," where "we begin to understand why hierarchical claims to the inherent originality or 'purity' of cultures are untenable" (Bhabha, *Location* 37) determines the non-fixity of the cultural identities involved in the cultural dialogue, recalling Harris's concept of the restless nature of tradition. Bhabha himself recognises this convergence and often quotes Harris, particularly in *The Location of Culture*, where he comments the resemblance of the image of the void and his own "third space" as a similar "cultural and historical dimension" (38). Despite Bhabha's recent tendency to overcome the "obsession" of identity[26] and some scholars' criticisms regarding the lack of cultural specificity of Bhabha's approach, it is still considered a valuable strategy and it is often linked, in addition to the direct references such as the one reported above, to Harris's "universalist" "cross-culturalism." While Bhabha, in agreement with orthodox post-colonial theory, rejects the term "universal," the effects of "hybridization" may at certain stages mirror the multiplicity of influences which constitute the post-colonial subject, as acknowledged by Harris's universalist view. However, Bhabha's concept is much more addressed to the ex-colonised, while Harris assumes the "cross-cultural" condition as a universal one which includes intuitive relationships with traditions as diverse as alchemy and Amerindian mythology, whose existence is not exclusively determined by the colonial encounter, but they emerge from "what I would call the unconscious," and pass "into the subconscious and into the conscious mind" (Harris, "Originality" 118). Consequently, Harris's strategy is based on recognition of unconscious/neglected possibilities rather than on the creation of a completely new identity and therefore intrinsically different from Bahbha's "hybridity." On the other side, their common recognition of history[27] as a fundamental ground and their valuing of non-official histories as a fundamental counterpart to the authoritative narratives of colonial origin is evident, especially when reference is made to "Signs Taken for Wonder," and to its deal-

---

26 "I'm tired of this notion of identity," unpublished lecture given at the Turin Book Fair (Salone del Libro), Torino, 7 May 2005.
27 Bhabha treats time itself in a similar way to Harris's, stressing the concept of "non-synchronous temporality of global and national cultures" (Bhabha, *Location* 218).

ing with the authority of European history and its possible alternative interpretations in different contexts such as the Indian environment in which the Anund Messeh anectode is set.

Instead of a deeper discussion of Said redirecting to the extensive critical literature published on his work. In this study, the inclusion of a variety of approaches with an emphasis on a post-colonial view is favoured, with the purpose of better representing Harris's unconventional approach and the multifarious, mixed influences which inform his thought.

3 – Jungian and Pre-Modern Influences

3.1 Jungian Influences

Harris has shown a certain reluctance to acknowledge direct connections between Carl Gustav Jung's writings and his own early work, up to the point of denying, on some occasions, any influence at all: "Jung never influenced me, but I had a dialogue with him" (interview by Riach 62). Whether Harris is completely sincere or is just trying to claim intellectual independence in the formulation of some common concepts, it is not the interest of this comparison to judge. The analysis of the relationship between Jung's thought and Harris's is important in either case, whether we consider the latter as a direct filiation or the two as separate theorisations which converged at a certain point in time. It is evident, and Harris does not deny this, that his views of tradition and of the human psyche bear great similarities to some concepts expressed in the construction of Jung's "Analytical Psychology," and he himself admitted that when he read "what he [Jung] had to say about the collective unconscious, it sustained and supported me" (interview by Riach 62).

It would have been otherwise impossible to refer to Harris's views about imagination, cross-culturality, memory, dream, human time and alchemical symbolism without calling into play Jung's extended analysis of the unconscious. Apart from slight discrepancies on a terminological level, mainly about the label of "collective unconscious" which is reformulated by Harris on a couple of occasions for unclear reasons,[28] all the themes and key concepts of Harris's philosophy listed above have a parallel formulation in Jung's writings. In this chapter the most important similarities will be analysed, while the differences and the particularities of Harris's theories will be mentioned and left to further discussion in the following chapters.

To begin with, it is useful to define the kind of approach selected for the discussion of Jungian theories. As elsewhere stated, this thesis is characterised by a purely literary approach and does not claim any specific competence on such complex and vast subjects as, in this case, psychology or "Analytical Psychol-

---

28 Here are two examples of Harris's doubts about Jung's definition, which will be analysed later in more detail: "C.G. Jung first used the term, 'collective unconscious.' I don't know if it is the best term. I would rather call it the world's unconscious" (Harris, "Judgment" 25). "I would not have called it the 'collective unconscious' at that stage. Even now, I tend to hesitate. I much prefer the term 'universal unconscious'. But 'collective unconscious' is also no doubt valid" (Harris, interview by Riach 62).

ogy." Therefore critical sources have been selected to fit this purpose, with the extended use of mainly introductory texts and applications of Jungian theories to literary criticism, while direct references to Jung's production, mainly to his *Collected Works,* will be limited to particular sections, especially those about archetypes and the collective unconscious.

As a starting point it is useful to refer to Kathryn Berthelsen's article "Surveying the Psyche: A Jungian Reading of Wilson Harris' *The Guyana Quartet*" (Berthelsen), where she offers a few interesting insights on the subject. It is the purpose of this chapter to expand these and other insights and also to bring to the surface some meaningful differences which arise from the different cultural backgrounds of the two writers, despite their mutual recognition of the numerous universal elements of the human experience.

3.2 Archetypal Images

The concept of archetype has often been used in the field of literary theory since Carl Gustav Jung himself addressed the subject a few times during his multi-faceted research activity.

According to Darrell Dobson,

> Archetypal literary theory begins [...] with Carl Jung, and he most clearly addresses the topic in *The Spirit of Man, Art and Literature*, which contains two essays (first published 1922 and 1930) about literary archetypal analysis and one discussion of James Joyce's *Ulysses.* (Dobson)

However, when archetypal literary theory is cited, very often Northrop Frye is considered as one of the main representative scholars. His *Anatomy of Criticism,* in Dobson's view, can be considered in the light of a preceding definition of archetypal literary theory which Frye had formulated in a review of some of Jung's essays:

> [Archetypal literary theory is] that mode of criticism which treats the poem not as an imitation of nature but as an imitation of other poems. It studies conventions and genres, and the kind of recurrent imagery which connects one poem with another. (Frye, "Forming" 616)

Despite being especially fit for his own work, Frye's definition does not take into account all the aspects implied in the use of the Jungian concept of archetype in literature and in literary theory; more specifically, "Frye uses the term archetype differently than Jung does. By archetype, Frye means only a recurring pattern" (Dobson). Frye's view is not irrelevant to this discussion; however, along with other types of mythological or archetypal theory, it can be considered as an aspect of the panorama of possibilities which arise in the application of Jung's original and more comprehensive conception of archetype. It is important to state it here because literary theory is not the only application of Wilson Harris's particular conception of archetype, which can be compared very closely to Jung's. It is therefore essential to define Jung's original concept which refers to a typical way of thinking and acting of humankind in general as an innate possibility of representation which precedes imagination and resides in the "collective unconscious." (Pieri, 62-76) The Jungian archetype has peculiar characteristics, as briefly reported by Dobson:

> The archetype is unknowable and irrepresentable; it is merely a shared impulse to create pattern; its nature can only be guessed at from an overview of its representations, all of which are located, specific and embodied in dreams, rituals, myths and art. As the 'archetype' is transformed into the 'archetypal image' it takes on the characteristics of the individual and/or collective into which it arrives. (Dobson)

It is clear how this formulation expands the meaning of archetype into an entity which comprises much more than the seeds of different patterns of psychic manifestations or, as in Frye's case, of literary production; while, on the other side, it differentiates the actual manifestations, or "archetypal images," which are, on the contrary, investigable. These archetypal images are co-substantial with the archetype, which is, in fact, "not a Platonic form that exists separately from its manifestations: it is the shared aspect of unique manifestations" (Dobson).

Harris's interest is centred mainly on the archetype as such,[29] and this can be inferred from the analysis of his fictional and non-fictional production which manifests a constant concern with the investigation of such common features of

---

[29] Harris often refers to the concept of archetype as "myth," in its wider meaning, especially in his early works when specifically Jungian terminology tends to appear less frequently.

human experience and, seen as a whole, gives the clear impression of a continuous re-working and reformulation around a central theme, which can be identified with a kind of quest, similar to the alchemical quest for the lapis which in turn inspired much of Jung's work. The theme of the quest will be discussed later on, while here I will concentrate on Harris's treatment of archetypal images and its relation with Jungian ones.

Significantly, in an essay re-printed in Andrew Bundy's collection *Selected Essays: The Unfinished Genesis of the Imagination* (1999), Harris directly quotes Jung and discusses what could be considered an example of archetypal image. In this essay, entitled "Merlin and Parsifal, Adversarial Twins," Harris refers to a legend in which the struggle between the figures of Parsifal and Merlin is represented: "In the Merlin/Parsifal legend a far-flung theatre slumbers which bears on a hidden self-confessional, self-judgmental rapport between all cultures" (59). His interpretation of this legend may appear, as will emerge later, as an attempt on his side to build an archetypal representation of the struggle between two forces which operate on a cross-cultural level. As usual, Harris is concerned with the discovery of common features among cultures, but he derives from this archetypal image of conflict a series of considerations which are mainly centred around literature and his own poetics.

The reference to Jung is essentially based on the recurrent allusion the Swiss scholar made to the legend of Merlin and to the "cri de Merlin." In one of these allusions,[30] while referring to an episode about a cornerstone which occurred during the construction of his Bollingen country retreat, he clearly opposes the figure of Merlin to that of Parsifal:

> Do you know what I wanted to chisel on the back face of the stone? '*Le cri de Merlin!*' For what the stone expressed reminded me of Merlin's life in the forest, after he had vanished from the world. Men still hear his cries, so the legend runs, but they cannot understand or interpret them.
>
> Merlin represents an attempt by the medieval unconscious to create a parallel figure to Parsifal. Parsifal is a Christian hero, and Merlin, son of the devil and a pure virgin, is his dark brother. In the twelfth century, when the legend arose, there were as yet no premises by which his intrinsic meaning could be understood. Hence he ended in exile, and hence 'le cri de Merlin' which still

---

30 It is actually Harris's same source, but in his essay he quotes only the first sentence.

> sounded from the forest after his death. This cry that no one could understand implies that he lives on in unredeemed form. His story is not yet finished, and he still walks abroad. It might be said that the secret of Merlin was carried on by alchemy, primarily in the figure of Mercurius. Then Merlin was taken up again in my psychology of the unconscious and – remains uncomprehended to this day! That is because most people find it quite beyond them to live on close terms with the unconscious. Again and again I have had to learn how hard this is for people. (Jung, *Memories* 228)

It is useful to report this whole quotation here to highlight the convergence between Harris and Jung not only on a conceptual level, but also in the evocative quality of the style. Moreover, the tendency to treat this theme as archetypal emerges from Jung's own words and from his insistence on its recurrence, and recalls other occasions on which he writes about Merlin as a realisation of the archetype of "the old wise man." It is not this last aspect which interests Harris the most, actually he focuses on the kinship of Parsifal and Merlin which sees the latter as a dark double. Curiously he quotes only a few lines of Jung's insight, but he investigates, nevertheless, the archetypal quality of this relationship as suggested by the whole passage above. As usual, Harris bends the material he draws from different sources to his peculiar interests, and in this case he joins together the mentioned theme with another Jungian concern, the need for a "new conceptual language":

> If the latest conclusions of science are coming nearer and nearer to a unitary idea of being... it seems to show that there is some possibility of getting rid of the incommensurability between the observed and the observer. The result, in this case, would be the unity of being which would have to be expressed in terms of a new conceptual language. (Jung, *Synchronicity*, *Collected Works* Vol. 8, 512)

Harris builds up a controversy using the Merlin/Parsifal archetypal image to link materialism and its relative literary mode, realism, with the figure of Parsifal and his own poetics with Merlin's:

> Jung ventures to say that a 'new conceptual language' is needed to breach that core-bias if a deeper hidden rapport is to come into

play between Parsifal (and all that Parsifal entails as a vessel of sovereign power) and apparently trapped Merlin (and all that Merlin entails as a vessel of shamanic lore and a visionary, stranger, self-confessional, self-judgemental orbit slumbering in the iron-clad but deceptive logic of ruthless materialism...). (Harris, "Merlin" 59)

Moreover, he interprets a passage of Jung's writings about synchronicity as addressing a kind of "psychophysical narrative" which " would bear on trials of the imagination involved in the re-birth of a genuine cross-cultural age within the body of civilization" (Harris, "Merlin" 61). It should be clear by now how Harris makes use of this archetypal image to support his own idea of literature as opposed to a conventional one which appears imbalanced towards Parsifalian aspects. However, he does not limit this reading to abstract literary theory. From the Merlin/Parsifal contraposition he finds support for his own fictional strategy:

I am sure that the mediation by sense organs (which Jung requires as indispensable to the new medium of imagination he addresses) is achievable in fiction as a threshold into altering the Parsifalian core-bias in civilization. Jung has not reflected as far as I am aware on how the 'sense organs' are fictionally, dialectically and numinously clothed and re-dressed within a self-judgemental, self-confessional art. Self-confessional, self-judgemental art is perhaps as close as we may come to a *fiction* of absolute knowledge which is redemptive in its insights into the interconnectedness of all species and beings and things. (61)

This can be considered one effective definition, amongst the many Harris has expressed about the fictional strategy that he has applied in most of his novels, but it also widens the concept of unity which Jung seldom extends to inanimate entities in such an extremely inclusive way as Harris does. This last aspect is even more evident if Harris's older essays, such as "The Phenomenal Legacy" (1970), are taken into consideration. Actually, his claim about the complete autonomy of his early theories from Jungian influences is supported by some evidence in the scarcity of terminological similarities which otherwise characterise the later "Merlin and Parsifal" (1996), and by the constant consideration of the contribution of landscape and man-made ruins to the "original unity or wholeness of being" (Harris, "Phenomenal" 65-66).[31] It is useful to quote here a critique by Syed Manzu Islam: "Indeed, the worst thing one could do is a Harrisian reading of Harris's own texts. Prompted by his passion for archetypes, Harris as a critic has produced some of the most shockingly reductive criticism that I have seen." (Manzu Islam 61-62) Suspending the judgement about the validity of such consideration, which is nevertheless founded in the opaqueness of several critical works by Harris, it is relevant indeed to acknowledge the sometimes extreme tendency of the Guyanese novelist to reduce his own reading of literary texts to their relation with some sort of archetype or myth, as evidently emerges from his main work of literary criticism: *The Womb of Space* (1983).

According to Russell McDougall's "Wilson Harris on the Frontiers of Myth-Criticism," the "scouting expedition" into the field of archetypal criticism carried out in *The Womb of Space* can be seen as the practical application of the concepts discussed in an earlier essay, "Metaphor and Myth" (1982), in which Harris for the first time explicitly "took the Jungian view – that myth is 'untamed and untam[e]able'" (McDougall, "Frontiers" 111), linking his concept of myth to Jung's archetype. On that occasion Harris clearly refers to the Swiss psychoanalyst in considering the sexed quality of the archetypal opposition of Anima and Animus:

> women of earth, fire, water whose conjunction within the harlequin body of creation may easily be suppressed by male hubris suspended on fortress heights. That such muses may themselves connive at, or ape, the investitures of male hubris raises the difficulty of true coniunctio or productive union, the complexity of dialogic heights in depths, depths in heights. (Harris, "Metaphor" 11)

Despite the presence of previous references to Jung's theories,[32] it is reasonable to agree with McDougall in marking "Metaphor and Myth" as a fixed point in Harris's process of acknowledgement of Jungian influences:

> The explicit sex-coding of myth in this essay was new to Harris's critical thinking. The epic hero hanging from the bridge represents "male hubris;" and the cosmos through which the rainbow

---

31 This last aspect will be dealt more in depth in the next chapters.
32 Direct reference to "the archetype of the collective unconscious" already appears in "Art and Criticism," the first essay in *Tradition the Writer and Society* (9).

arcs [sic] is coded by a Jungian identification of Unconscious Soul with the Great Mother. We do, I think, see the beginnings of a Jungian idealisation of the feminine principle here in Harris's non-fiction for the first time. (McDougall, "Frontiers" 113)

3.2.1 Archetypal Images in Earlier Novels

Harris resorts to archetypal imagery in both his non-fictional and his fictional works, with the result of blurring the boundaries between the two, and, with the latter, he seems to adopt a more systematic strategy much earlier in time. Berthelsen's reading of *The Guyana Quartet* effectively supports this view. In her article, she outlines a number of themes and features which strictly interconnect Harris's quartet, especially *The Palace of the Peacock* (1960), to Jungian theories. In partial contrast with Syed Manzu Islam's opinion, mentioned in section III.ii, she reports Andrew Bundy's dismissal of exclusively post-colonial critical approaches when analysing Harris's work:

> While conscientiously we might make comparisons with these critical approaches and Harris's own theories, such stances are likely to be less productive than reading Harris in the light of traditions of the imagination (literature, philosophy, anthropology, analytical psychology) that act as 'parallel texts' to his work. (Bundy 10)

However, Berthelsen takes up the suggestion to apply a Jungian reading to Harris's earliest fictional works, which among the more than twenty he had published at the time of writing, are the least intertwined with theoretical writing:

> Harris' [sic] writing takes on a profoundly psychological dimension when one considers it in relation to Jung's seminal work with the collective unconscious, archetypes and the restorative processes of alchemy and active imagination. [...] particularly *The Guyana Quartet*, sets aside conventional realism (i.e. fiction that obeys the logic of the conscious mind) in favour of a world governed by unconscious elements. (Berthelsen)

As to the parallels with alchemy and active imagination, they will be discussed separately, as with dream elements, while the use of archetypes and archetypal images will be considered here to be extended, in spite of Islam's warning, to some later novels, such as The *Infinite Rehearsal* (1992), *Jonestown*

(1996) and *The Mask of the Beggar* (2001), which develop this hybrid mode to an even greater extent.

The first element Berthelsen highlights is water, which is usually associated with "the unconscious and the fluid body of non-formal, dynamic intuitive wisdom" (Berthelsen). Water is, in point of fact, intrinsic in the very name of Guyana, as Harris points out in the introductory note to *The Guyana Quartet*,[33] and its role in his symbolic world of fiction is quite strikingly connected with Jung's vision of the unconscious as a world of water:

> For what comes after the door is, surprisingly enough, a boundless expanse full of unprecedented uncertainty, with apparently no inside and no outside, no above and no below, no here or there, no mine and no thine, no good and no bad. It is the world of water, where all life floats in suspension; where the realm of the sympathetic system, the soul of everything living, begins; where I am indivisibly this and that; where I experience the other in myself and the other-than-myself experiences. (Jung, *Archetypes*, *Collected Works* Vol. 9i: 21-22)

The fictional strategy Harris adopts to better represent intuitive processes and the unconscious results in an extensive use of dream sequences, and this particular aspect will be analysed in more detail later on, along with the emerging concept of the unity of "everything living"; here some of the archetypal images recreated by Harris will be outlined.

According to Berthelsen,

> Oudin and Ram enact the roles of slave and master in *The Far Journey of Oudin*; Donne and Mariella, the conqueror and conquered in *Palace of the Peacock*; Magda and Cristo, authority figure and inexperienced youth in *The Whole Armour*; Fenwick and Poseidon, the "civilized" modern man and ancient noble "savage" in *The Secret Ladder*. The clash also occurs between archetypes of nature, such as the struggle between water, whose psychological implications have already been mentioned, and the bush, which buries every tributary in its 'grave of wilderness' [Harris, *Guyana* 368]. (Berthelsen)

---

[33] "Guyana is derived from an Amerindian root word which means 'land of waters'" (Harris, *Guyana* 7).

Following Berthelsen's analysis, the relationship between identity and rootlessness can be seen as a recurring theme in *The Guyana Quartet*, and it is expressed through archetypal or symbolical images such as the mixed crew of *The Palace of the Peacock*, but the feminine figures which appear in the four novels are presented as the best example because they can be considered as different manifestations of "goddesses of identity," an archetype regarding identity and reconciliation. In her discussion of the theme, an interesting convergence of post-colonial and Jungian strategies is used to represent Mariella as "the last remaining member of an ancient 'consciousness of race'" which is to be seen in the context of "Guyana's struggle for a reconciled postcolonial self." (Berthelsen) Similarly she interprets the other woman characters in the quartet, Beti, Magda and Sharon as images related to identity. What is interesting to notice here is the fact that all four women can be seen as partially different archetypal images, or slightly different myths, of a single archetype, or Myth: "when one myth is finished, another myth begins containing the same meaning, but with changed details." (Berthelsen) Berthelsen continues by bringing to the surface other archetypal readings, such as "reiterations of the savior archetype" or the Merlin/Parsifal opposition discussed above, as realised in the Donne/I-narrator couple (*The Palace of the Peacock*), or Beti's opposition to Ram (*The Far Journey of Oudin*), or Fenwick/Poseidon (*The Secret Ladder*), while *The Whole Armour* seems to elude a simple analysis.[34] All these archetypal oppositions evolve, in the end, towards a form of unity, which Berthelsen poignantly refers to as an alchemical process: "while these unresolved archetypes appear repeatedly throughout *The Guyana Quartet*, Harris also embeds in the text a mechanism for unifying these opposing images: alchemy" (Berthelsen). As already stated, this topic will be dealt later on, when further discussion of Berthelsen's view will bring new useful elements.

3.2.2 Doctor Faustus and *The Infinite Rehearsal*

Moving to Harris's later novels it is relevant to reconsider the Faustian themes emerging from *The Infinite Rehearsal* introduced in the first part of this book (I.iv). At this point the figure of Doctor Faustus can be discussed under the light

---

34 Berthelsen actually includes *The Whole Armour* by considering the village as a place of Parsifalian influence and the jungle linked to the figure of Merlin. While this interpretation is perfectly acceptable on a general basis, *The Whole Armour* seems to fit less easily in the pattern she has drawn for the discussion of the other three novels, for the main reason that the opposition is realised in two divided spaces rather than in two characters.

of Jungian archetypal theory, in relation with Goethe's original character. The original Faust, however, must not be considered as the only source for Harris's character: Doctor Faustus appears as a synthesis of different features of Goethe's Faust and Mephistopheles, while including, as his name suggests, elements from Marlowe's famous play. This conflation of the two principal literary representations of the archetype of Faust in European literature is actually declared by Harris when he has Robin Redbreast Glass saying: "*Faust* – both Goethe's and Marlowe's – had been a priceless possession in my grandfather's stock of books" (*Infinite* 186). In addition, the name of Harris's character – Doctor Faustus – clearly refers to Marlowe's protagonist, while its features and his role in the novel directly recall Goethe's Mephistopheles. Moreover, Harris's usual process of appropriation of literary and traditional elements must be taken into account: despite the direct references to tradition, Harris's version of the archetype is substantially different from its models. Once again this is made clear through Robin's words: "my grandfather's revised text of *Faust*. He read *Faust*, he loved *Faust*, and he rewrote it in his own image."(Harris, *Infinite* 183).

It is necessary, at this point, to present in a few lines the main characters related to Doctor Faustus in *The Infinite Rehearsal*. It has already been mentioned in the course of this discussion how Wilson Harris recurs to the multiplication of characters and narrators to blur identities and to suggest a fundamental unity of experience. This is also the case with *The Infinite Rehearsal,* where the reader is already puzzled in the first page – a note to the book signed by Robin Readbreast Glass. This note introduces the story as a "fictional autobiography" which, according to Robin, has been stolen and published by a certain W.H., whose entire name is never mentioned, although it is easily interpretable as a meta-fictive reference to the real author himself. On the other side, the acronym alludes to more problematic elements which seem to relate to autobiographical episodes or real situations connecting the fictional city of Skull and the country of Old New Forest to the Guyanese reality, while "at the same time, the author follows a deliberate strategy of defamiliarization" (Creighton 197) which results in the perception of Guyana as "a microcosm standing for the world at large" (Maes-Jelinek, *Naked* 6). The political allegories inscribed in the episodes regarding Tiresias Tigers and the great strike of the Animal Bands (section IV), clearly refer to the Guyanese political situation in 1948 (a theme Harris had already fictionalised in *The Eye of the Scarecrow,* 1965) albeit they defy simple interpretations. The various references to historical facts, such as the bombing of

Hiroshima or the Chernobyl disaster,[35] all add up to a series of dates and facts which concur in increasing the number of precise temporal and spatial connections, an unusual feature for a typical Harrisian novel. It is possible to read this as a response to some criticisms Harris had received around the time of writing about being completely detached from any socio-political reality, being too concentrated on the mythical and archetypal quality of his characters. It is particularly evident in *The Infinite Rehearsal* that Harris's fictional strategy is not aimed at a sterile idealisation of characters or at some obscure allegorical representation. The proliferation of doubles and alter-egos is justified by Harris's project of investigating archetypes which are in fact grounded in the reality of the historical world, archetypes whose immanent realisation and effect can be associated to precise historical facts.

On the widest scale, the character of Doctor Faustus works exactly in this way: as an actual character, he might embody numerous potential references to reality, but as an archetypal image its main function is the representation of a principle which underlies various realisations of power, the ambivalence of knowledge and technology. In a more specific analysis of the novel, as quoted above, the figure of Faust readily appears in the first pages, when Robin Redbreast Glass refers to Marlowe's and Goethe's as the objects of his grandfather's rewriting. Curiously, in his book *Memories, Dreams, Reflections* (1973), Carl Gustav Jung remarks the importance that Faust had in his life by covertly referring to the legend which saw his own grandfather as Goethe's natural son: "Jung used to speak of this stubbornly persistent legend with a certain gratified amusement, for it might serve to explain one subtle aspect of his fascination with Goethe's Faust; it belonged to an inner reality, as it were" (Jung, *Memories* 36).

At this point in Harris's novel, Faust is still a distant figure in the work of Robin's grandfather, but he is addressed as "the Beast of immortality, the Beast of the circus and of the machine" (Harris, *Infinite* 186). Therefore, it is possible to argue that Doctor Faustus is represented from the very beginning of *The Infinite Rehearsal* as a reformulation of the archetype of materialism and technological hubris Harris embodied in Parsifal in the essay discussed above. At this stage, it might appear feeble as a connection, but in the course of the whole novel, the Parsifalian element of the character emerges with indubitable

---

[35] "Harris catalogs everything from manmade disasters like the atomic bombing of Hiroshima and Nagasaki and the Chernobyl meltdown to the political nightmares [...] of Beirut, Belfast and Jamaica" (Johnson, "Translation" 132-133).

strength. The interest in again analysing this archetype lies in the recognition of the subtle nuances as well as the clear differences that emerge in the continuous reworking of a theme or a figure (an archetype through archetypical images, such as the idealisation of the Fludd/Kepler dispute discussed in chapter 1) which characterises the whole of Harris's production and is particularly relevant for a novel expressing this very concept in its own title.

Those differences and nuances might be better understood if considered in relation to the other character of the archetypal image chosen as a reference, Merlin, by trying to identify a corresponding figure in the novel. It must be said, however, that the typical fluidity of Harrisian characters often does not allow us to re-discuss a formerly emerged opposition in exactly the same terms, due not only to the evolution of the "archetypal character" itself but mainly to its interaction with other characters. This is the case of Ghost, which in a way could be seen as the "Merlin" opposer of "Parsifal"–Doctor Faust, while, as a spirit, it intrinsically eludes fixation or embodiment. The principal oppositions that can be found in *The Infinite Rehearsal* are reflected in all their layered complexity through Robin Redbreast Glass, whose name seems to suggest both "the vulnerable fragility of man" (Creighton 197) and "reflection and transparency" (Maes-Jelinek, "Re-visionary" 349). As already mentioned, Robin himself is immediately presented in an adversarial relationship with the alter-author W.H., but in the second part of the novel he is reflected in another alter ego, Peter, one of the children drowned with Robin in the first performance of his death. It is AD 2025 and Harris further complicates the pattern of oppositions:

> Now, however – in AD 2020 – though I remained as young as ever (my hair was immaculately black and I was dressed to a t or a T in the paradox of time/Time) I knew that W.H. himself had vanished and that someone else – some other ageing mask – played the role of authorship/characterschip in my book, as if I were he, and he me. (Harris, *Infinite* 229)

Adversarial representation of the characters and the author alike is inscribed in Harris's fictional project which, in specific formulations, seems to support this Jungian/archetypal reading:

> Fiction reveals its truths, its genuine truths that bear on the reality of persons, the reality of the world, when fiction fictionalizes au-

thors and characters alike. Thus is archetypal myth resurrected. (Harris, *Infinite* 220)

However complex, in line with Jung's definition of archetypes as inevitably dual[36], Harris's approach to the fictionalisation of archetypal images is almost systematically realised through the embodiment of their opposite qualities in opposing characters. His exploration of archetypes, however, is not simply dualistic: each character can be seen as part of a dualistic opposition, while it may acquire a different function in relation with another, giving life to a complex, multi-voiced representation. This is the dynamic which sees Robin opposed to the immigration officer Ulysses Frog in the first part of the book, while a few pages later the axis is shifted between Frog and Ghost, who becomes in his turn a pole in the opposition with Doctor Faustus. Among the various facets explored by Harris, the relations which include Doctor Faustus emerge more strongly, as Doctor Faustus is a pivotal figure in the novel, especially when the axis which sees him on one side and Ghost on the other is considered. In the light of the aforementioned formulation of the archetype of Merlin and Parsifal, it is possible to recognise the reflection of the theme of the opposition between Western history and technological hubris, re-staged in the Doctor Faustus character, and the non-Western, specifically Caribbean history and spirituality encapsulated in Ghost, which/who significantly "appeared out of the sea"(Harris, *Infinite* 175), echoing Walcott's famous poem *The Sea Is History* (1979).

All the characters seem to be conscious, to a certain extent, of their mythical/archetypal role – "for they (Peter and Emma) were themselves characters of myth" (Harris, *Infinite* 229) – but Doctor Faustus and Ghost embody the two extremities of the archetypal opposition represented in the Jungian archetype of the old sage, about the problem of knowledge, further developed by Harris with the Merlin/Parsifal duality, or the spiritual/technological dichotomy. In *The Infinite Rehearsal*, all the negative effects of the Faustian technological hubris are listed, conceptualised as "the mystery of deprivation" and "*illiteracies of the heart and mind*" or historicised in the episodes of the "wreck of civilisation" as performed in Alice and Miriam's theatre of time. On the other hand the fascination with Doctor Faustus is never denied, as it appears in Peter's behaviour in the second part of the book or in some ambivalent definitions: "Beast is also the hunted victim thoughtlessly exploited by man, 'Beast-morsel, Beast-fish, Beast-grain,

---

36 "Just as all archetypes have a positive, favourable, bright side that points upwards, so also they have one that points downwards, partly negative and unfavourable." (Jung, "Phenomenology," *Collected Works*, Vol. 9 i: 226-227).

Beast-shrimp,' the Beast that feeds and clothes man" (Maes-Jelinek, "Immanent" 339), and moreover the dangerousness of a spiritual hubris is no less underrated, as Hena Maes-Jelinek highlighted: "Despite Faust's defeat, Glass is nevertheless being cautioned against the possible deception and hubris of spirituality itself" ("Immanent" 340).

3.2.3 *Jonestown* and the Shape of Evil

Archetypal reading can be quite effectively applied to a later novel, *Jonestown* (1996). The novel is based on the massacre of Jonestown, Guyana, in which more than 900 people died in a sort of ritual which involved the drinking of cyanide mixed with a sweet drink known as "Kool-Aid."[37] Harris explores the enigma of this episode by freely revisiting the facts through the memory of a fictional survivor, Francisco Bone, who took part in the founding of the community along with Deacon, another completely fictional character, and Jonah Jones, based on the People's Temple leader Jim Jones. The reference to the actual tragedy, however, is transfigured by Harris into a much wider reflection on the enigmas which characterise the history of Central and South America: "Harris is not interested in revisionist history, of the 1978 events or any other; but in revisiting, imaginatively, the death of that community, he derives from its parallelism to other past events and myths its relevance to the contemporary world of the late 1990s" (Burnett 216).

---

37 The massacre of Jonestown is the culminating episode of the history of the Peoples Temple, a religious organisation founded in 1955, in California, headed by the controversial figure of Reverend Jim Jones. The enigmatic character of this religious movement and its tragic end have generated various interpretations, up to the point of suggesting a direct involvement of the CIA, as the promoter of a "mind-control" experiment (Vankin and Whalen 1995). Besides these conspirational theses, the relationships of Jim Jones with certain US politicians (G. Moscone, First Lady R. Carter) have raised deep controversy. Before 1977, he enjoyed vast popularity and he even became executive director of the Indianapolis Human Rights Commission in 1961; later, some negative rumours were spread, but only in November 1978, after all the members moved to Guyana to found the utopian Peoples Temple Agricultural Mission (an attempt to flee from journalistic accusations), was a serious investigation carried out by US congressman Leo Ryan, with tragic consequences. The political implications of the massacre have been discussed most notably by Shiva Naipaul in *Black and White* (1980). Recently a comprehensive documentary by Stanley Nelson produced for American Experience in association with the BBC, *Jonestown, The Life and Death of Peoples Temple* (2006), was shortlisted for an Oscar nomination. A useful resource is maintained online by the Department of Religious Studies at San Diego State University <http://jonestown.sdsu.edu>.

As discussed in the first chapter, Michael Mitchell has identified trinity as the main archetypal shape sustaining the Bone-Deacon-Jones relationship, and the mandala represented in the Axiom of Maria Prophetissa as a good image for the inclusion of Mr. Mageye. While this reading allows several concepts to be clearly outlined, it could be further complicated by referring to Jung's interpretation of trinity in Western culture, with particular attention to the function of its Eastern quaternal counterpart, the mandala. Jung has shown on various occasions his professional concern with the "archetypal shape" of the trinity, mainly drawing on Christian or proto-Christian sources, integrating them with expanding concepts borrowed from eastern, mainly Indian and Chinese, philosophies and religions. Jung's treatment of the subject is vast and elaborated, therefore a necessary simplification will be performed here to delineate a few key concepts for the interpretation of *Jonestown*'s characters. The main sources for this book are principally derived from Vol. XII, XIII and XIV of Jung's *Collected Works* for the alchemical problems, while the problem of evil and those related to triads and mandalas are formulated on the basis of Vol. IX (part I and II) and "A Psychological Approach to Dogma of the Trinity" (Jung, *Collected Works* Vol. 11, 107-200).

From these sources it is possible to choose a direction in Jung's analysis of the problem of trinity as related to the nature of evil following a pattern of theorisations which draw back to the discussion of the problem of the same and the other as presented by Plato in the *Timaeus*. In this collection of dialogues can be found one of the first examples of the discussion of this theme in relation to the numbers 1, 2, 3 and 4: "The genesis of the elements also forms an important section of Plato's *Timaeus* where the subject is developed mathematically" (*Dictionary*, Alchemy 028).

The associations Jung builds using the numbers three and four may vary depending on the main subject of his analysis. They might be related to the sexing of some psychological aspects such as the Animus, which is associated with the masculine and the number 3, or the Anima, feminine and linked to 4, but they are mainly used in the analysis of the unity of the self. In his analysis of the dogma of trinity, Jung highlights the partiality of the Christian symbol based on the number three and integrates it with the image of the mandala, linked to the number 4, which is, in his opinion, better suited to represent totality. Jung mainly refers to the tradition of alchemy, quoting the "Axiom of Maria Prophetissa" as a hermetic formulation of the symbolic function of the number four, which he extensively discusses in "The Problem of the Fourth" (Jung, "Problem," *Collected Works* Vol. 11, 164-192). This axiom simply states that: "One becomes two, two becomes three, and out of the third comes the one as the fourth" and it has been considered in relation to the process of individuation in general: "Jung used the axiom of Maria as a metaphor for the whole process of individuation. One is the original state of unconscious wholeness; two signifies the conflict between opposites; three points to a potential resolution; the third is the transcendent function; and the one as the fourth is a transformed state of consciousness, relatively whole and at peace" (Sharp). Not so simple are the implications of this statement for the exemplification of the human cognitive process as expressed by Jung in relation to his description of the dogma of the Trinity, when he represents the figures of the Father, the Son, and the Holy Spirit (ghost) as the various stages of the recognition of the self: the reflection of the one that becomes two and the conscience of the self as a third separate entity. The lack of a symbol for the unconscious part of the self, which is its own mirrored but inverted image, leads Jung to consider the quaternity of the mandala as a better symbol for totality. As a consequence, the image of goodness, represented in the vertex of the triangle of trinity as Christ, is reflected in the fourth vertex of the mandala as the anti-christ, therefore solving the controversy of the nature of evil that Jung had already analysed in relation to the pre-Nicean doctrines. It seems to emerge that the *privatio-boni*, which constituted the basis of the definition of evil for early Christian orthodox doctrines, did not satisfy Jung who, in agreement with W. Pauli, tried to demonstrate the existence of evil in positive terms rather than in the negative concept of the lack of good.

In this context, Michael Mitchell's reading of the three main characters of *Jonestown* appears truly engaging, but it reveals the same unsatisfactory limit which Jung saw in the christian symbol of trinity, as long as Mr. Mageye is not considered. It could be useful, here, to insist on this fourth character, which may perform, in the complex vision of Harris, the function of the reflected 1, thus completing the representation of a unified whole. It is supportive of this view that *Jonestown* has often been described as "self-referential" and characterised by "self-reflexiveness" (Simon 207), and Hena Maes-Jelinek confirms this approach: "A major aspect of Bone's quest, especially in 'Foundation of Cities,' is its self-reflexiveness" (Maes-Jelinek, "Tricksters" 432). If we borrow Mitchell's vision, it is possible to refer to Jim Jones as the main vertex of the trinity, without associating him to any specific figure of the Christian dogma of trinity,[38] and

---

[38] The fluidity of Harris's characters applies also to the triadic figure they come to represent, with the result of a sort of interchangeability of the various vertices of the

Bone and Deacon as the other two. By introducing Mr. Mageye, a new symbol, the quaternal mandala, is formed where Jim Jones takes the function of the one and Mageye of the four. However, being one the inverted reflection of four, according to Jung's interpretation, it may seem sensible to associate the visionary, Western religious leader to the evil vertex, and the visionary, pre-Columbian shaman as the good one. This might result in a too simple opposition which sees a post-colonial subject as the innocent victim of an evil coloniser, but considering the premises of Jung's analysis of the self as a totality, where these opposites are necessary and their existence is completely and 'positively' recognised, the reading presented above may reflect Harris's own concept of the complex interrelation between coloniser and colonised that could bring to positive solutions even after the experience of such traumas as the ones realised in the disappearance of Native American cultures or in the middle passage. It is, in fact, through Mr. Mageye's visionary camera that a comprehensive vision of the past, which includes all the elements of pre-Columbian culture, including the "quadraties of Mayan mythography" (Burnett 228) associated by P. Burnett to Jung's mandalas, can be glimpsed at, revealing a hopeful perspective after the terrible tragedy brought by single minded fanaticism symbolised by Jones. As discussed in the section on Henry Paget's view of Harris's philosophy, the construction of the self emerges as central, and this is even truer in *Jonestown*: "Civilization has not solved (and I believe never fully will) the mystery of consciousness. [...] for example, that Francisco Bone in Jonestown, conscious of himself as a diminutive surviving entity of holocaust, says of himself 'one is a multitude'" (Harris in Simon 210). The individuation of both the "evil-technological" Western tradition and the "good-natural" pre-Columbian one which concur in the formation of the post-colonial self[39] must not, therefore, support a biased view, as both traditions are complex, multiple and ambiguous, like the Doctor Faustus character as described in *The Infinite Rehearsal*. Besides these few aspects, *Jonestown* reveals an intricate fabric which allows "simultaneous possibilities of flourishing into a poly-history" and valorises its presence in this discussion, for "[...] the novel belongs to those narratives identified by Linda Hutcheon as 'historiographic metafiction'" (Concilio, "Cryptic" 242). Therefore, as already mentioned in the first chapter, it is important to inscribe all these archetypal representations in a pro-

---

triad. Therefore, Jones, Bone and Deacon can be considered in turn as Father, Christ and Holy Ghost, despite the usual association of Bone with Christ.

[39] The term post-colonial is here considered in its widest meaning, including the Western self, which, in some way, has been affected by the colonial experience.

ject in which their main function is that of a kind of historical revision through multiple lenses, performed with ethereal allegories, as will emerge in the section about the collective unconscious: "Jonestown lay still submerged in the collective unconscious! it had not yet been built in 1954. This was true but I could see it lifting on to a wave of the future" (Harris, *Jonestown* 197).

3.2.4 *The Mask of the Beggar* and Ulyssean Images

Another Europe-based pool of archetypes providing Harris with the basic material for his visionary fiction is certainly the world of Ancient Greece, in particular Homer's epic, which seems to play a prominent role in Caribbean culture, as Walcott's *Omeros* (1990) demonstrates. This should not sound strange if one considers the importance the sea plays for the two cultures, the Greek and the Caribbean, and the presence of *The Odyssey* in many different literary traditions. It is in fact this epic work of Homer's which offers Harris one archetypal figure often recurring in his works: Ulysses, Odysseus. It is not, however, the figure of Ulysses as a whole which will be discussed here, rather the role he plays in a particular section of the *Odyssey*: the moment he returns home after his long absence. After twenty years of wandering Ulysses comes back to Ithaca disguised as a beggar. The figure of the disguised Ulysses provides an allegorical image to Harris to represent the "legacies" of past or eclipsed cultures over the present, which are revealed to those who recognise the profound language of the imagination, such as the beggar's real identity, only disclosed to Telemachus's eyes.

It is possible to read *The Mask of the Beggar* as one of Harris's most clearly autobiographical novels, because of the connections he draws between his own step-father's disappearance in "the ocean of the forest" (Harris, *Beggar* 3) and the disappearance of Odysseus. The loss of his step-father in the interior of Guyana is a fact often recorded in reference to Harris's life and it is a recurring element throughout his work. It is however in an autobiographical essay that Harris reveals the importance of this episode:

> In an autobiographical essay, Wilson Harris describes the strong emotional impact he experienced as a child of eight when news reached his mother that his step-father had disappeared in the rainforests of Guyana. On the same day, his mother opened a large black trunk that had belonged to his real father, who had also disappeared in the Guyanese interior, from which she extracted a copy of *The Odyssey* and a wooden horse "carved from

a Greenheart tree" [Harris, 122]. Harris writes about the first event of that memorable day:

> My step-father's disappearance in that immense interior when I was a child was the beginning of an involvement with the enigma of quest and journeys through visible into invisible worlds that become themselves slowly visible to require further penetration into other invisible worlds without end or finality. [Harris, 122] (Maes-Jelinek, "Carnival" 377)[40]

This aspect reveals a deeper insight when it is compared with Krishna Ray Lewis's consideration about some autobiographical elements in *The Carnival Trilogy*:

> Holquist, Bahktin's translator, reminds us of life's dialogism: "In order to forge a self, I must do so from outside. . . I author myself." And Paquet has argued that in West Indian autobiography there is the "intention of something other than autobiography. . . Autobiographical self as subject is transformed into cultural archetype." Thus Ghost is spoken for through the voices of several narrators. (Lewis 89-90)

Krishna Ray Lewis highlights the archetypal function of the autobiographical aspect of some of Harris's novels, which sees the reflection over the self and personal experience, as parallel with the process of recognition of a cultural consciousness and identity, in line with Henry Paget's interpretation of Caribbean poeticism. At the time of writing, *The Carnival Trilogy* may have been the clearest manifestation of this tendency to problematise individual experience and cultural identity through Homeric imagery, especially regarding the rewriting of *The Odyssey* in *The Four Banks of the River of Space*. Moreover, Harris readily acknowledged the strong relation of his view of myth with the modernist's and Joyce's, especially in *The Infinite Rehearsal*, as Hena Maes Jelinek ("*Carnival, The Infinite Rehearsal,* and *The Four Banks of the River of Space*" 388) points out in her critical insight on Harris's admiration for the Irish writer, quoting this passage from Harris:

---

40 The quotes in Maes-Jelinek's text refer to Harris's autobiographical essay, "Wilson Harris: An Autobiographical Essay," in *Exploring the Palace of the Peacock*, ed. Adler Joyce Sparer.

I saw the new moon like a curved fingernail in the late, afternoon Old New Forest sky. I stared at it with intensity. As if my hollow voyager lost and lost and found again and again had pared it from ancient Homer's webbed hand with immeasurable Joycean delicacy and drawn it on the sunset sky. (Harris, *Infinite* 3)

However, with the publication of *The Mask of the Beggar* in 2003, Harris brought the investigation of these themes to a deeper level, as Zulfikar Ghose notices in his review of *The Mask of the Beggar,* managing to intermingle the fictional qualities of his own writing with an unusually intelligible critical insight, in spite of Syed Manzu Islam's opinion. This novel appeared to be the perfect closing for the writer's career, a view supported by the author himself on several occasions, but the recent publication of *The Ghost of Memory* (2006) confirmed the ongoing process of revision typical of Harris's literary approach. Nevertheless, *The Mask of the Beggar* possesses peculiar qualities in relation to Harris's whole literary production, which can be defined, both the single novel and the complete work, as "a philosophical journey down towards the roots of consciousness" (Maes-Jelinek, "Carnival" 388). A similar opinion is expressed by Ghose:

> The final novel [*The Mask of the Beggar*] can be seen as a summation of what Harris has been voicing (in that peculiarly personal rhythm of his prose) in all of his work since *Palace*, immersing the reader in dimensions of time and space that are dreamlike, unsettling, and yet profoundly real. [...] a kind of aesthetic summation of Harris's career. (Ghose)

Ghose expresses some reserve on the excessive "abstract generalization" that the novel's summing quality often generates; he nevertheless recognises the unusual clarity of some passages, especially in the introductory note: "The text of the book is preceded by a note in which Harris presents an uncharacteristically direct statement about his ideas and how they are to be understood in his work" (Ghose). A long quotation from the introductory note is therefore useful:

> In *The Mask of the Beggar* a nameless artist seeks mutualities between cultures. He seeks cross-cultural realities that would reverse a dominant code exercised now, or to be exercised in the future, by an individual state whose values are apparently universal. He senses great dangers for humanity in this determined and

one-sided notion of universality. He senses unconscious pressures within neglected areas of the Imagination that may erupt into violence. The roots of consciousness are his pursuit in a quantum cross-cultural art that brings challenges and unexpected far-reaching, subtly fruitful consequences.

The West has implicit governance of the world in politics, economics, social and cultural values. This is a well-known fact. It may have started with the Conquest of the pre-Columbian civilizations of the Americas in the sixteenth century and the decline of the ancient civilizations of China and India.

The Mask of the Beggar is based on the disguise Odysseus adopts on returning to his kingdom in Ithaca. It is changed, however, into a holed or fissured face in which Chinese, Indian, African and European immigrants may be invoked in Harbourtown, an imaginary gateway into South and Central America. Quetzalcoatl, an ancient god of the Americas, comes into focus in an unusual way that adds mutual and implicit distinctions between figures that appear:

Well-nigh forgotten, ancient pre-Columbian imageries are explored. They offer new perspectives. European codes begin, it seems, to suffer a measure of transfiguration as they face faculties and creativities beyond their formal traditions. (Harris, *Beggar* vii-viii)

Fundamental concepts of Harris's philosophy are expressed here with rare clarity: the mutuality of historical and cultural processes above all, such as the insect-eaten books in Carpentier's *The Lost Steps* (1953): when "European codes" come into contact with the pre-Columbian world of the Amazon and Central-South America, they suffer radical "transfiguration," but they nevertheless participate in a mutual process of creativity "through cross-culturalities in Space and Time" (Harris, *Beggar* ix).

The Greek myth of Odysseus is not an exception, it is transfigured and reduced to the common archetypal ground of human experience through the image of the beggar's mask:

His crew, who had been lost or drowned, were alien and invisible then. But did they not lurk in the holes and crevices of his mask? They were unconsciously/subconsciously there. You will find it

3 Jungian and Pre-Modern Influences 97

> as well in Pre-Columbian, ancient masks, in the oceans of forest of South and Central America, alternative faces secreted in one mask, the faces sometimes of alternative natures whose subtlety we have long forgotten to read. No wonder the Beggar, in one shape or form, endures. (Harris, *Beggar* 4-5)

Ulysses's image intermixes with absences, invisible subjects/objects of history who gather under the mask of a Beggar: the archetypal image of a lost father, in a way, the image of the quest for identity. It might even be interpreted as a realisation of one aspect of Jung's archetype of the Old Man, meaning: "the Beggar's mask that remains a subtle opening into the origins of meaning" (Harris, *Beggar* 13).

The archetypal world arising from a "profound, universal understanding" operated by "the inexplicable mind of the imagination" (Harris, *Beggar* 5) escapes history's "linear, one-track plane" (Harris, *Beggar* 9) by presenting a reality in which time and space are flexible: "I died in 1952 and yet I speak in 2000 (after my death) and in 1850 before my birth)" (Harris, *Beggar* 8). The narrating I who begins as the mother of the artist-child who recognises the Beggar, progressively overcomes the gender division and becomes, as usual, a voice that defies individuality, this time not through the intervention of several alter-egos, but with a gradual descent into the meanders of an "extended consciousness." In such a context the rhythmic repetition of profound questions such as "what is art? or even "what am I?" assumes a central role in the process of conscious reflection, but one question is more relevant than others to this discussion: "what is memory?" Memory, as the basis for history, has a particular function in the world of the archetypes. It is not only a memory of the past, it is also an active agent in the present and a numinous foresight into the future, in a complete flexibility, circularity of time, "open-ended *stillness* of flying Time" (Harris, *Beggar* 48), "the strangest blend of today and of a well-nigh forgotten yesterday in an abyss of Imagination" (Harris, *Beggar* 94). It is a "collective memory" (Harris, *Beggar* 17), "a precarious identity of opposites, such a precarious art of collective memory" (Harris, *Beggar* 19), This collective memory is to be found in the image of the mask:

> The skeleton on which I place the Beggar's Mask gives me bumps, holes, crevices from which to make the diverse racial figures of humanity we have imprisoned in our minds *as though they were separate, absolutely separate, entities.* [...] I hope to

> look at a long tradition of *unawareness* of models we have neglected that bear acutely on us and on our unity of origins, despite appearances, in them... (Harris, *Beggar* 68)

As Hena Maes Jelinek cleverly notices, "in most of Harris's fiction, especially the later novels, fissures, splits, holes and gaps are recurring images parallel to chasms in the landscape or the abysses of history" (Maes-Jelinek, "Mask" 455). The quest for wholeness which characterises many of Harris's novels is therefore impossible and unattainable, but through the splits and the holes, through the "wounds" of history, we can glimpse at a reality, only partial in our perception, which is the substance of myth, whose unity can be described only through different realisations of partial stories, partial archetypal representation of a whole expanded "collective unconscious" which comprises, as will be extensively discussed, landscape, trees and animals in a sort of "world's unconscious":

> Already in *Tradition the Writer and Society*, Harris suggests that when Ulysses is tied to the mast of his ship to listen to the Sirens, the mast "becomes an extension of his body" and he talks of "a community of animate and inanimate features" (52-53). This is a recurrent feature in his fiction. (Maes-Jelinek, "Mask" 456)

3.3 Archetypes, the Collective Unconscious, the World's Unconscious and the Quest for Unity

After these few examples, it may be easier to understand and to explain the reluctance showed by Harris when references were made to Jung's theory of the "collective unconscious" mentioned at the beginning of this chapter. Many common positions have emerged from the analysis of three particular novels, and the influence Jungian theories bear on Harris's literary evolution cannot be denied. However, the consideration of the wider scope of the term preferred by the Guyanese writer can be useful for the definition of his peculiar philosophy and his approach to history and time. First, a systematisation of the concept of "collective unconscious" as the womb of the archetypal representations used by Harris and Jung will finally determine to what extent the work of Harris can be inscribed in an exclusively Jungian perspective. Secondly, the discrepancies and the inclusiveness of Harris's own vision of a "world's unconscious" will be delineated to be extensively discussed in the following chapters, regarding both their cultural origins and their effect on the writer's philosophy and poetics.

Here, it is useful to recall and expand the definitions of archetype and archetypal image discussed in the first part of this chapter. According to the handy *Jung Lexicon: A Primer of Terms & Concepts,* archetypes are the pool of "primordial, structural elements of the human psyche" (Sharp). This might be seen as part of the deepest layer of the human psyche which sees, in Jungian terms, the conscious ego at the opposite side, followed by progressively deeper layers – the self-image, or Persona; subconscious memories; denied psychic material, or Shadow; gendered opposition, or Anima / Animus and finally the realm of universal and archetypal processes labelled "collective unconscious." As already mentioned in section III.ii, the archetypes are unknowable and irrepresentable, and their existence can only be inferred through the analysis of archetypal images, "the form or representation of an archetype in consciousness" (Sharp). Jung gave various definitions of archetypal image, but in literary contexts the terms – archetype and archetypal image – sometimes are not clearly distinguished, therefore a closer analysis might be helpful. First, it must be made clear that images are the basic elements of consciousness: "Archetypes... present themselves as ideas and images, like everything else that becomes a content of consciousness" (Jung, "Nature of the psyche" § 435). Secondly, the nature of archetypes must be acknowledged as predominantly extra-conscious, as their "effects" (archetypal images) are the only knowable manifestations: "Archetypes are, by definition, factors and motifs that arrange the psychic elements into certain images, characterized as archetypal, but in such a way that they can be recognized only from the effects they produce." (Jung, "Trinity" § 222 [note2]). On the basis of these statements, a definitive approach to the nature of archetypes can be found again in Jung's own words: archetypes are not "a question of inherited ideas but of inherited possibilities of ideas" (Jung, "Anima Concept" § 136). That is to say: archetypes are not actually perceivable elements, but potential entities "[The archetype is] a dynamism which makes itself felt in the numinosity and fascinating power of the archetypal image" (Jung, "Nature of the psyche" § 414).

Moving on to the core of the question, particular attention should be given to the adjective "inherited," because it points to the main question of the definition of the level of reality (not only psychic, but also biological, as will be seen later on) of the "collective unconscious." Archetypes are, in fact, not "individual acquisitions but, in the main, common to all, as can be seen from [their] universal occurrence" (Jung, "Anima Concept" § 136). There is a deep level in the individual which is therefore linked to all the other individuals both in space, that is to say regardless of specific cultures, and in time: ever present in different historical eras. This level is labelled by Jung with the expression "collective unconscious," a term which draws back to Lévy-Bruhl's studies about the "savage mind" and specifically refers to the formulation of the concept of "collective representations." (Levy-Bruhl ch. 1) However questionable,[41] Lévy-Bruhl's studies about the psyche of the "savages" represented a fundamental contribution to the evolution of psychoanalysis, with the formulation of such concepts as "collective representations" and "participation mystique," whose influence can be seen both in Jung's vision of the "unus mundus" and in Harris's extended concepts of the "universal unconscious" and the intuitive imagination. A brief definition of "collective representations" can be useful to understand Jung's borrowing of the term to refer to the reality of the archetypes as a whole:

> According to Levy-Bruhl, [...] the social group constructs mental processes in a different manner which is imposed on the individual who constitutes a part of the social group. Levy-Bruhl has labelled this phenomenon as 'Collective Representations.' The reason as for the differences in mental processes is, thus, collective and sociological and a collective psychology may be constructed for each society. (Serper)

Collective representations, therefore, shape the mental processes of the individuals of a particular social group, who show, as a consequence, common mental processes in the interaction with reality which are socially constructed in time. Jung's vision of a much wider social group, which comprises all the human beings, justifies the term collective, while "unconscious" refers to "the totality of all psychic phenomena that lack the quality of consciousness" (Sharp). Actually Jung considers the "collective unconscious" as "a structural layer of the human psyche containing inherited elements, distinct from the personal unconscious," (Sharp) adding the characteristic of inheritance mentioned above. The "collective unconscious" acts at a "structural" level, outside consciousness (although elements may become conscious under particular conditions), and it is commonly shared among human beings, inherited through the centuries: "the

---

41 Sir Edward Evan Evans-Pritchard had already criticised Lévy-Bruhl's assumption that the savage mind (besides the inability to differentiate the supernatural from reality) did not address contradictions at all, while, in Pritchard's opinion, it addressed it in different ways other than logic and speculation, typical of the Western mind. Successively, Lévi Strauss addressed the problem in his *La pensée sauvage* (1962), drawing similar conclusions.

collective unconscious contains the whole spiritual heritage of mankind's evolution, born anew in the brain structure of every individual" (Jung, "Structure of the Psyche" § 342). It is clear, at this point, that these theories can be seen as deep influences in Harris's vision of extended cross-culturality, considering the tendency of the elements of the "collective unconscious" to manifest themselves in literary terms:

> An archetypal content expresses itself, first and foremost, in metaphors. If such a content should speak of the sun and identify with it the lion, the king, the hoard of gold guarded by the dragon, or the power that makes for the life and health of man, it is neither the one thing nor the other, but the unknown third thing that finds more or less adequate expression in all these similes, yet – to the perpetual vexation of the intellect – remains unknown and not to be fitted into a formula. (Jung, "Child" § 267)

Among all the similarities emerging in the analysis of the psychological concept of archetype and of its anthropological realisation in a kind of "savage mind," there are two questions of ambiguity: one concerning Harris's substantial agreement with Evans-Pritchard's and Lévi-Strauss criticisms of Lévy-Brühl's formulation, and one about Jung's concept of the heritage contained in the "collective unconscious." As to the first, it must be acknowledged that the Guyanese writer, in spite of his similar cross-cultural approaches, explicitly distances himself from the French anthropologist, as poignantly noticed by Hena Maes-Jelinek: "I must point out that Harris distances himself from structuralism" (Maes-Jelinek, "Future" 7 [note]). Actually, Harris often refers to Lévi-Strauss's work recognising its value as a relatively unbiased study of Amazonian cultures, but he criticises his structural method on the basis of his own conception of myth: an "untamable force or *unstructured* mediation between partial systems" (Harris, "Carnival" 132. Emphasis in the original). According to Harris, "what we can salvage from structuralism at his best, I think, is the community beneath static systems whose 'articulacy' is biased" (132). In conclusion, Western interpretations of the "savage mind," although they reach with Lévi-Strauss a considerable level of unbiased analysis, do not completely express, for Harris, the potential implications of a different system of thought such as the Amerindian-Amazonian-South-American one, deeply based on the actual perception of a mythical and archetypal reality, offering us "some mysterious evolution of structures of ancient myth within our psyche [...] and disclos[ing] unsuspected inner/outer dimensionalities that one may call 'unfinished genesis of the imagination'" (Harris, "Composition 17).

Particularly the concept of "participation mystique," which has been relegated by Lévy-Bruhl to a manifestation of a less developed mind immersed in superstitious beliefs, is reinterpreted by Harris, mirroring the general criticism by Lévi-Strauss, as a cognitive approach radically different from Western logic, with a dignity of its own. Especially concerning the aspect of "participation mystique" which relates to natural phenomena and environment, Harris seems to reverse Lévy-Bruhl's judgement that posits the unreliability of a cognitive process "in which the subject cannot distinguish himself from the thing" (Samuels, Shorter, Plauts 105), by praising the possibilities of an intuitive approach to knowledge. As will be clarified in the last chapter, the mutuality of subject and object inserted in a system which contemplates the livingness of natural environment and landscapes is highly valued by Harris as a perspective which can go beyond exclusively human perception into a universal, and mystic to a certain extent, relationship with an extended reality whose temporal dimension subverts the linearity of Western historical approach, a "phenomenon of simultaneity" (Harris, "Quetzalcoatl" 187), inscribed in "a mythical thought [...] attuned to the natural and cosmic worlds, to their rhythms and metamorphoses" (Maes-Jelinek, "Future" 6).

As to the second ambiguity, it must be made clear that when Jung links the 'collective unconscious' to the individual psyche, he tends to consider the biological aspect of this inheritance, therefore limiting it to humankind: "Archetypes are systems of readiness for action, and at the same time images and emotions. They are inherited with the brain structure - indeed they are its psychic aspect" (Jung, "Mind and Earth" 53). However, in the same passage, there is a sentence that may give rise to much wider interpretations: "they are thus, essentially, the chthonic portion of the psyche... that portion through which the psyche is attached to nature" (53). This apparent contradiction is the point from which Harris's interpretation of the common psychic elements of experience departs from Jung's. As discussed above, Harris's vision should not be considered as a reformulation of Jung's insight, but rather as an expansion: reaffirming the psychic reality of a common human experience, Harris extends the participation to all beings, whether animate or inanimate, ranging from the animal and the vegetal world to the "absent-present" function of disappeared populations, up to the inclusion of the whole South-American landscape:

> In some essays I said that I don't know if the word "collective" is the best word, that one could say "universal" unconscious, but I must make this very clear here. When I speak of the unconscious I'm not only speaking of the human unconscious but of the unconscious that resides in objects, in trees, in rivers, I'm suggesting that there is a psyche, a mysterious entity, that links us with the unconscious in nature. (Harris, "Composition" 19)

This inclusion may draw on non-Western elements that contribute to Harris's philosophy, such as the Amerindian legacies and the pre-Columbian traditions to which he often refers. The discussion of these sources, however, deserves a separate analysis, and it will constitute the core of chapter 4. Here, it is important to investigate the method Harris uses to integrate this view to his writing, with particular attention to Jungian connections. As early as the publication of *Tradition the Writer and Society* (1967), Harris showed a distinct approach to the matter that had already emerged in his early fictional production, paying tribute to Jung's achievements:

> the association of life and environment is a deep process immensely altering or breaking the shape of things in 'the domain of the specific and esoteric' (Malraux) or in the 'archetype of the collective unconscious' (Jung). (Harris, "Art" 9)

This is much more evident in later interviews, a means that, despite the apparent obscurity, Harris often uses to convey complex concepts in a somehow less cryptic way than in his critical essays. This is the case with the view of unity which forms the basis of his concept of "the world's unconscious" and its manifestations:

> Well, as I tend to see it at this point in time, there is a kind of wholeness, but one can't structure that wholeness. One knows it's there and one moves into it ceaselessly, but all the time one moves with partial images. Now the partial image has within it a degree of bias but it also represents a part of something else, so that there is a kind of ceaseless *expedition* into wholeness which has to do with the ways in which one consumes – metaphysically consumes – the bias in the partial image and releases that image as a part of something else which one may not be immediately aware of in that context. (Harris, interview by Jane Wilkinson 30)

In this passage it is possible to read various connections with the definition of archetypes and their manifestations as mentioned above, especially regarding the partial nature of the archetypal images (partial images) through which we come into contact with the reality of the "collective unconscious," here referred to as "wholeness." Moreover, the ambiguous nature of archetypal representations is also taken into account, by mentioning their "degree of bias," and even the function of opposites is addressed ("to consume the bias") although in different terms than the Jungian process of *coincidentia oppositorum*, which Harris often freely borrows.

It is possible, on the other side, to read this as a "high-level" description of Harris's own method of bringing up unconscious material in his writings ("something else which one may not be immediately aware of") through the intentional use of paradoxes and juxtapositions, which practically mirrors the psychic double function of archetypes. Even clearer connections can be seen in the parallel function of dream as the liminal experience between consciousness and unconscious as used by both Harris and Jung, and in the metaphoric function attributed to the quest, whether for the Philosopher's Stone, the Holy Grail, or El-Dorado, in the representation of the "impossible dream, impossible quest for wholeness" (Harris, *Infinite* 173) performed in the search for recognition of "the self," which is always provisional and continuously questioned. Among those quests, it is important to comment on the common choice of both Jung and Harris of the alchemical process as an effective metaphor, as particularly emerges in *Psychology and Alchemy* and in *The Palace of the Peacock* (1960). Harris often refers to alchemy, but, for the sake of brevity, a short example will suffice here:

> What I would say straight away is that the alchemical imagination functions in this way, in my judgement. You know the alchemists believed in what they call the *nigredo* phase, which meant the unknown land - they were entering the unknown land and therefore it was a kind of darkness. Now as they explored that, a kind of illumination came into being which they called the *albedo* phase, or the dawn, dawning light, and then that moved on into the phase they called the *cauda pavonis*, the colours of the peacock. Now the thing is that the *cauda pavonis* phase can come back into the *nigredo* phase and *that* is enriched and it moves on... So it's a continuous kind of cyclical thing which could be expanding, if you like, but every time it is as if the *nigredo* phase alters its shape and form as it moves back into the

albedo phase. In other words the 'labels' of alchemy are a *threshold* into being, into a *de-centred Being* through which we break the tyranny of one-sided existence, one sided charisma or centrality. (Harris, interview by Jane Wilkinson 34)

This is again linked with Jung's interest in alchemy on various levels. First, Harris and Jung both recognise an "unexpected affinity between individual dream symbolism and medieval alchemy" (Fordham), and secondly they accord a profound symbolical value to the quest for the philosopher's stone, which can parallel the quest for wholeness mentioned above. Frieda Frordham, in her introductory work, seems to support this view, although she exclusively refers to Jung. Nevertheless the connections with Harris, particularly with the process described above and effectively fictionalised in *The Palace of the Peacock*, can be easily perceived:

> The individuation process is sometimes described as a psychological journey; it can be a tortuous and slippery path, and can at times simply seem to lead round in circles; experience has shown, however, that a truer description would be that of a spiral. In this journey the traveler must first meet with his shadow, and learn to live with this formidable and often terrifying aspect of himself: there is no wholeness without a recognition of the opposites. He will meet, too, with the archetypes of the collective unconscious, and face the danger of succumbing to their peculiar fascination. If he is fortunate he will in the end find 'the treasure hard to attain,' the diamond body, the Golden Flower, the lapis whatever name and guise have been chosen to designate the archetype of wholeness, the self. (Fordham)

According to Fordham, this is the ground over which Jung finds the most significant links with the history of religion, mythology and alchemy, and it could be said the same for Harris, who reformulates the parallelism Jung built with pre-modern religious thinking by frequently citing "the memory theatre," as discussed by Frances Yates in *The Art of Memory* (1960), and her interpretation of Titian's painting *The Allegory of Prudence*.[42] Moreover, as already mentioned,

---

42 Harris constantly refers to Yates's book, but here this short reference is included with the only aim of identifying his main source for pre-modern thought. Any discussion of Frances Yates's complex book is avoided, like several other important

he considers himself "a kind of Christian Gnostic" (interview by Riach 57). Along with these, Harris repeatedly links the power of intuitive knowledge to scientific theories such as quantum mechanics, for the possibilities of different layers of reality (parallel universes) it suggests, and chaos theory, for its ability to consider patterns of regularity within complex, seemingly random systems.[43] Both these directions will not be discussed here in depth, while the main urgency which underlies Harris's metaphors will be finally differentiated from Jung's.

In an interview given in 1990, Harris complained that "there has been a complete disregard for the unconscious" (interview by Riach 35) in the literary world, expressing his concern about one of the central ideas that, according to P.T. Zabriskie, "shaped Jung's view on life, art, and history":

> Our conscious minds are *not* the sole captains of our ships or even of our thoughts. Individually and collectively, we are continually being influenced, for better an worse, in our thinking, our feelings, our behavior, and our perceptions, by energies of which we are much of the time unconscious. (Zabriskie 3)

According to Fordham's view, "The individuated person, [...] through his acceptance of the unconscious has, while remaining aware of his unique personality, realized his brotherhood with all living things, even with in organic matter and the cosmos itself" (Fordham). This cannot however be considered the orthodox interpretation of Jung's theories about the "collective unconscious"; Harris is aware of this and frequently highlights his extended concept by proposing, even if not systematically, a terminological differentiation. Finally, despite the initial assumption with which Harris denied any direct influence from Jungian theories, he is completely aware of the convergences and differences between his formulation of "universal unconscious" and Jung's:

> This is the mystery of one's peculiar dialogue with the past and it proves or validates what C.G. Jung calls the 'collective unconscious' and its eruption within processes of hard work, concentration and creativity, into the subconscious and conscious. Jung by

---

influences, for methodological reasons.

43 A similar view of the function of the metaphoric use of the concept of chaos and chaotic systems can be found in Antonio Benítez-Rojo's *La isla que se repite: El Caribe y la perspectiva posmoderna*. 1989. Trans. as *The Repeating Island: The Caribbean and the Postmodern Perspective*. 1996.

> and large applied his concept to the human psyche and faculty. I sense the collective or universal unconscious extending into voices that echo within the roots of nature as from the ancestral dead, from rivers, from rocks, from birds and other species, from the rhythm of landscapes, skyscapes, etc. (Harris, "Profiles" 201)

The implications of this expanded view for Harris's interpretation and fictionalisation of time and history will be discussed in depth in the conclusive chapter, while parallel origins of this concept and different metaphors for the alchemical quest of unity, such as the El Dorado legend, will be investigated in the next chapter in relation to non-European sources.

4 – Pre-Columbian Legacies

Wilson Harris moved from Guyana to Britain in 1959 at the age of 38; at that time he had only published a collection of poetry entitled *Eternity to Season* (1954), but he had been extensively writing essays, poems and short stories for Caribbean journals, essentially *Kyk-Over-Al* and *Bim*, since the mid 1940s. These early writings already bore the signs of the fundamental experience which characterised, through continuous re-elaboration, the whole body of Harris's philosophy: the exploration of the Guyanese (British Guiana at that time) interior. In T.J. Cribb's "T.W. Harris – Sworn Surveyor" (1993) precious information is reported about this period of Harris's life which the Guyanese novelist often refers to, seldom giving precise clues. According to Cribb, Harris was being trained around 1939-1940 as an official surveyor, a figure ideally related to late eighteenth-early nineteenth century explorers such as Robert Schomburgk and Alexander Von Humboldt, who will be presented later in this chapter. At the time of Harris's training, however, the profession had changed significantly, astronomic and ethnographic concerns still formed part of a surveyor's tasks, "but more frequently work had to do with topographic, engineering, and cadastral surveying, in all of which Harris was trained." (Cribb, "Sworn" 34). This kind of specific education can be seen as the source of Harris's interest and competence in scientific matters as expressed in the frequent analogies he draws between his philosophy and complicated issues of physics such as quantum mechanics and chaos theory. A confirmation can be found in a rarely concise autobiographical account of his early education at Queen's College in Georgetown:

> I left at the end of 1938 with credit or distinction in English, Latin history and mathematics. The last was not my favourite subject, but I could enjoy the elegance of geometric and algebraic proportions, and at a time – when unemployment was endemic in the colony – it became the basis upon which I was able to study the trigonometric properties of land surveying. (Adler xii)

On the other hand, it is the actual experience of the rain forest, the people and the landscapes of the Guyanese interior that stroke Harris the most and started a process which can be still traced in his evolving philosophy even after more than sixty years. It is important to ground this process in real experience, because Harris is often criticised for his tendency to over-intellectualise, while the roots of his interpretation of pre-Columbian traditions, which substantially inform his philosophy and concur in the formation of the Guyanese self, are strongly connected with his personal, direct experience of the peoples and landscapes of the interior of the country.[44] In "A Talk on the Subjective Imagination" (1973), reprinted in the precious *Explorations, a Selection of Talks and Articles* (1981), Harris goes back to his early years in Guyana and re-elaborates his contact with this new reality which has evolved in such a deep relation with his literary work:

> I was born on the coastlands of Guyana and one is aware that one has there a heterogeneous body of peoples, peoples whose antecedents came from Africa, form India, Europe, and so on. And apart from that there is a very significant Amerindian presence, people who are descended from the pre-Columbian world. One of the sad things is that most of these people live within a context in which the issue of community remains alien or hidden away. This is something which came home to me in a peculiarly symbolic way on my first expedition into the interior of Guyana, in which I was aware of an enormous difference between the landscape of the coastlands and the landscape of the interior. I had penetrated 150 miles. It seemed as if one had travelled thousands and thousands of miles, and in fact had travelled to another world, as it were, because one was suddenly aware of the density of the place. One was aware of one's incapacity to describe it, as though the tools of language one possessed were inadequate. (Harris, "Subjective Imagination" 58)

Harris's strong rejection of realism, his intricacy of style and several recurring thematic elements in his work can be referred to the formative experience of the exploration of the Guyanese interior, although they are further complicated by previous related experiences or later studies and reinterpretations.[45] The the-

---

44 In support of this view, it may be useful to report Cribb's extremely detailed reconstruction of Harris's surveying records in which curiously the names of the characters of Donne's crew in *Palace of the Peacock* are listed: "A. da Silva, W. Schomburgh, [...] A.Carroll, G. Vigilance., L. De Souza [...] Here, then are the originals for the characters in *Palace of the Peacock,* and with Schomburgh we come to full circle, for according to Harris he was a grandson of the romantically inclined Richard Schomburgk the botanist and explorer, who had an affair with a creole woman in the 1840s. Once again we find that novels which have repeatedly been read as purely conceptual in their generation have a basis in experience" (Cribb, "Sworn" 38).

45 The tragic disappearances of Harris's father and successively of his step-father in the jungle strongly affected his view, as already mentioned in 3.2.4. Moreover, later

matic issues can be effectively analysed following two interconnected lines: first, a detailed analysis of the Amerindian cultures which characterise Harris's Guyanese background will be carried out with particular attention to the novels which directly re-interpret Amerindian elements; secondly, an extended discussion of some aspects of other American cultures, particularly Maya and Inca, will be offered with precise reference to the intuitive thread which Harris has woven between the South-American Amerindians and some of the great pre-Columbian civilisations. Particular attention will be paid to historical aspects and conceptions of time, in order to bring to the surface a relationship with animals, landscapes and the natural world which is rooted in the common experience of the rain-forest landscapes. Harris's interpretation of nature, its larger time scale and circularity, in relation to human time and history, will be the object of the fifth and final chapter.

4.1 Amerindians

4.1.1 Guyanese Society

As mentioned in III.ii.a, Guyana is often linked to the etymological origin of the term, meaning "land of waters";[46] however, it is commonly referred to as "the land of six peoples," borrowing the title of Michael Swan's essential book *British Guiana: The Land of Six peoples* (1957). This last definition relates to the former one for its stressing the liquid, unfixed quality of Guyanese social identity, which is usually divided in six different ethnic groups. The Indo-Caribbean community being the largest (43.45% of the entire population) and Afro-Caribbean the second largest (30.20%), the remaining four groups share a much smaller percentage which sees, in decreasing order, the people of mixed origin (16.73%), the Amerindians (9.16%), the Chinese and the Portuguese (0.20% each) and lastly the White with a mere 0.06% (Population & Housing Census 2002). Since 1980 (previous census), noticeable changes have occurred, especially regarding the foreseeable increase of people of mixed origin and a sensible decrease of the Indo-Caribbean component, but the most interesting evolution is the positive trend in Amerindian communities, which are demographically becoming more important. This variety of ethnic groups, investigated through many of E. Mittelholzer's novels, such as the Indo-Caribbean-centred *Corentyne Thunder* (1941), has been constitutive to Guyanese society since the

---

interest in quantum physics contributed to complicate his approach to these issues.
46 "Guyana is derived from an Amerindian root word which means 'land of waters'" (Harris, *Guyana* 7).

early colonial period, as a consequence of the frequent change of ruling nation which saw the alternation of Spain, France, the Netherlands and Britain. In 1957 Swan already recorded a similar situation:

> It would take, I imagine, half the lifetime of a social anthropologist to define the structure of Georgetown society accurately; to plot the relationships between the various peoples, the Chinese, Indians, Negroes, coloured people, high coloured people, British and Portuguese, not to mention the results of miscegenation between them all, would require the subtlety of a Guianese Proust. It is a subject which has, in fact, preoccupied the Guianese novelist, Edgar Mittelholzer, in many of his novels. Subtleties of social position exist largely among the 'coloured' people, that is to say people who have European blood, whether or not it is dominant. Out of a total population of 435,000 there are roughly 50,000 people, mostly living in Georgetown, who come into this category. (Swan, *British Guiana* 49)

Further on, he links the "miscegenation" to a frequent attitude of white colonial rulers who, apart from institutional slave-trade or indentured labour,[47] personally contributed to the definition of what has defiantly been considered by postcolonial intellectuals as an intrinsic, positive quality of all Caribbean society: hybridity or "mestizaje." Swan continues:

> It is surprising that a greater miscegenation has not taken place since inter-breeding between colonists and slave girls was practised from the beginning of colonization. As late as 1806, when Staunton St. Clair, a British army officer, arrived in the Colony, there were few European women there. 'The first thing generally done by a European on his arrival in this country,' he wrote, 'is to provide himself with a mistress from among the blacks, mulattoes, or mestees, for here they are to be found of all the different shades of colour.' (Swan, *British Guiana* 49)

This is the background from which the need for reconciliation that characterises Harris's thought sprouts. Along with post-colonial issues regarding a wider

---

47 After the abolition of slavery in 1838, indentured labourers (from Madeira and Portugal, Africa but mainly India) were brought to Guyana. Chinese people were deported mainly between 1834 and 1865. The process lasted up to 1917.

scope of coloniser-colonised relationships, the need for a common ground is immediately evident in such a multi-cultural country. Harris's strategy is no less multi-faceted, but the analysis of his concern with the recuperation of Amerindian traditions will here be favoured, without denying the interest he showed in incorporating other groups.[48] Despite the demographic trend, the Amerindian component of Guyanese culture has often been neglected, favouring the more evident (and violent) opposition of the two main groups. However, the original inhabitants of the interior never completely disappeared as did the Carib, Taino and Arawak in the main islands of the Caribbean: they have substantially maintained their ancient traditions, thanks to the almost exclusively coastal settlement of the colonial activities. Harris's main fictionalisation of Amerindian tradition can be seen in the rewriting of Carib myths in *The Sleepers of Roraima* (1970) and Arawak myths in *The Age of the Rainmakers* (1971). However it is the heritage of those neglected cultures as constitutive of Harris's philosophy which will be analysed in more details, by acknowledging, as far as possible in a literary study, its sources in actually observed Amerindian cultures.

4.1.2 Amerindians: Historical and Anthropological information

Except for archeological studies, which will be discussed later, the first information available to Westerners about Guyanese lands date back to Columbus's third voyage, in 1498, when he sighted Guyanese territories, and anchored off the coast. In his detailed *The Search for El Dorado* (1978), John Hemming quotes Columbus's first impressions of the new land and its people:

> he found the land to be 'the loveliest in all the world, and very populous' and contacts with the natives were friendly. 'They came out in hordes to the ship, and many of them wore pieces of gold at their breasts and some had pearls around their arms.' (Hemming 2)

The volume of water of the Orinoco deeply impressed Columbus and led him to think of the new land as a "vast continent," yet he was reluctant to admit it might not be Asia. Successively, he headed northwards, past the mouth of the Orinoco river, towards the Gulf of Paria through what is known today as the Co-

---

48 The all-encompassing quality of Harris's fiction is well known and its universal scope does not exclude any social group, however it may be useful to report at least his fictionalisation of the Indo-Guyanese, *The Far Journey of Oudin* (1961), and his portrait of the social turmoil of 1948, *The Eye of the Scarecrow* (1965).

lumbus Channel, without further explorations. Nevertheless, the kingdom of Spain claimed the new lands, and the reign of Nueva Grenada, which already comprised present-day Venezuela, was extended past the Orinoco mouth. During the 16th century, explorations[49] were carried out by Spanish adventurers such as Diego de Ordáz, Francisco de Orellana and Gonzalo Ximénez de Quesada, the first governor of the reign, to which the first organised expeditions for El Dorado can be traced.[50] The early encounters between Europeans and Amerindian peoples seem to confirm Todorov's theories about the misunderstandings generated by lack of communication (*La conquête de l'Amérique*), as it appears from the reports by Ximénez de Quesada and his designated successor Antonio de Berrío. From these accounts, as reported in Dr. Luís Orama's *En pos del Dorado* (1947) and José Rafael Lovera's *Antonio de Berrío: La obsesión por El Dorado* (1991), the myth of El Dorado may have generated from this kind of misunderstanding. The tendency to fulfil the desires of their "hosts" appears as a natural attitude on the side of the aboriginal peoples, as emerges from the account of Domingo de Vera Ibargoyen, one of Berrío's officers; while the Spaniards' ambition seems to grow uncontrolled to the point of requiring from Berrío, on Quesada's side, the oath to pursue "por el resto de la vida, a la conquista del Dorado" (Orama 13). These misunderstandings add up to the various preconceptions, of medieval origin, that peopled the Europeans' minds about wonderful creatures living in remote places, as in the case of Ibargoyen's report about the "cacique" Morequita's allusion to a nearby tribe whose individuals sported such massive shoulders that their head did not even come out of the chest (Lovera 150). These seem likely to be the prototypes of headless people such as those listed in *Mandeville's Travels*, a fantastic report about the rarities of the world published in the mid-14th century in England,[51] which probably was

---

49 In Hemming's work an important 16th century German expedition lead by P. von Hutten is also reported.
50 Several hypotheses were formulated around the legend of El Dorado, some identifying it as a lake (Pizarro), Lake Parime, or as a golden city (Raleigh); according to Hemming (120) the legend supposedly originated in Quito around 1540 and referred to a "golden man." However, it was under the reign of Quesada and Berrío that the legend widely spread.
51 "And in another isle toward the south dwell folk of foul stature and of cursed kind that have no heads. And their eyen be in their shoulders" (de Mandeville).

As an example of Mandeville's influence in British literature the following passage from *Othello* may be cited: "And of the Cannibals that each other eat, / The Anthropophagi, and men whose heads / Do grow beneath their shoulders" (Shakespeare, *Othello* I.iii. 142-144).

Walter Raleigh's most authoritative source when he set sail for his first exploration of "the large rich and beautiful empire of Guiana." Towards the end of the century, anticipated by a brief episode which saw William Hawkins's involvement in slave-trading activities (Adelaide-Merlande), the famous incursion of Sir Walter Raleigh took place and the English first came into contact with the Guyanese Amerindians and the land of the El Dorado. Raleigh, one of Queen Elizabeth's favourite courtiers, was an English adventurer who saw in the new lands freshly discovered by the Spanish an enormous golden mine, mainly because of the exaggerated accounts that reached 16th century Europe. He thought of Guyana as an easy opportunity to gain richness and fame, blinded by a burning ambition which emerges from his own account of the expedition, *The Discovery of the Large, Rich, and Beautiful Empire of Guiana, with a Relation of the Great and Golden City of Manoa (Which the Spaniards call El Dorado)*, published in Richard Hakluyt's *The principal Navigation, Voyages, Traffics and Discoveries of the English Nation* (1598-1600). This is not the first Western text which deals with the indigenous populations, but its diffusion and importance in the English literary panorama deserves particular attention. When Raleigh refers to the newly "discovered" land, he summarises many of the psychological features which characterise the coloniser's mind, including the association of the land with a virgin woman and the anxiety to take advantage and exploit its paradisiac abundance, mirroring the penetration of the rain forest with sexual intercourse, a sort of predatory desire for possession:

> Guiana is a country that hath yet her maidenhead, never sacked, turned, nor wrought; the face of the earth hath not been torn, nor the virtue and salt of the soil spent by manurance. The graves have not been opened for gold, the mines not broken with sledges, nor their images pulled down out of their temples. It hath never been entered by any army of strength, and never conquered or possessed by any Christian prince. (Raleigh)

His encounters with the aboriginal peoples were marked by his obsession with gold and by his political strategy; however, they reveal the typical attitude of the Europeans that essentially lasted for centuries, especially regarding Cannibalism:

> Of these people those that dwell upon the branches of Orenoque, called Capuri, and Macureo, are for the most part carpenters of

canoas; for they make the most and fairest canoas; and sell them into Guiana for gold and into Trinidad for tabacco, in the excessive taking whereof they exceed all nations. And notwithstanding the moistness of the air in which they live, the hardness of their diet, and the great labours they suffer to hunt, fish, and fowl for their living, in all my life, either in the Indies or in Europe, did I never behold a more goodly or better-favoured people or a more manly. They were wont to make war upon all nations, and especially on the Cannibals, so as none durst without a good strength trade by those rivers; but of late they are at peace with their neighbours, all holding the Spaniards for a common enemy. When their commanders die they use great lamentation; and when they think the flesh of their bodies is putrified and fallen from their bones, then they take up the carcase again and hang it in the cacique's house that died, and deck his skull with feathers of all colours, and hang all his gold plates about the bones of this arms, thighs, and legs. Those nations which are called Arwacas, which dwell on the south of Orenoque, of which place and nation our Indian pilot was, are dispersed in many other places, and do use to beat the bones of their lords into powder, and their wives and friends drink it all in their several sorts of drinks.

These encounters reveal an ambiguous attitude, praising the virtues of the Amerindians while condemning Cannibal practices and covering, at the same time, the extremely violent attitude which Raleigh did not spare even his fellow Europeans. This was exacerbated by his profound hatred of the Spanish, who happened to be killed in peaceful contexts, such as reported by J. Rafael Lovera about Berrío's welcoming of Raleigh's men who were offered shelter and food and in return massacred the delegates: "a los catorce que estaban comiendo les dieron de alabardazos y puñaladas, y sin poderse valer los unos a los otros, los mataron" (Lovera 338). Such unusual behaviour was determined by a precise political strategy: Raleigh was trying to gain indigenous peoples' confidence to drive the Spanish out of Guyana and to reassure the Queen about the prospect of an easy conquest. Besides political considerations, the quoted passage is important because it is one of the first descriptions of Guyanese peoples in the English language, and it already gives some useful information about their culture, such as the Macureo's ability in carving canoes and Arawak (Arwacas) traditional costumes, while the cannibal practices mentioned may refer to Carib tribes rather than Arawak. Raleigh's expedition, at first, seemed to gain great success and to open the way to English colonisation; however, after Charles Leigh's attempt at establishing an agriculture-based colony (1603), which came to an early end with his death in 1604, the interest of English colonists in Guyanese territories seemed to disappear. At home, Raleigh did not enjoy the same favours at court, especially after Queen Elizabeth's death, and he was imprisoned in the Tower of London. However; he was not taken aback by the situation: first, he managed to be freed and then set sail for another expedition in 1617, to gain King James's favour. This time he was not as fortunate as twenty years before and the Spanish could maintain their position in the land; when he got back to England he was finally beheaded, on request of the Spanish ambassador offended by Raleigh's attempt.

In the meantime, the Dutch had established a flourishing commercial relation in the region, without excessive friction with the Spanish. Kyk-Over-Al, the oldest European fort in Guyana was built by the Dutch in 1616 on a little island in the mouth of the Mazaruni River. The 17th and the 18th centuries saw an escalation of warfare in the Caribbean, especially in the islands, involving France, Spain, England and, to a lesser extent, the Netherlands, while exploration and ethnography of the Guyanese region were characterised by a lower priority on each nation's side, also due to the partial loss of interest in the frustrating search for El Dorado. The situation in Guyanese territories can be summarised by reporting the return of the English in 1630 in present-day Suriname, with a stronger presence after 1646. In 1781 the French drove the English out of Demerara, Essequibo and Berbice and founded Georgetown, which went to the Dutch with the Treaty of Versailles in 1783 and prospered under the name of Stabroek. In 1796 the lands and the city finally went back to the British, who reunited the provinces and established the colony of British Guiana in 1831. The historical context, which witnessed such frequent turnovers, determined the relative lack of both literary and scientific information about the Guyanese Amerindians, with the exception of the mentioned sources and other few accounts, such as those reported in Peter Hulme and Neil Whitehead's *Wilde Majesty: Encounters with the Caribs from Columbus to the Present Day: An Anthology* (1992). In this seminal work, which is mainly centred in the Caribbean islands, two interesting and contrasting episodes about Guyana can be singled out. In the account of the voyage of the Olive Branch, published between 1605 and 1625, William Turner, a member of the crew, presents the Amerindians as friendly and peaceful, while his fellow sailor John Nicholl reports a less favourable situation: friendly at first, the Amerindians violently attacked them and few could escape. Despite the contradiction, these last experiences deliver useful information about cultural aspects, such as witnessing the use of cassava root as food, a fundamental element in today's Guyanese-Amerindian diet: "a roote of a tree whose juice is poyson: but [...] the flower doth make an excellent kind of bread" (Hulme; Witehead 69).

An interesting but isolated case of literary interest in the Guyanese reality is Aphra Behn's *Oronooko*, set for the largest part in Suriname, published as early as 1688. However, the information about the Amerindians is flawed by the proto-novel's exoticism to the extent of rendering the Amerindian characters in a manner exclusively functional to the basic idealised opposition of a natural, unspoilt world and European "civilised" corruption. Before the 19th century, few other works dealt with the indigenous peoples of the Guyanas; worthy of mention is Fray Antonio Caulín's *Historia Corográfica, Natural Y Evangélica de la Nueva Andalucía, Provincias de Cumaná, Nueva Barcelona, Guayana y Vertientes del Río Orinoco*, published in 1779, while in the course of 1800 a series of works denote a progressively reviving interest. A recent article by Arlene Munro published in the online version of *Kyk-Over-Al*[52] partially reconstructs the increasing literary interest around Guyana during the early 19th century:

> When the British gained control of the colonies of Demerary-Essequibo and Berbice in 1796 several British expatriates came to the colony of British Guiana to work in various capacities. Among these were George Pinckard, Thomas Staunton St. Clair, Henry Bolingbroke, Robert Schomburgk, Rev. Edwin Wallbridge, and Rev. Henry V. P. Bronkhurst. These men were professionals and wrote about their journeys and experiences in British Guiana. Their books are a valuable source of information on the social and economic life of the colonies during the eighteenth and nineteenth centuries and are written from a Eurocentric perspective. At that point of history, books were written by Europeans whose social position and financial resources enabled them to publish books. The coloured masses were still labouring in the canefields. (Munro)

---

52 *Kyk-Over-Al* takes its name from the mentioned Dutch fort in Guyana; it is the only survivor of the three pioneering Caribbean journals born in the 1940's, *Bim* and *Focus* being the other two.

Munro introduces a few cases, but many more could be analysed, especially scientific explorations such as Charles Waterton's *Wanderings in South America* (1812-1824) or the passages regarding South America in Charles Darwin's *The Voyage of the Beagle* (1838), but for the sake of brevity only the most significant will be given further attention, with the intent of better analysing the important anthropological and literary works of the late 19th and early 20th centuries.

Alexander von Humboldt's *Personal Narrative of Travels to the Equinoctial Regions of America* is an early example of a naturalist-scientific approach to the Guyanese landscapes and peoples, and allows some clear insight in the Amerindian cultures encountered. It is curious how a definition given in this book could relate to Harris's approach to Guyanese traditions: "Guiana, that land of fiction and fabulous tradition" (Humboldt § 2.19). Humboldt's empiricism allows him to assume a detached attitude towards the 16th century legends about the El Dorado and to observe a fairly different reality:

> I found no cavity (druse), no crystallized substance, not even rock-crystal; and no trace of pyrites, or any other metallic substance. I enter into these particulars on account of the chimerical ideas that have been spread ever since the sixteenth century, after the voyages of Berreo and Raleigh, "on the immense riches of the great and fine empire of Guiana." (Humboldt § 2.19)

Although he does not dismiss the possibility of the presence of gold in the Guyanese territories on the sole basis of his own observation, his detached attitude allows some uninflated information about the Amerindian cultures to pass through, such as the useful description of general clothing habits:

> When we speak in Europe of a native of Guiana, we figure to ourselves a man whose head and waist are decorated with the fine feathers of the macaw, the toucan, and the humming-bird. Our painters and sculptors have long since regarded these ornaments as the characteristic marks of an American. We were surprised at not finding in the Chayma Missions, in the encampments of Uruana and of Pararuma (I might almost say on all the shores of the Orinoco and the Cassiquiare) those fine plumes, those feathered aprons, which are so often brought by travellers from Cayenne and Demerara. These tribes for the most part, even those whose intellectual faculties are most expanded, who culti-

> vate alimentary plants, and know how to weave cotton, are altogether as naked,* as poor, and as destitute of ornaments as the natives of New Holland. (* For instance, the Macos and the Piraoas. The Caribs must be excepted, whose perizoma is a cotton cloth, so broad that it might cover the shoulders.) The excessive heat of the air, the profuse perspiration in which the body is bathed at every hour of the day and a great part of the night, render the use of clothes insupportable. Their objects of ornament, and particularly their plumes of feathers, are reserved for dances and solemn festivals. The plumes worn by the Guipunaves are the most celebrated; being composed of the fine feathers of manakins and parrots. (Humboldt § 2.19)

Several other interesting examples may be extracted from Humboldt's account; however a number of them are particularly important because they directly relate to some of Harris's readings of Amerindian cultures. The next episode testifies the cruel habit of abandoning twin babies in the forest, which could be linked to Harris's reading of the myth of "bush babies" in *Yurokon*, which will be discussed later:

> When twins are born, false notions of propriety and family honour require that one of them should be destroyed. [...] To avoid the disturbance of conjugal tranquillity, the old female relations of the mother take care, that when twins are born one of them shall disappear. If a new-born infant, though not a twin, have any physical deformity, the father instantly puts it to death. (Humboldt § 2.20)

Humboldt despises the practice, yet he does not condemn it as criminal for the natives' practical and social reasons are supported by their "candour and simplicity of manners" (Humboldt § 2.20). As appears from this last quotation, he is not alien to the biased view of a Western-minded scientist, even though he reveals a paternalistic attitude rather than the bigotry common to many of his contemporaries.

This is also evident in his interpretation of the native's religious and philosophical beliefs. To my knowledge, Humboldt's observation of the Cassiquiare river petroglyphs is the first available[53] to the Western world and his interpreta-

---

[53] Actually, Humboldt mentions two previous reports: Hortsmann's Rupununi

tion anticipates some concepts which inform both Denis William's and Wilson Harris's readings of Amerindian philosophy. Humboldt identifies a "quadrilateral plot of a thousand square leagues," delimited by the rivers Cassiquiare, Atabapo, Orinoco and Rio Negro, where

> as in other parts of Guiana, rude figures representing the sun, the moon, and different animals, traced on the hardest rocks of granite, attest the anterior existence of a people, very different from those who became known to us on the banks of the Orinoco. (Humboldt § 2.24)

In a wider context he observes:

> I have lately verified this curious fact, which is recorded in the journal of the traveller Hortsman, who went up the Rupunuvini, one of the tributary streams of the Essequibo. Where this river, full of small cascades, winds between the mountains of Macarana, he found, before he reached lake Amucu, rocks covered with figures, or (as he says in Portuguese) with varias letras. We must not take this word letters in its real signification. We were also shewn, near the rock Culimacari, on the banks of the Cassiquiare, and at the port of Caycara in the Lower Orinoco, traces which were believed to be regular characters. They were however only misshapen figures, representing the heavenly bodies, together with tigers, crocodiles, boas, and instruments used for making the flour of cassava. It was impossible to recognize in these painted rocks (the name by which the natives denote those masses loaded with figures) any symmetrical arrangement, or characters with regular spaces. (Humboldt § 2.24)

These petroglyphs, as will shortly be discussed, are part of precious archeological evidence which helped the multiple genius of Denis Williams to formulate a convincing hypothesis about the origin of the Amerindian tribes of modern Guyana. Moreover, their discovery generates in Humboldt an interpretation, denoting this time his Christian-Westerner arrogance, which raises nevertheless a

---

petroglyphs and the "piedras pintadas" observed by the missionary Fray Ramon Buen. Moreover, the Casiquiare canal, although part of the broader Guyanese basin, must not be confused with the Kassikaityu river, which is, as will shortly be clarified, the main site for ancient petroglyphs in proper Guyana.

fundamental issue for the analysis of Harris's work, as anticipated in section III.iii about Lévy Bruhl's "savage mind":

> The human race, when in an uncultivated state, believes itself to have sprung from the ground; and feels as if it were enchained to the earth, and the substances contained in her bosom. The powers of nature, and still more those which destroy than those which preserve, are the first objects of its worship. It is not solely in the tempest, in the sound that precedes the earthquake, in the fire that feeds the volcano, that these powers are manifested; the inanimate rock; stones, by their lustre and hardness; mountains, by their mass and their solitude; act upon the untaught mind with a force which, in a state of advanced civilization, can no longer be conceived. This worship of stones, when once established, is preserved amidst more modern forms of worship; and what was at first the object of religious homage, becomes a source of superstitious confidence. Divine stones are transformed into amulets, which are believed to preserve the wearer from every ill, mental and corporeal. (Humboldt § 2.23)

In this passage, besides the statements denoting Humboldt's biases, it is possible to read the idea of "living landscape" and the particular rapport with nature which Harris links with Amerindian culture. This will be analysed in due place, mainly in the last chapter; here it is useful to highlight an even more startling coincidence which sees the "intuitive thread" Harris draws between Meso-America and Guyana reflected in the consideration of a typically "scientific mind" with deep European roots. Regarding Guyanese manufacture, Humboldt notices the diffusion of Jade objects, to the point of defining these hard stones as "the green stones of Guiana" and he wonders about possible links with Meso-American civilisations:

> Although a distance of five hundred leagues separates the banks of the Amazon and the Orinoco from the Mexican table-land; although history records no fact that connects the savage nations of Guiana with the civilized nations of Anahuac, the monk Bernard de Sahagun, at the beginning of the conquest, found preserved as relics at Cholula, certain green stones which had belonged to Quetzalcohuatl. This mysterious personage is the Mexican Bud-

dha; he appeared in the time of the Toltecs, founded the first religious associations, and established a government similar to that of Meroe and of Japan. (Humboldt § 2.23)

Humboldt concludes that trading contacts may have occurred between the Meso-American table-land and the Amazonian basin; however, this may work as a spark to ignite Harris's ideal link with Maya culture, as will be analysed in IV.ii.

Historically, Anthony Trollope's *The West Indies and the Spanish Main* (1860) may be of interest, especially regarding the social composition of the coastal settlement of early British Guiana, and the disillusion due to the hard climatic condition of the colony. Similarly, *Twenty Five Years in British Guiana* (1898), written by the Governor Henry Kirke, is rich in sociological information; it would be excessive to report long passages here, except for a couple of interesting comments about Amerindians. According to Kirke, they were a lucky stock at that time because nowhere else had the natives been treated better than in British Guiana and they even "enjoy some advantages denied to the colonist. The Indian pays no tax of any kind" (Kirke 148). The record of some of the rules which defined the Amerindians' coastal life is much more interesting : "the wife of one of our governors was much scandalized at meeting one of this parties [...] So she persuaded her husband to issue an order that all indian women landing in the town should be presented with a petticoat each" (Kirke 148).Other important works which at least partially deal with Guyanese Amerindians are W.H. Hudson's *Green Mansions* (1904) and Arthur Conan Doyle's *The Lost World* (1912), and successively Evelyn Waugh's works of the thirties such as *A Handful of Dust* (1934) and his travel accounts, especially *Ninety-two Days* (1934). Later, the Guyanese writer Edgar Mittelholzer dealt with the ambitious project of representing all the components of Guyanese society in his historical fiction, with particular attention to the Amerindian element, resulting in the publication, among others, of *My Bones and My Flute* (1951), *Shadows Move among Them* (1951) and the famous *Kaywana Trilogy* (1952-58). These pioneering works deserve a dedicated analysis and will not be discussed in depth.

4.1.3 Harris's Main Anthropological Sources

Robert Schomburgk's work, despite its earlier publication, certainly deserves a closer look, for it represents the fundamental surveying expedition for the mapping of Guyanese territories and for its importance in Harris's fictional imagery. As already mentioned, a character in *The Palace of the Peacock* is named

Schomburgh, possibly after Harris's fellow surveyor as revealed by T.J. Cribb, but much more probably after Robert Schomburgk, whose account of his exploration of the Guyanese interior was published in 1840. *A Description of British Guiana* can be considered as the first scientific survey of Guyanese territories and functioned as a source for all successive mappings of the land, almost certainly including Harris's. It deals with "whatever relates to the physical structure, natural productions, and present and future capabilities of the colony of British Guiana, including the statistical information I have been able to procure" (Schomburgk 1). The amount of data is therefore vast and varied, and Schomburgk declares its impartiality by acknowledging as leading motivation "the pursuit of science alone" (1). It may thus be read as a fairly objective representation, were it not for the unexpected intrusion of the revived legend of the El Dorado and Lake Parima when he comes to a depression of the land: "may not we connect with the former existence of this inland sea the tale of the lake Parima and the El Dorado?" (5).

Nevertheless, the information Schomburgk gathers about the Guyanese Amerindians is extremely valuable, for it delivers fairly objective statistical data, along with personal commitment in the ethnographic study of these populations. The first important fact recorded may be related to the positive demographic trend mentioned at the beginning of this chapter, for the Amerindian population of the first half of the 19th century appeared to Schomburgk's observation to have "dwindled to an inconsiderable number" (42). With compassionate look, revealing his fundamentally paternalistic attitude, Schomburgk laments how the arrival of the Europeans, even in recent times, had had effects similar to the violence of the first conquistadores: "it is a melancholy fact, but too well founded, that wherever Europeans have settled, the extermination of the native tribes has succeeded their arrival" (48). Besides, he draws a comprehensive map of the collocation of the various tribes over the Guyanese territory, listing all the major groups: Arawak, Warrau, Carib, Akawoi, Taruma, Macusi, Arecuna, Wapisiana, Atorai, and Wai-wai. Among these, Schomburgk finds interesting similarities, especially regarding language: "the analogy in the roots of the Carib, the Macusi, and the Arecuna, the Wapisiana, and the Parauana, leaves little doubt that these nations descend from the same stock" (48), anticipating later classifications and Denis Williams's hypothesis of a common origin. Finally the total number of Amerindian individuals is estimated at seven thousand.

The statistical and scientific value of his work, however, is strictly linked to the rhetoric of the second wave of English imperialism, and Schomburgk's paternalistic considerations about the Amerindian's good nature and their presumed need of civilisation reveal his commitment to the British imperialist ideology; one should not forget that his expedition was officially supported by the Royal Geographical Society:

> I speak from experience, if I assert that the Indian is as capable of progressive improvement, and the establishment, among his tribe, of social order, European arts, and christian morals, as were the teutonic races in their infancy, who emerged progressively from the greatest barbarism to the bright station which they at present occupy among the most civilised nations of Europe. (51)
>
> Would it not be worthy of an enlightened government, not only on religious, but likewise on political grounds, to advise some plan for the amelioration of their forlorn situation? (56)

Despite its official character, Schomburgk's was a pioneering exploration and opened the way to future ethnographic expeditions which revealed a revived interest for Guyana, both scientific and economic. The late 19th and early 20th centuries did not witness a new rush for the El Dorado, although pork-knockers still sift the sand of Guyanese rivers in search of a few nuggets, but a strong interest in bauxite extraction and sugar-cane production which procured financial support for further explorations. Many of these encounters are recorded in Mary Noel Menezes's extremely useful *The Amerindians in Guyana 1803-1873* which testifies with several official documents the activity of missionaries, ethnographers and government functionaries among the Amerindians in the 19th century and delivers a valuable, although often distorted, amount of information about Amerindian costumes. Among the ethnographers, Sir Everard Im Thurn gained wide respectability with the publication of *Among the Indians of Guiana* (1883) and offered a model for the process of settlement of Guyanese Caribs: "Sir Everard Im Thurn offered evidence that the Acawoi arrived simultaneously with the earliest European settlers" (Schomburgk 3).

The first theories about the origin of the Amerindians in Guyana have recently been questioned by Venezuelan and Guyanese scholars, such as Domingo P. Sánchez and Denis Williams. Sánchez credits the anthropologist Kay Tarble with a valuable hypothesis: "Tarble propone (Table 1985:65) un nuevo modelo de expansión de los Caribe, en el cual ubica a los Proto-Caribe, en las zonas de las Guayanas, 'A partir de los 3000 A.C.' según las evidencias arqueológicas y la información lingüística disponibles" (Sánchez). This theory is even further developed by Denis Williams, a fundamental figure in Guyanese Art and Science. He moved to London in 1950, and there he gained worldwide consideration as a painter exhibiting, since 1955, his much admired works about plantation societies of the Caribbean. However, the European experience was not positive and lead Williams to an abrupt change: he went to Africa for ten years (Sudan and Nigeria), where he started studying the African forms of art under a historical-anthropological perspective. During this period he wrote a first work of fiction, *Other Leopards* (1963), much praised by Harris as an example, by a Caribbean writer, of "a novel which refuses to exploit realism" (interview by Munro and Sander 46). In 1968 Williams felt that his life had come to a new turning, and he went back to Guyana to live and work in an Amerindian village in the interior, where he had the opportunity of studying Amerindian artifacts, culminating in the publication of *Image and Idea in the Arts of Guyana* (1970) and the Guyanese based short story 'The Sperm of God.' In 1974 he left for Georgetown, where he concentrated on archeological studies. He was appointed Director of Art for the Ministry of Education, Social Development and Culture in Guyana in 1977. Wilson Harris wrote about him:

> Denis Williams' migration from a realm of brilliant painting to literature and archaeology was natural and right for him within his pursuit of symbol and actuality. His final sanctuary lay in exhaustive analyses of the skeleton of history of South America, Guyana, to which he returned in the late 1960's. (Williams, *Prehistoric* xxi)

The variety of Williams's background allowed him a different look into archaeology and anthropology as well as into Guyanese culture, and his works represent the main source of information on Amerindian history along with Walter Roth's. Despite their importance, non-fiction works by Williams are not easily found and his posthumous *Prehistoric Guiana*, published by Ian Randle Publishers in 2003, is a precious document. Although the book mainly presents Williams's archeological achievements, it should not be considered as merely technical: substantial information is included about Amerindian culture and Williams's interpretations are often interconnected with Harris's fictional re-elaborations. Deep investigations of "shell mound complexes, petroglyphs, pictographs, stone tools and weapons, earthworks, pottery, artificial depressions, rock alignments, rock circles and related structures, and human burials" (Williams, *Prehistoric* 6) allow Williams to confirm and extend Kay Tarble's hypothesis, dating the presence of human activity in South America "in excess of 12,000 years ago" (62), and more precisely, "human occupancy of the Rupununi Savannas [...] around 4000 b.p." (58).[54] Various opinions have been expressed about the genealogy of Guyanese Amerindians despite general agreement on the grouping of the different tribes:

> The Amerindian population of Guyana is usually divided by anthropologists into three tribal families, Arawakan, Cariban and Warrauan. The Arawakan stock in Guyana comprises two tribes: The Arawaks (Lokono) and the Wapishanas. There are six Cariban tribes: the Akawois. Patamunas, Arekunas, Makushis, Caribs and Wai-Wais. The Warrau tribe is the only representative of the Warrauan group in Guyana. (Edwards-Gibson 162)

Williams does not oppose this classification, but formulates the hypothesis that the peoples of Guyana may have shared a common origin in the Amazon basin before 4000 b.p., challenging the previous conviction, derived from Im Thurn's intuition, of a fairly recent migration from the Caribbean islands. Williams's theories are important because they postulate a common origin of the Guyanese Amerindians from a rain-forest culture[55] based on a special relationship with the environment, offering a historical background to Harris's view of living landscapes, and possibly bringing together Amerindian cultures and Meso-American traditions. The fundamental role of a sustainable rain-forest economy for Guyanese Amerindians and the extended concept of a similar global relationship with the environment is clearly summarised in the following passage:

> Guiana occupies somewhat more than a quarter of the area of the rain forests of the Amazon Basin and boasts an antiquity directly associated with the Early Man migrations into the southern continent 12,000 or more years ago. The development of archaeology in the Guianas must therefore be seen as apposite to global concerns regarding the recoverable history of the rain forest and

---

54 The river Kassikaityu mentioned above for its petroglyphs flows in the southern part of the Rupununi Savannas.
55 With the exception of the Warrau, believed by Edwards and Gibson to be indigenous of Guyana and alien to rain-forest culture, Williams's view agrees with recent anthropological achievements. Menezes's model slightly differs in splitting Wapisiana (Wapishiana) and Arawaks in separate ethnic groups.

its sustainable exploitation, as well as to problems centering on the past and future of its non-immigrant populations. (Williams, *Prehistoric* 6)

On several more occasions Williams highlights the necessity of recovering "the cumulative heritage of adaptation to specific ecological zones in the mosaic of the Tropical Forest environment [which] did not long survive the incursion of Europeans" (*Prehistoric* 405) further fortifying the link with Harris's conceptions, which will constitute the core of the last chapter.

Among specific anthropological works, it is worth mentioning Peter Rivière's *Individual and Society in Guiana* (1984) for the condensed information about anthropological studies of the Guyanese Amerindians that, except Roth's works of the early 20th century, started in fairly recent times: "intensive anthropological fieldwork in the region dates only from the 1930s with Gillin's study (1936) of the Barama River Caribs. After that there was a slight hiatus until Butt, Fock, and Yde started work in the 1950s" (Rivière 1). However, Rivière's most interesting statement regards the Amerindian's concept of time, which may offer a reason for the fundamental role played by myth in their societies: "Guiana society exists with a narrow time scale, and the difference between a synchronic and a diachronic view is not great" (102). This may be interpreted as a different realisation of the "absolute past" Bakhtin theorised as a prerequisite for the epic and mythical narratives, and will be discussed in the last chapter.

Three earlier works deserve special attention for their approach to Amerindian cultures from a less technical point of entry: W.H. Brett's *Legends and Myths of the Aboriginal Indians of British Guiana* (1898), Walter Roth's *An Inquiry into the Animism and Folk-Lore of the Guiana Indians* (1915)[56] and T. Koch-Grünberg's *Indianermärchen aus Südamerika* (1920)[57] will be discussed here in chronological order.

Besides the scientific commitment of the explorers, the religious zeal of Christian missionaries reached the remotest branches of the Amazon basin. The oldest printed collection of Amerindian folk-tales is the result of the fascination of one of these missionaries, William Henry Brett, with Arawak, Warau and Carib cultures of the Guyanese region of the great savannah:

---

[56] Among Roth's works, this collection of myths and folk tales may be considered as less technical.
[57] Koch-Grünberg's work will be analysed on the basis of the Italian edition of this text, due to the limited availability of the original and the lack of any available English translations.

in 1840, the Revd. W. H. Brett of the Society for the Propagation of the Gospel had begun his missionary labours among the Arawaks and the Caribs in the Pomeroon and Moruka rivers, at Caracaburi and Waramuri respectively. His service to the Indians became a 40-year saga of missionary enterprise unsurpassed by any other missionary in British Guiana. (Menezes xxiii)

Published in 1880, *Legends and Myths of the Aboriginal Indians of British Guiana* is a collection of Amerindian beliefs rendered in verse. According to the online editor, M. Weimer, "the entire book is written in very regular meter. The relentless rhythms and rhymes, are combined with the sometimes ridiculous portrayal of the Natives as late Romantic 'savages'" (Brett). It is evident, in fact, that Brett's attitude is deeply biased because of his religious beliefs and his devotion to British-imperialistic ideals; nevertheless, he may be considered a pioneering ethnologist-anthropologist for being the first to record Guyanese folk tales, which can still be critically recovered from his text. The book is structured in five parts which respectively deal with Arawak, Warau, Carib, Acawoi and mixed provenance legends. Despite the mentioned problems of interpretation, some important common features of Amerindian mythologies can be found, especially regarding metamorphosis involving humans and animals such as jaguars, crocodiles and vultures, either in verse form: "We change as we like, and we do it with ease. / Some appear as bush-hogs, / Some as jaguars or dogs; / While some, as large snakes, love the rivers and bogs" (Brett 79); or in notes and comments: "The legend ends with the conflagration of the house of the royal vultures, who, 'hemmed in by crowds of hostile birds, are unable to use their wings, and forced to fight and die in their human forms'" (30). Other recurring elements are bones, whether animal or human, associated to musical instruments or to cannibal practices: "Men beat the drum, or sound the flute (The thigh-bone of some human foe)" (103). Instruments made from bones, and particularly bone-flutes, are actually one of the most frequently recorded artifacts of the Guyanese Amerindians and they have often been used by Harris as complex metaphors, as already mentioned, since *The Palace of the Peacock*.

Another frequent theme re-elaborated by Harris is cannibalism and Brett does not miss the opportunity for fuelling the tradition of condemning accounts that goes back to Columbus: "Human bones - of all sizes laid bare! / Skulls, in fragments long buried, were cast up to view, / And all the long bones had been split open too, / For the marrow, by savages there" (33). Evidence of cannibalism have frequently been discussed among anthropologists with opposite conclusions, which can be summarised by Marvin Harris's materialist interpretation as nourishment in famine periods or élite food and William Arens's negation of any case of institutionalised cannibalism, confirmed by the lack of first-hand observations of the phenomenon. Among the Caribs, with due care, it appears from second-hand sources that a kind of ritual cannibalism may have existed. Harris seems to credit this view, but problematises the practice by stressing its spiritual, archetypal dimension: "'The Caribs ate a ritual morsel', I said, 'on the eve of battle'" (Harris, *Jonestown* 16).

> It is not inconsistent, therefore, that we may discern, in the rubble of the Carib past, signs akin to a new ominous but renascent consciousness at the time of the Spanish conquest. That new darkness or dawning renascence lay not simply in the ritual morsel of the enemy they devoured or the flute they fashioned from his bone, but from a sudden upsurge of bush-baby spectres which rose out of their cooking pots like wraiths of smoke or sparks of fire. Certain Vestiges of legend – in this context – have come down to us and the bush-baby syndrome corresponds to a figure C.G. Jung calls the *puer aeternus* – the immortal or archetypal child of dreams. The immortal wraith which the Caribs glimpsed as they crouched over their campfires, and consumed a morsel of the enemy, carried therefore overtones of eclipse at the hands of Spain, overtones also of a new dawn, and of a host native. (Harris, "Amerindian" 169)

In the second part of Harris's complex reference to Carib mythology and to the effect which it may have performed in the post-conquest formation of a "native" identity, which he links to the archetypal imagery discussed in chapter 3, the figure of the 'bush-baby' is introduced. The origin of Wilson Harris's idea of "bush-baby omens" may be traceable in Brett's rendering of the Warau story of Korobona. To my knowledge, Harris, despite attributing it to the Caribs, never linked his reference to any traceable legend,[58] but it is possible to infer that Humboldt's quoted report and the story of Korobona listed in Brett's and Koch-

---

58 Hena Maes-Jelinek links Harris's interpretation to a legend reported by Roth (179) which involves Yurokon in the story of a baby thrown in a boiling pepperpot. Despite the presence of several elements cited by Harris, the legend does not seem to be his only source and it will be discussed in relation to the figure of Yurokon. (Maes-Jelinek, "Novel as a Painting" 229-235).

Grünberg's collections (Roth reports substantially different versions)[59] may also have entered Carib's culture and contributed to the background of Harris's interpretation.

Korobona was a young Warau woman who bathed in a portion of a lake prohibited to women and was taken by a water spirit. She became pregnant and brought a girl to life. When her brothers discovered it, they threatened her with killing the baby, but in the end she managed to keep her. Time passed and Korobona, bathing in the same lake, was taken again by the spirit. Being pregnant one more time she ran into the forest to hide her child from her brothers. However they finally found her and killed the baby. She buried the corpse, but thanks to her loving care, he came back to life and grew much more than normal children. The story continues with the brothers chasing the big child and cutting him to pieces. Korobona buried him again and watched overveiled the corpse in the forest. During the mourning she heard a voice coming from living flowers saying her son would rise again to avenge his murder. In fact she saw a mighty man, all armed, and with fairer skin than the Waraus: this was the first Carib warrior who came to slaughter the Waraus (Brett 64-74; Koch-Grünberg 6-9).

The immortal bush-baby who comes back as a warrior for revenge may have been interpreted and archetypally reformulated by Harris to symbolise the process which sees the coming of the Spaniards in a circular process: the end of an era (or culture) as the beginning of another, "as though the guilt of the victor stands on the threshold of a creative breakthrough in the darkening consciousness of the victim as prelude to the birthpangs of a new cosmos" (Harris, "Amerindian" 169). At the same time, Yurokon, as will be discussed later, offers a different interpretation, being often associated with a spirit of the forest which shows similar aspects to the bush-baby.

Another typical feature of Amerindian culture can be usefully highlighted in Brett's work: the evil spirit Kanaima. Kanaima, which gives the name to Lucius Canaima, a character in Harris's *The Four Banks of the River of Space* (1990) and the title to a short story first published in 1964, is a recurrent figure in every collection of Amerindian folk stories. It is the name by which Guyanese tribes refer to a primordial evil spirit that performs various symbolic roles, and it is believed to be the main cause of death: "From the base of high Roráima /   To the widespread Eastern sea, / Votaries of dread Kanáima / Track their victims se-

---

[59] Roth reports both Warau and Carib versions which, however, prove to be very different from Brett's and Koch-Grünberg's. For the sake of brevity only the "cross-referenced" one is reported here.

cretly. / Deadly vow must each fulfil, / Real or fancied foe to kill" (Brett 153). The figure of Kanaima deserves a deeper analysis and will shortly be discussed in relation to Roth's extensive information.

Moving to Koch-Grünberg's *Indianermärchen aus Südamerika*, it must be pointed out that the date of publication (1920) may be misleading for a parallel analysis of Roth's *An Inquiry into the Animism and Folk-Lore of the Guiana Indians* because the basic material with which Koch-Grünberg compiled the collection had already appeared in the volumes entitled *Zwei Jahre unter den Indianern. Reisen in Nordwest Brasilien*, written in 1903-5 and published in 1910. This is important because, along with Brett's and Schomburgk's, Koch-Grünberg's work is cited among the main sources in Roth's introduction. Therefore, a few words may be spent on *Indianermärchen aus Südamerika* and some of its peculiar aspects, while a more comprehensive discussion about the legends will be carried out in relation to Roth, for these are often simple transcriptions of the previous version.

Differently from Brett's poetic interpretation, the legends reported in *Indianermärchen aus Südamerika* appear as, according to the editors of the Italian version, quasi-literally translated from the original languages (Koch-Grünberg 3). It is hard to check how faithful this transliteration may have been, for the languages of the tribes involved have not yet been systematised, but the cross-check with Schomburgk and Roth seems to reveal at least a general consistency. The folk-tales collected by Koch-Grünberg show, better than others, the general interrelationship between the animal world and the humans, reporting several episodes in which animals behave as if they were humans and they are approached as such by the human characters: such is the case of the man who took a howler monkey or the girl who loved a sloth. Frequently the jaguar seems to be able to imitate the voice and the appearance of various living forms, humans included. Transformations, however, are the most frequent and they occur in both ways: the Haimara fish have such big and beautiful eyes because once they were people from an Arawak village who mistreated a spirit of the forest; a Brazilian man, instead, had a woman who once was a vulture. The close relationship with the animal world is not limited to such wondrous episodes: the origin of agriculture is related to the discovery of the tapir's secret: a prodigious tree which gave all the fruits in the world. Sadly, it was to be cut down because men could not reach the fruits, but the *bunia* bird showed them how to plant the seeds and grow trees and crops.

Besides these stories, many legends deal with the figure of Makunaima. Makunaima is a very important character in Amerindian mythology, but a detailed discussion is not particularly relevant in the context of this thesis, except for what concerns the legend of "Makunaima and Pìa." Moreover, the attention this figure has received in literature, particularly in Mario de Andrade's *Macunaíma, O Herói sem Nenhum Caráter* (1926), in Harris's *The Age of the Rainmakers*, and in *The Ventriloquist's Tale* (1997), a novel by the Guyanese writer Pauline Melville, invites to a brief presentation. According to Roth, who quotes Schomburgk,

> Makunaima, or Makonaima, the alleged God [ScR, II, 225, 515] or Supreme Being [IT, 365] of the Akawais, the Maker of Heaven and Earth [ScR, II, 319] of the Makusis, was one of the twin children of the Sun—in this particular all the traditions concerning him are in agreement. He and his brother Pia may be regarded as both Akawai and Makusi heroes. The name itself, Makunaima, signifies "one that works in the dark." [HiC, 244] (Roth § 29)

The story of "Makunaima and Pìa," as first recorded by Koch-Grünberg, has some relevance to the discussion because it may support the mentioned link Harris draws between Amerindian and Meso-American cultures. In this case, the twins, sons of the sun, may be connected, following Harris's intuitive method, to the Hero Twins of the *Popol Vuh*, the sacred book of the K'iche Maya of the post-classic period, which are themselves related to the sun: all share a central role in their respective mythologies as trickster gods and creators.

Still, one general aspect, as emerging from Koch-Grünberg's collection, deserves a brief discussion to better introduce the theme of the relationship between man and nature: the recurrence of the image of the flood and the consequent repeopling of the world. Legends about the flood or 'great waters' seem common to every tribe in the Amazonian basin and to many other peoples worldwide, as theorised by Lévi-Strauss,[60] but the Makusi and Tamanac are peculiar versions and the most relevant part is the way the earth is populated anew.

---

60 The French anthropologist analysed non-Western mythology on a wider scale focusing on the definition of the mind processes of the savages (*La pensée sauvage*, 1962) and challenging Lévi Bruhl's conclusions discussed in section 3.3: "In opposition to the theories formulated by influential predecessors, such as Lucien Lévy Bruhl, he has revealed that these 'primitive' modes of thought are neither

Von Humboldt had already recorded the Tamanac legend in the early 19th century:

> When the Tamanacs are asked how the human race survived this great deluge, the age of water, of the Mexicans, they say, a man and a woman saved themselves on a high mountain, called Tamanacu, situated on the banks of the Asiveru; and casting behind them, over their heads, the fruits of the mauritia palm-tree, they saw the seeds contained in those fruits produce men and women, who repeopled the earth. (Humboldt §2.19).

Roth, about a century later, briefly reports the Makusi's variation, whose first recording he attributes to Schomburgk's, with a slightly different ending: "According to the Makusi tradition, Makunaima sent great waters: only one man escaped... this one man who survived the flood threw stones behind him, and thus peopled the earth anew [ScR, II, 320]" (Roth §58).

These two brief examples may meaningfully represent the tendency among Guyanese Amerindians to consider themselves as part of a whole creation which does not distinguish between animal and human world, including even the vegetal world and quite astonishingly the inanimate world, which is often represented as animate, at least in older times or on special ritual occasions. The very origin of man is related, in the two legends reported above, to the seeds of a palm-tree or to rocks. The implications of this world view and their possible different interpretations as evidence of a "savage mind" will be analysed in due place; here, it is fundamental to discuss Roth's comments of these manifestations, which he interprets as forms of animism.

---

radically different (prelogical, prerational) nor fundamentally more archaic than our 'civilized' ways of thinking. Indeed, Lévi-Strauss is careful to present these 'primitive' modes of thought not so much as the attribute of so-called primitive societies, but as an aspect of the way in which all human beings think" (Murray, *Encyclopedia* 421). He dealt in detail with Amazonian mythology essentially in *Tristes tropiques* (1955) and in *Le cru et le cuit* (1964). Lévi-Strauss studied Guyanese-Amerindian folk tales, but mainly focused on Nambikwara and Yanoami tribes of Brazilian Amazon, and his main concern was the theorising of a specific approach to mythology which would expose the structural, universal interrelationship of human mythology. In this context he observed the deluge as a recurring mythical theme. Here, however, the aim of this analysis is to frame a mythical tradition regarding specific tribes and cultures, therefore his work will not be discussed in depth.

Regarding the first creation of mankind (i.e. before the flood), Roth affirms that according to Amerindians, generally "man was either brought here from Cloud-land, etc., or was created here; in the latter case, from Animals, as Tigers, Snakes, from Plants, or from Rocks and Stones" (141). This is expanded in a more extensive consideration:

> the Indian seemingly can conceive of man's origin only from something already existing in the world of nature immediately surrounding him. And so, in considering the reputed origins of the various tribes, the belief becomes more and more prominent that Mankind – and by Mankind each Indian means the original ancestors of his own people – was originally derived, with or without the assistance of pre-existing agencies, from various animals and plants, from rocks, stones, and rivers. (52)

In Roth's work there is a tendency that distinguishes it from the other collections and accounts analysed above: it is enriched by a vast amount of hypotheses and considerations about the various legends collected which is not based on qualitative judgements nor evidently biased by a presumed cultural superiority, but inspired by a rigorous comparative study. In a vast number of these statements a direct link with Harris's imaginative interpretations can often be discovered. The theme of extended animism introduced above is one of them, but in addition a parallelism can be drawn following three main lines: the imaginative recuperation of ritual cannibalism and other traditional Amerindian elements; the idea of a living nature linked to the spiritual quality of certain rocks; and the figure of Yurokon. The last two will lead directly to the main object of the next subsection: Harris's view on the legacies left by Meso-American cultures.

4.1.4 The Amerindian Legacy: An Imaginative Reading

It is necessary here to relate the issues which emerged in the discussion of Amerindian legends and cultures to Harris's ideas, with special regard to Roth's conclusions. It will be best to start by considering some of Harris's critical writings which deal with these themes in a rather more linear way than the novels cited above, which will subsequently be considered. Many references to Amerindian cultures are found in essays which deal with the themes of history and the recuperation of past, eclipsed cultures; as these will be extensively discussed in the final chapter, here the main focus will be on the elements strictly linked with the works presented above with the aim of stressing the foundation of Harris's interpretation on actual anthropological achievements, rather than, as often theorised by Harris scholars, on exclusively imaginative elements.

A whole critical work was dedicated to this issue on the occasion of the 1970 Edgar Mittelholzer Lectures, revised and republished in 1995. *History, Fable and Myth in the Caribbean and Guyanas* deals with a vast amount of influences which contributed, in Harris's view, to the formation of the Caribbean self; of these, the Amerindian one is especially considered, receiving a separate chapter. In "The Amerindian Legacy" the first issue discussed by Harris is cannibalism. The recurrent references to the symbol of the Carib bone flute have been repeatedly cited; here he explains the associations which underlie this symbol. Referring to Michael Swan, Harris borrows the definition "transubstantiation in reverse" to indicate Carib cannibalism and stresses the possibility that the stories reported by the Spaniards about cannibalism may have largely been "a smokescreen for their own excesses" (Harris, "Amerindian" 168). The process of transubstantiation is better explained by Harris in "The Schizophrenic Sea," where he quotes Swan again:

> In the light of oral traditions and of significant and varied parallels between Yurokon and the origins of Carib cannibalism in Roth's researches into the animism of the Indians, Swan has no alternative but to state that 'the object of [Carib] cannibalism was a kind of transubstantiation in reverse: the bone [flute] contains the living spirit of the dead... [it was the source of] prophecy and witchcraft... [and] transference of spirit. (Harris, "Schizophrenic" 106; annotations and ellipses in the text quoted from Swan are by Harris)

As emerges from the quoted passage, Harris's reading of the possible custom of cannibalism among the Guyanese Amerindians is not based on any real evidence, but it acquires a historical value in the context of Harris's philosophy of history. The recuperation of past cultures does not interest him at a purely factual level; it is the sensibility expressed in these eclipsed traditions which informs his fiction, inserted in a historical project which aims at the integration of all the features concurring in the building of the Caribbean self which may be left out of official, scientific historiography.

This very attitude characterises his recuperation of Amerindian legends as a whole and it may be effectively exemplified by another interpretation of a recurring myth: the foodbearing tree. As mentioned above, this tree is the central feature of the myth regarding the birth of agriculture; it has, however, various realisations in the three main collections cited. The common elements are the tree, its discovery, its destruction and finally the growing of plants from the seeds of its fruits. Harris offers a version of his own[61] that does not match any of the above:

> The foodbearing tree of the world in Arawak and Macusi legend reaches to the sky of fiction across the forgotten ages, but we become suddenly aware of it as creation bridge or myth between sky and earth at a time of catastrophe when a new genesis or vision has become necessary.
> It is a time of war. The rainbow compression of a tree is set on fire by the Caribs when the Arawak seek refuge in its branches, upon which stand multi-coloured birds and fruit overcast in the wake of the fire by a cloud of smoke. [...] The fire rages and ascends even higher to drive the Arawaks up and up until there is no further escape, they burn and rise into a spark in the sky of fiction. That spark becomes the seed of the garden of the Pleiades.
> The foodbearing tree, therefore, is re-dressed, the blackened fruit unravelled into a garden in the sky of fiction. The most curious enigma of all is the reconciliation that the Caribs and Arawaks appear to achieve, a treaty of sensibility that borders on *coniunctio* between sky and earth. (Harris, *Womb* 50)

In this visionary passage, many heterogeneous images from different legends and beliefs come together in a synthesis whose reflection of a real tradition is arguable, to say the least. It is possible that Harris could refer to a precise myth; however, this interpretation is a perfect example for the fictional process he applies. The important presence of the Pleiades, of the Milky Way and Orion (often linked with Makunaima) among the legends of the Amerindians is well documented by numerous stories gathered by Brett, Koch-Grünberg, or Roth. The same could be said of the foodbearing tree, the related discovery of agriculture and the Arawak-Carib rivalry; nevertheless, none of the elements of Harris's re-elaborations can be considered as evidence for any actual observation or comparative investigation, thus bearing little scientific or anthropological relevance. Yet, according to Harris, his synthesis conveys some aspects of a living tradition

---

61 This legend is also imaginatively reinterpreted by Harris in his 1978 novel *The Tree of the Sun*.

which could not be effectively recovered but through the imaginative power of fiction which allows him to testify the process of conflicting opposites resulting in an alchemical *coniunctio*, a new creation, which in this case he reads in the Amerindian legacy of reconciliation, a "treaty of sensibility" with the cosmos. The same could be said of other features of Amerindian culture, such as *couvade*,[62] the practice in which the father of a newborn child is revered and served as if he were the one who brought the creature to life; this allows Harris to relate, in the first story of *The Sleepers of Roraima* (1970), his ideas of mutuality in birth and death to a non-European tradition.[63] According to Menezes's definition, Couvade is

> a custom among most primitive people connected with the birth of a child. After the birth the father takes to his hammock and receives the congratulations of his friends, while the mother continues with her daily routine. *Couvade* underlines the basic, physical relationship between father and child. Although South America is the centre of *couvade,* it is a widespread custom among other peoples – emphasizing also the bond of sympathy between husband and wife. In Guyana, *couvade* is practised by the Arawaks, Warraus, Caribs, Macusis and Wapisianas. (Menezes 296-297).

Harris, as usual, is interested in the mythical and psychological symbology intrinsic in the practice and offers, in a note at the opening of *Couvade*, a personal view:

> The Caribs have virtually disappeared as a people though their name is attached to the islands of the Caribbean sea and remnants of their mythology can be traced deep into the South American continent. This story is based on their little-known myths – the myth of *couvade*.
>
> The purpose of *couvade* was to hand on the legacy of the tribe – courage and fasting – to every newborn child. All ancestors

---

62 A play by Michael Gilkes titled *Couvade* was published in 1974 with an introduction by Harris, in the context of a nationalist project of including Amerindian myths in the formation of national Guyanese sensibility.

63 A different fictionalisation of the same themes can be found in the first pages of *The Dark Jester* (2001) where the image of the Rondanini Pietà is discussed with reference to a Byzantine Icon.

> were involved in this dream – animal as well as human, bird as well as fish. The dust of everything, cassava bread (the Caribs' staple diet), the paint of war, the cave of memories, were turned into a fable of history – the dream of *couvade*. (Harris, *Sleepers* 13)

The issues raised by Harris in this note are also related to *Yurokon* and to his whole approach to Amerindian mythology; however, the main theme emerging in *Couvade* is strictly linked to the interpretation of the observed practice as a symbolic ritual for the transference of valuable qualities and of tradition to a newborn child. This acquires a special meaning when referred to the main character of the short story: a young orphaned Amerindian in present day Guyana who asks his grandfather about his roots. With the common stratagem of dream narrative, Harris faces the dilemma of the passing of a tradition which refers to a "virtually disappeared" people (by the hand of the European conquerors and by ethnic intermixing with Arawaks) to individuals, such as himself, who are no longer physically part of it and yet perceive the intuitive links with these "living absences." This is once again the core of Harris's fictional-historical operation, for nothing else than fictional reinterpretation of Amerindian myth can better testify their vitality and feed the mythical tradition at the same time. Through this process, he manages to represent what has been defined by Gary Crew as the "eternal present" (Crew 218-227) of *Couvade*, which can be read as a sort of "timelessness" allowing the myth to live in between the Bakhtinian "absolute past" symbolised by the cave "old as the womb – old as the guacharo bird" (Harris, *Sleepers* 20) and the symbols of modernity represented by an "aeroplane whose sun glasses falling from the sky belonged to his own masked parents" (20).

The mythical landscape that derives from this conception of time and fiction does not only witness the time leaps well known to Harris's readers which link past, present and future, but it allows the fictionalisation of the living quality of Amerindian landscape without exoticism or presumed superiority, for, in Harris's view, it is not enclosed in a fixed genre of a civilised people who cannot produce epic anymore (the image the modern West has conveyed of itself), but a living agent in the dialogue with everyday life. The Amerindian culture does not need a distant past to conceive and perceive the constant agency of nature, and the use of a kind of mythical epic mode is still available as a way to describe reality and integrate, as in Harris's case, Western and scientific cognitive instruments. This is particularly evident in the novel entitled *Tumatumari* (1968), in which an engineer, Roi Solman, dies drowning in the Tumatumari falls, in the interior of Guyana. Already in the title, an Amerindian word meaning "the place of sleepers, the sleeping rocks" (Harris, *Tumatumari* 24), Harris starts stressing the importance of the landscape for the interpretation of the events. In the novel Roi Solman and his wife Prudence live by the river near the village of Tumatumari, at that time still surrounded by Amerindian settlements. Roi is a surveyor, working for an electrical company which is evaluating the hydro-electric possibilities of the numerous falls in the Tumatumari zone. He plays, therefore, the role of a symbol of a technological society which tries to exploit natural elements to produce energy and comes into contact with a different, the Amerindian, world, which seems at first completely detached from Roi's life, despite his earlier intuition, prematurely terminated by his death, of its fundamental importance. However, through the eyes of his wife Prudence, the reader progressively discovers the profound intervention which the social and natural environment performs over the psyche of the two "outsiders." The main theme is actually the psychic transfiguration which takes place in Prudence's mind after the loss of a stillborn child, shortly followed by the death of her husband. This mental metamorphosis significantly includes the reconstruction of her father's death: the historian Henry Tenby, who introduces a fundamental undertone to the surface of the events by offering a constant contrast to Prudence's imaginative memory. In her mind, inanimate elements of the surrounding environment acquire a life of their own, akin to that aliveness observed in the animism of Amerindian mythology; particularly rocks seem to reveal a fundamental agency, from the very episode of Roi's death on: "[he] was decapitated by the Rock which rose to meet him out of the falls...." (Harris, *Tumatumari* 19). This is the beginning of a mental process which brings Prudence to a new consciousness:

> The metamorphosis was so remarkable it seemed to her fresh ammunition of wilderness. As if every given state of things began to alter – the fertility of the rain forest and the barren reaches of poles of desert were ignited by an element far older, though frailer, than uniformity or persuasion the hairspring of life.... The stilts of earth danced within this refractive sun. (21)

Life and the fertility of the rain forest are represented through the symbolic figure of Rakka, Roi's Amerindian mistress, who bears in her womb the child of the electrical engineer. The new sensibility with which Prudence comes into contact is considered by Harris as a typical quality of the Amerindians of Guy-

4 Pre-Columbian Legacies 141

ana who offer a contrasting, yet integrative view of reality to Roi Solman's technological hubris and Henry Tenby's Western approach to history: a synergy often defined by Harris as a "treaty of sensibility" well exemplified in a dialogue between Prudence and Roi:

> 'I demand to know what's all this fuss about the wretched Indians....Who are they...?'
> ' For God's sake' – he was peevish – 'wretched or not, they're the conscience of our age....In this part of the world anyway....'
> (Harris, *Tumatumari* 34-35)

Besides acknowledging the importance of the direct encounter of the symbolic Amerindian and Western characters, it is my intention to stress the "phenomenal legacy" of the new conscience Prudence acquires. By referring to a "phenomenal legacy" a series of concepts is called into play; in this case it is useful to refer to the precise aspect of the gateway offered by the encounter with the Amerindians towards the wider concept expressed by Harris in "The Phenomenal Legacy":

> what I would like to do is to direct a certain critical light upon the residue of experience we all share. [...] Our awareness of the riddling archetypal mystery of life [...] the man-made ruin and the 'faults' of landscape enter into a new, sometimes extreme original unity or wholeness of being. ("Phenomenal" 43-45)

Resorting to the terminology used in chapter 3, it may be argued that the living rocks of Tumatumari may be the archetypal images of the archetype consisting in that "wholeness of being" to which Harris refers in the passage above. They may function as the perceivable manifestation, a phenomenon, of a vaster reality, at first neglected by the Western characters, but successively acknowledged thanks to the gateway offered by Amerindian sensibility.

Tumatumari, as well as *The Age of the Rainmakers* and *The Four Banks of the River of Space*,[64] offer multiple images for the active quality of rocks and stones, through expressions such as "sleeping rocks," "rock womb," "architecture of the

---

[64] The theme of rocks as a principal element in the history of South-America and the Caribbean is widely extended, Walcott's interpretation of Caribbean history and Carpentier's *Los Pasos Perdidos* (1953) may suffice here as citations. Harris has shown his interest in several novels, but for reasons of of space only *Tumatumari* is analysed here.

tides" (a particular behaviour of non-tidal Amazonian rivers involving a seemingly active role of rocks), etc., which can be linked to Harris's interpretation of the famous petroglyphs of Guyanese archaeology: the "Timehri" rocks discovered by Denis Williams in the early seventies. This interpretation is based on the imaginative approach which extends Denis Williams's interpretation of the "Timehri" petroglyphs into a philosophical speculation on the role of landscape in a kind of world's consciousness (or world's unconscious).[65]

Harris's meaningful reading of those archeological findings is worth quoting for it may suggest a bridge between the "rocks of history" (*Tumatumari* 72) of Tumatumari and the main theme of the last chapter of this study:

> Timehri may be translated not only as 'the mark of the hand,' but as ' the hand of God.' There is an odd humour in the word 'Timehri' which is obviously the Anglicised version of an Amerindian root word. As though one were involved in a secret or unwitting pun on TIME. What is time? Time identified with space in Einsteinian mathematics. But space, in the phenomenology of consciousness, has many objects within it, many draperies, many variable garments and shapes. [...] The mark of the hand, therefore, the hand of God upon rock, is a confirmation of our intercourse with living time. The mark is mysterious. It hints at a language or text that existed before human discourse. Yet it engages with human discourse to enrich the language of the imagination. (Harris, "Aubrey" A 222)

As Louis James aptly notices, "the mystery of 'Timehri' has featured in Wilson Harris's work since *Tumatumari* (1968)" (James 50) and, although it is reprised and expanded in *The Four Banks of the River of Space*, it already offers the elements to speculate on the "magical proportion of time" suggested by the discourse of the living landscape engaging human concepts of time and history, as it emerges from several of the novel's images such as "Ceremony of the Rock" and "Rocks of History." A deeper investigation of the historical implications will be offered in the last chapter.

As a final discussion the myth of Yurokon, in Harris's interpretation, will offer a link with the Meso-American sub-section. Yurokon is a recurring figure in the three collections of legends presented in the course of this chapter, but more

---

[65] For the discussion of the seemingly incongruent use of the terms 'unconscious' and 'conscious,' refer to sub-sections 1.3 and 3.3.

than any other theme discussed it is rooted in a real anthropological hypothesis about the common features of Amerindian and Meso-American cultures, alluded to by von Humboldt, developed by Schomburgk and supported by Roth. Moreover, this mythical figure is central to Harris's general reading of the Amerindian legacy as emerges from the short story published in *The Sleepers of Roraima* (1970), and from the wide critical attention it has received. In *Yurokon* Harris seems to concentrate many of his favourite themes regarding the recuperation of tradition: it is his main fictionalisation of the mentioned concepts about the Amerindian bone flute and cannibalism; at the same time it is an allegory of "tradition as a living though often unacknowledged reality underlying conventional and unquestioned orders of existence" (Maes-Jelinek, "Novel as a Painting" 230), and some aspects may be interpreted as an emanation of Harris's alchemical interests in the possibilities of rebirth from conflicting situations. Lastly, the development of the hypotheses about the nature of the name Yurokon helps us to understand the theory of the cited intuitive thread with Meso-America. The first theme, already partially discussed, appears immediately when the young Yurokon, a present day descendent of the Caribs, asks his uncle about the origin of his tribe's name:

> 'Are we really huntsmen of bone?' Yurokon asked down at his uncle and through the sky as he sailed in space. [...] 'We became huntsmen of bone when we ate our first Spanish sailor,' his uncle replied to the intricate sticks of the sky. 'For that reason we are sometimes called cannibals.' (Harris, *Sleepers* 66)

Here the theme of identity linked to cannibalism is introduced and investigated through Harris's usual visionary language, which achieves, more than the mentioned diatribes between anthropologists, to expose the core of the matter. Hena Maes-Jelinek correctly highlights the fact that the Caribs "were themselves fierce conquerors before being conquered by Spain" ("Novel as a Painting" 231), but she interprets the related bush-baby legend as a "myth [...] linked with a strong sense of guilt among the Caribs" (231). Contrastingly, Harris's quotation of Swan about cannibalism given above may suggest the interpretation of this sense of guilt as a result of the encounter with the Spanish: whether it was practised or not, cannibalism has been perceived as a deplorable practice only after the encounter with an alien culture which had already theorised the eating of human meat as the symbol of an evil nature. The resulting situation has historically witnessed the moral justification for the exploitation of "evil populations," on one side, while, psychologically, it continues to generate a sort of guilt in the exploited: "'How can you say such a thing?' Yurokon cried, descending from the kite to earth in a flash and stopping dead" (Harris, *Sleepers* 66).

This is supported in the story by the rival presence of a Christian missionary, Father Gabriel, who contributes to Yurokon's confusion generating a "discrepancy between ancestral and Christian allegiance" (Crew 222). However, Harris's view offers a way out of the closure of this opposition: the ritual morsel was a spiritual practice no less deplorable than the Christian counterpart, being merely a reversal of transubstantiation, and the bone flute was seen as a creative counterpart for death as it emerges from symbolic chasms: "innocent evil [Caribs] and maleficent good [Europeans]" (Harris, *Sleepers* 73). The changing perspective allows him to visualise the intrinsic closure of a fixed concept of identity, be it an uncritical recuperation of idealised roots or the externally imposed inferiority and guilt. In support of this it is possible to borrow from *Couvade* the concept of fluent identity attributed to the Carib tribes which expands and explains the image of "the cauldron [...] within which [...] innocent evil and maleficent good, were living morsels of divinity in their native organ":

> "we called ourselves feathers of the toucan long long ago," the old man said, "before we became fishermen of night and our enemies (the fishermen of night) became huntsmen of night." [...] dusty feathers of the toucan, misty fishermen of night, black huntsmen of night. They were one and the same – the cruel tricks and divisions of mankind, the cruel ruses and battles of mankind. (73)

In opposition and conflict a creative spark may be found, igniting a kind of evolution similar to that expressed in the Korobona legend reported in 4.1.3, which attributes to an Arawak woman the origin of the first Carib warrior who started the Caribs' violent assimilation of the Arawaks.[66] The principle of "birth-in-death" (72) is exemplified in the myth and in the modern reformulation of Yurokon, who, in this sense, can be considered the first "native," being the heir of the tragic encounter of Europeans and Amerindians. His legacy, however, includes new possibilities embodied in his Carib bone flute with which to play the four European movements of a cross-cultural symphony:

---

66 This is also the object of "I, Quiyumucon," the other story included in *The Sleepers of Roraima*.

the story has four movements like a symphony. The tension between two different tones and the resolution of this tension at the end, typical of symphonic structure, find a correspondence in the confrontation between Caribs and Spaniards resolved in the denouement. (Maes-Jelinek, "Novel as a Painting" 231)

It is the "unwritten symphony of the wind" (Harris, *Sleepers* 69) which Yurokon associates with "all the wild warring elements, [...] *broken water* [...] *broken fire* [...] broken atmosphere [broken] land" (69-70). This is a music whose substance sprouts from the living landscapes of Amerindian myth shaped through traditional European symphonic form, reflected in the four sections of *Yurokon*, which correspond also to the fourfold process of alchemical individuation (see 3.2.3), to the fourfold vision of Blake's imagination,[67] and the fourfold images of the Maya cosmic tree, which will be discussed in 4.2, and lead to a continuously evolving conciliation between opposed cultures which may be considered Harris's central philosophical achievement.

On the other hand, the name of Yurokon, the Guyanese spirit of the forest, offers an intuitive pillar to the bridge thrown by von Humboldt's observation of the distribution of jade stones suggesting an ancient and living connection between Guyanese Amerindians and Meso-American peoples, including Maya, Toltecs and Aztecs. Harris has often expressed his fascination with the possible etymological correspondence first alluded to by Roth; it is however in "The Schizophrenic Sea," first published in *The Womb of Space* (1983), that he clearly presents the most complete discussion. The presence of an Amerindian character in Edgar Allan Poe's *Arthur Gordon Pym* is the starting point for Harris to analyse the work as an example of "a pre-Columbian bridge of myth that runs through the Americas" (Harris, "Schizophrenic" 105).

Von Humboldt's intuition about the possible commercial links of the Guyanese Amerindians with Toltecs and Maya may have started a tradition which reached Walter Roth when he reasoned about the name "Yurokon":

It will be noticed how the term Yurokon, in the form of Hyorokon, Hyrouca, Yolok, Iolokiamo, Iya-imi, is spread throughout

---

[67] Michael Mitchell links Harris's approach to Amerindian culture (its multifaceted nature as opposed to the linearity of official history) to William Blake's poetic definition of his imaginative way of seeing (as opposed to the "Single Vision" of orthodox European Enlightenment): "unfamiliar ways of seeing, such as those Blake sets out in a letter to Thomas Butts: Now I a fourfold vision see,/ And a fourfold vision is given to me" (Mitchell, "With Covered Eyes" 108).

the extent of the Guianas, while in the form of Juluca [...] it is met with on the islands, as the personification of the Rainbow. I have also shown the probability of its identity with the Shadow Spirit [...]. Equally striking is its resemblance to the word Huracan, the name given by the Aztecs to the autumnal equinox. (Cordonazo de San Francisco). Huracan means the Spirit (corazon) of the Sea, the Spirit of Heaven and Earth: the Nahuas were unable to conceive of the author of the universe except in a cataclysm. Cyclone, Hurricane, or Cordonazo de San Francisco are names of the same phenomenon. Hurakan of the Quiche myths is the Kukulcan of the Maya, the Quetzalcouatl (morning-star) of Mexican mythology. Yawahu, the Arawak generic term, includes the Tukuyuha, the Ekkekuli or Manahau, and the Mansinskiri Spirits, the Tukuyuha being subdivided into Konoko-(Tu)kuyuha and Adda-(Tu)kuyuha, according as they are more specially associated with the bush and forest, or trees, respectively. (Roth 94)

In a process of intuitive play with words similar to that applied to "Timehri," Harris picks up Roth's observations and expands and transform them into "a rainbow arc across Mexico into the Caribbean and Guianas" (Harris, "Schizophrenic" 105). He refers to this intuitive link in several essays and inserts it as a background in numerous works of fiction in the course of his long career, especially *Companions of the Day and Night* (1975), *Jonestown* (1996) and *The Dark Jester* (2001); a meaningful and representative explanation can be found once again in "The Schizophrenic Sea":

I spoke earlier of a pre-Columbian bridge of myth that runs through the Americas [...].

For the purposes of this exploration we may approach the bridge where it is identified with a rainbow arc across Mexico into the Caribbean and Guianas. The masquerading figure associated with the Caribbean and Guianas is Yurokon. He is fourth in a series of masquerading 'block' gods (twinships of space, in my estimation) upon and beneath that rainbow arc. The first is Quetzalcoatl (bird and snake mask) followed by Kukulkan and Huaracan (both of which sustain species of twins of heaven and earth). These mutate into, or are succeeded by, Yurokon (as Roth's inventory of masquerading features suggests) where the bridge arches into the Caribbean and moves into South America. (105-106)

From this passage, Harris's extended interpretation of the relationship of Central and South-American mythologies emerges in all its fertile ramifications, a pregnancy which leads the Guyanese writer to advance the arguable anthropological theory of the Meso-American provenance of the Caribs: "You must remember that the Caribs voyaged across oceans. We don't know where they came from. I would tend to think they have connections with ancient Mexico" (Harris, "Absent Presence" 81). On one side, this assumption clearly conflicts with Denis Williams's theories about the origin of Guyanese Amerindians, which have been considered as the most authoritative at the time of writing. On the other side, paradoxically, it has also been suggested how they may support Harris's general concept of a unitary cultural genesis. Nevertheless, despite the superficial incongruence over the exact circumstance of contact, the connection between Carib (or Guyanese Amerindians) and Meso-American cultures is particularly fruitful at a literary level. Considering that this minor incongruence does not outweigh the several cultural connections presented above, which date back to von Humboldt's observations, a further speculation may be introduced. Whether the Caribs came by sea or by land, there are many undeniable cultural features which link the populations of Meso-America, South-America and Guyanas. It will be suggested in the last chapter that the intuitive link drawn by Harris is not only supported, albeit partially, by anthropological theories, but it may be reflected in the particular relationship with nature and the surrounding rainforest landscapes that these cultures have similarly developed. The aim of the discussion will be to bring together the animism and living landscapes of the Guyanese Amerindians and the Aztec, Inca, but principally Maya environmental beliefs on the basis of recently emerged historical-archeological studies which see a sustainable rain forest economy as the fundamental quality of the Maya society, allowing new hypotheses on its enigmatic decline. This will offer a rich ground for the discussion of one of Harris's latest concerns: his own vision of environmentalism.

4.2 Meso-American and South-American Main Civilisations

4.2.1 The Maya

It would be impossible to account for all the literature published about the Maya civilization since the discovery of America. Even more difficult would be the direct analysis of the few Maya codices which survived the burning zeal of European missionaries[68] or the interpretation of the many sculptures and stelae which fortunately still testify this millenary culture. Therefore, a precise line will be followed, favouring those historical-archeological achievements which seem more relevant for this study, with particular reference to David Freidel, Linda Schele and Joy Parker's comprehensive *Maya Cosmos* (1993) regarding the cosmic and religious aspects, and Arthur Demarest's more technical *Ancient Maya* (2004) for the latest theories about environment-related issues. The European approach to Maya culture has been strongly characterised by the flawed image which emerged from the first Spanish accounts, such as Diego de Landa's *Relación de las Cosas de Yucatán* (1566), which is nevertheless a valuable record of Maya traditions. At that time no doubt was advanced about the original inhabitants of the numerous abandoned cities of the Yucatán, as a consequence of direct information by the local population of Maya descent. Later, various theories sprouted among Western scholars to explain the mysterious origins of the cities: "fanciful speculations began about lost races or tribes of 'mound builders' from Israel, Egypt, or from the imagined lost continents of Atlantis or Mu" (Demarest 33). During the late eighteenth and nineteenth centuries, more systematic investigations were carried out: the Anglo-Saxon world was particularly conditioned by the work of the American writer John Lloyd Stephens and "his gifted artist," Frederick Catherwood, who contributed to define "the popular image of the 'lost jungle cities' of the Maya" (Demarest 31). The deriving view was not based on improbable hypotheses such as those of the previous century, but, despite the artistic achievements and the precision of its inspirers, it contributed to construct an unrealistic romantic image of the Maya which still haunts today's studies. The great archaelogist epigrapher and ethnohistorian Eric J. Thompson was not immune to this "orientalist" view and his, otherwise seminal, *The Rise and Fall of Maya Civilization* (1954-1966) and *Maya History and Religion* (1970) contributed to convey the distorted image of "the most civilised of peoples" subsisting "almost exclusively on 'slash-and-burn' jungle farming" (Demarest 44). Thompson's work is very important, especially *Maya Hieroglyphic Writing: Introduction* (1950), for the comprehension of Maya inscriptions but, according to Arthur Demarest, it was also misleading because "the hieroglyphs of the Maya writing system that had been deciphered at that time were those glyphs dealing with Maya calendrics and astronomy" (44), and only later

---

[68] "While the Inquisition burned most of the Maya books and persecuted their users, three did survive amongst the booty sent back to Europe" (Demarest 192-193).

were they correctly interpreted as mere temporal reference points for the following text, which dealt with historical or mythic accounts. The early interpretation of Maya culture was therefore characterised by the importance given to their concept of time and their astronomy, generating a biased view of them "as a peaceful, highly civilised society dominated by a priestly scientific elite" which may simply have reflected "the social milieu of early Maya studies, with its gentlemen scholars and explorers sponsored by the best museums of Europe and the North American Ivy League" (Demarest 44). This approach overemphasised some features of Maya culture which often coincide with Harris's imaginative reading; however, he is never idealising pre-Columbian cultures in a fixed, exclusively positive frame, as will clearly emerge in his different approach to the cyclical concept of time of the Maya and to the similar Aztec one.

From the 1950s onward through the 1990s a more critical process has enriched the knowledge about the Maya world, to the point of allowing more balanced and solid interpretations. As a consequence, thanks to other eminent scholars such as Michael Coe, a more or less standard timeline for Meso-American settlements has been produced. In a few words, Demarest adopts a division which sees a paleo-Indian period followed by an Archaic one; early, middle and late Preclassic; a Classic period, including a Terminal one (in which a presumed "collapse" took place); and finally a post-Classic period reaching 1542, the symbolic date for the establishment of the Viceroyalty of Peru and the definitive end of the pre-Columbian era. If compared to Denis Williams's, Demarest's figures for the arrival of human beings on the American continent are less precise, allowing a wide margin for the presumed passing of the Bering Strait: "at about 12,000 BC, 40,000 BC, or even earlier" (Demarest 53). However, they are much more precise and similar when it comes to fix the first evidence of "bands of paleo-Indian hunters" in the region of Meso-America around 10,000 BC, which corresponds to the period Williams theorised for the presumably unified Amerindian culture of the Amazon Basin. A detailed survey of all the mentioned periods would be excessive here; the identification of the typical flourishing period of the main Meso-American cultures will suffice. The Omlecs, in whose large and round sculptures Harris sees the evidence of supposed early contacts with negroid peoples,[69] started flourishing in Veracruz and

---

[69] Referring to Irene Nicolson and Ian Van Sertima, Harris reports the theories advanced on the possibility that "Africans visited America long before Columbus. The impressive Negroid features of Olmec sculpture seem African" (Harris, "Absent Presence" 91).

Tabasco during the middle Preclassic, between 1000 and 400 BC. The Late Preclassic saw the rise of the great urban centre of Teotihuacan in the Valley of Mexico, between 400 BC and 300 AD, the time in which the Teotihuacan pyramids were built.[70] The kingdom of Teotihuacan survived as an influential "colossal neighbor" (Demarest 105) of the Classic Maya up until the 7th century AD. Those centuries also saw the early steps of the proper Maya civilisation which reached its peak during the Classic period (between 300 and 900 AD) and which suffered an enigmatic decline during the Terminal Classic (800-1000 AD). However, the Maya culture, despite a widespread belief, did not completely disappear; just the political organisation of the Lowland great cities such as the Classic Palenque or Tikal crumbled for unknown reasons, surviving in resized proportions in the Highlands with the late K'iche Maya of the Guatemalan highlands. As will be discussed shortly, this summarised timeline is a relatively uncritical, but useful, approach to the evolution of cultures which still exist today and did not witness the romantic total collapse which has fascinated many historians, Harris included.

The principal features of the Maya culture which can be useful to better understand Harris's reinterpretation are mainly related to their conception of time, to their cosmology and to the relationship with nature, which can be read either as a religious approach derived from cosmology or as a fundamental economic/ecologic strategy. First of all, the calendric system of the Classic Maya should be briefly explained. According to Demarest, the calendar was based on the precise astronomical observations: "Maya mathematics and astronomy carefully recorded and documented units of cyclical time as measured against the redundant and periodic movements of the sun, the moon, Venus and the stars" (Demarest 192), and it was based on a particular mathematical system: "Maya recording and calculations of time used a modified form of the base twenty (vigesimal) mathematical system with place notation and the use of zero" (193). These observations and calculations were organised in a count which started from the day of creation which, according to the inscriptions at the site of Koba, was fixed "on the day 4 Ahaw 8 Kumk'u [...]. In our calendar, August 13, B.C. 3114" (193). Time was counted from the date of creation on the basis of two annual calendars: one, the Haab, a "'vague solar year' of eighteen months (Winals)" (193) with the addition of five "unlucky" days (Uayeb) to adjust it with the solar 365 days; and a second annual round of 260 days, sometimes called

---

70 The protagonist of Harris's *Companions of the Day and Night*, Idiot Nameless, is described while he is falling from the Teotihuacan pyramids.

Tzolkin, which marked the most important sacred recurrences. This second set of circular dates was formed by an inner circle of thirteen numbers, "thirteen [being] a sacred prime number" (194), and an outer one of twenty named days (8 Ahau, 9 Imix etc.); their combination repeated only after 260 days. The conjunction of the Haab with the 260-day calendar gave the widely known fifty-two year cycle named by the scholars as the "Calendar Round" because the same sequence of combination of the three circles repeated itself only after fifty-two complete rotations of the Haab. In late Classic and post-Classic periods, sometimes a sort of "Short Count" was adopted by neglecting the 260-day reference, thus approximating the date in a way similar to the Western "Monday July 10," causing some difficulties to modern interpreters. Thus, the complete calendar resulted in a forward count in units based on the modified vigesimal (base 20) system as mentioned above. The days (Kin) were recorded within a count of months (Winal) of twenty days each, which were in turn grouped in a year (Tun), a set of 18 Winals. A group of twenty Tuns formed a K'atun which in turn, after twenty cycles, formed the Bak'tun, "the largest unit commonly used in Maya calendrics" (Demarest 194), 394.5 of our years. According to Demarest, one could therefore fix the Classic Maya period between the eighth and ninth Bak'tun, supporting the intriguing views which consider the disintegration of some of the lowland kingdoms accelerated by the "psychological impact" of the end of a great cycle: the ninth Bak'tun.

The riddle of the disappearance of the Maya is not the only element which links Harris's work to Meso-American concepts of time: as Paula Burnett poignantly points out in her "Memory Theatre and the Maya," the very concept of circularity is central to Harris's view of history. Since to the Maya "time only *appears* to move in a straight line," while in reality it runs over "ever larger circles within circles of time" (Freidel, Schele, and Parker 63) their historical and philosophical systems consequently differ from Western, linear approaches on the fundamental grounds of the systematisation of time and the interpretation of the past, which have been chosen to analyse Harris's thought. A brief presentation of the Maya system for the recording of time is therefore the necessary starting point to contextualise Paula Burnett's assumption that the Maya "regarded history as a cycle" (Burnett 220), and to ground the parallel philosophical consequences. The mentioned system may not by itself justify this, as long as we consider the neglected "non-linear" traditions concerning alchemy and archetypes within European, fundamentally "linear" culture, but similar approaches to Maya metaphysics have been commonly shared by most Mayanists, thus supporting the centrality for Maya culture of cyclicity and its derivations. According to Demarest, "the ancient Maya cyclical vision of time necessarily implied that to understand the repeating cycles of time was to know the future, as well as the past" (192) consequently providing "a close connection to the ancestors as it structurally linked the present, past, and future" (193). A more comprehensive statement finally suggests, in a fairly direct way, the connection with the constant concern of this study about Harris's fictional use of time: "Given the ancient Maya cyclical concept of time, insights into the past and predictions of the future were virtually synonymous" (Demarest 191).

In this light, the unity of past, present, and future, which allows Harris's characters to swing between different eras, may be related not only to his own fictional strategy (which, as the intellectual intuition of a single writer, would make this strategy merely functional to his project of recovering of American eclipsed cultures), but also to Amerindian and Maya cultures, testifying its direct derivation from non-European traditions, never completely faded. Burnett's general interpretation may thus acquire in this context a more specific reference: "The significance of such thinking to Harris's fiction is central to its address to chronicity. The tyranny of single conceptual systems (typical of modern Western culture) is unmade in its multiplicity of approach and openness to plurality of ideas" (Burnett 220). Far from denying the intrinsic cross-cultural and open quality of Wilson Harris's fiction, which derives the "plurality of ideas" cited by Burnett from multiple different sources, I suggest that the "chronicity" which informs Harris's philosophical interpretation of time and history can be effectively rooted in one particular tradition which, though widely extended through the Americas, has one of its historical manifestations in Maya culture. This may be the same tradition to which Freidel, Schele, and Parker refer when they summarise their twenty-year dedication to Mayan scholarship:

> We firmly believe that the Maya vision celebrates a way of conceiving the world that lives in the hearts and minds of the firstcomers to this hemisphere, a vision that is the natural legacy of all the American peoples and that can help to unite them in purpose as we face the challenge of rethinking our relationship to the life system that spawned us all. (13)

While meaningfully glossing the general considerations concerning the pre-Columbian legacies about time emerging in Harris's thought as a whole, they introduce the theme of relationship with "the life system that spawned us all" which will shortly be discussed.

Before that, it is necessary to exemplify the concepts analysed above in their fictional realisation in some of Harris's novels. It must be acknowledged that, at a deeper level, his approach to time and the concept of "timelessness" characterises the whole of his work (e.g. the time-travelling ability of several characters). However, in *Companions of the Day and Night* (1975), *Jonestown* (1996) and *The Dark Jester* (2001), this is especially investigated in relation to Meso-American Maya and Inca cultures. Due to the organisation of this study, which contemplates a separate sub-section for the Inca and a consequent generalisation, here the examples will refer exclusively to these three, with particular attention to *Jonestown* for its substantial inclusion of Maya-related elements.

Already in the letter by Francisco Bone addressed to a fictional editor, characterised once more by the already familiar W.H. acronym, fundamental statements appear about the way in which references to pre-Columbian cultures should be read. First, Bone makes clear that his own fiction is "archetypal" (in the sense discussed in chapter 3) and so are the characters; then the narration is patently inserted in Harris's usual recourse to dream "logics" by referring to Bone's fictional work as a "Dream-book" (4). The original aspect of Jonestown, as anticipated, is the direct connection of these familiar aspects of Harris's fictional strategy to Meso-American, specifically Maya, culture:

> I was obsessed – let me confess – by the cities and settlements in the Central and South Americas that are an enigma to many scholars. I dreamt of their abandonment, their bird-masks, their animal-masks... Did their inhabitants rebel against the priests, did obscure holocausts occur, civil strife, famine, plague? Was Jonestown the latest manifestation of the breakdown of populations within the hidden flexibilities and inflexibilities of pre-Columbian civilizations? The Maya were certainly one of the great civilizations of ancient America and the fate of their cities – such as Palenque, Chichen Itzá, Tikal, Bonampak – has left unanswered questions. Teotihuacan in Mexico raises similar enigmas. The unsolved disappearance of the Caribs in British Guiana is another riddle of precipitate breakdown. And there are many others. (4)

The fascination with those unresolved riddles of history is the main theme of *Jonestown* and it is the ground on which the 1978 episode is related to ancient Central and South-American history, but the fact of resorting directly to the cyclical conception of time developed by the Maya for the re-staging of past events (a fictional alternative to 19th century realism, a historical alternative to Western linear History) is extremely meaningful for the interpretation of Wilson Harris's work as a whole. Thanks to this direct reference, the constant strategy of Harris's "timeless" fiction realised in the "eternal present" of Amerindian myth or in the osmotic relationship of Maya past, present and future reveals its debt to a precise tradition in the panorama of Harris's cross-cultural sources. Moreover, it testifies the aliveness of this specifically American tradition through the effectiveness of its philosophical achievements as applied to historical fiction writing: "It is essential to create a jigsaw in which 'pasts' and 'presents' and likely or unlikely 'futures' are the pieces that multitudes in the self employ in order to bridge chasms in historical memory" (Harris, *Jonestown* 5). In order to account for the "living absences" neglected by the official scientific discipline of history, the novelist concerned about historical matters can resort to alternative representations of time which exceed their sterile metafictive function by contemplating a different reality through the lenses of the enigmatic but undeniable legacy of pre-Columbian traditions. In Bone's words (which more than ever overlap with Harris's), "Maya 'twinships' between the buried past and the unknown future – which are regarded as bewildering to the Western mind – seemed of burning and invaluable moment to me in their bearing on factors of originality and living time" (Harris, *Jonestown* 6). This originality is expressed in the possibilities which derive from the Maya approach to time and history:

> To sail back into the past is to come upon 'pasts' that are 'futures' to previous 'pasts' which are 'futures' in themselves to prior 'pasts' *ad infinitum*. There is no absolute beginning, for each 'beginning' comes after an unwritten past that awaits a new language. What lies behind us is linked incalculably to what lies ahead of us in that thee future is a sliding scale backwards into the unfathomable past within the Virgin womb of time. (Harris, *Jonestown* 5)

The importance of this aspect of Harris's philosophy of history is even greater when compared to essentialist recuperations of pre-colonial cultures which have often led to sterile contrasts with Western achievements, such as a kind of exotic primitivism or some extreme assumptions of the Négritude movement, Kamau Brathwaite's idealisation of Africa or Rastafarian harsh scorn of Babylon (the West, technology) as a whole. In Harris's cross-cultural view, the features of each tradition are not reduced to fit a static image of a whole; rather, they contribute to an ongoing dialogue with contrasting traditions to eventually find a momentary synthesis.

Such behaviour is meaningfully exemplified by the convergence of ancient Maya achievements ("celestial mathematics") with present-day Western scientific theories (Chaos theory) about mutuality and interconnectedness: "I voyaged between Maya twinships of pasts and futures and the Mathematics of Chaos" (Harris, *Jonestown* 5). This intuitive link between his own reading of Maya culture and Chaos theory is not always clearly expressed by Harris; however, it might be better understood in relation to the essay "Apprenticeship to the Furies" in which this clarifying passage is included:

> The Ancient Maya possessed a concept of blended pasts and futures. Eric S. Thompson, an American scholar, points out in his book *Maya Civilization* that this concept baffled the European mind, though I would think that Chaos mathematics – a new phenomenon in European science – has edged a little closer into its potential significance for the modern mind. Long before I knew it the idea was intuitively alive in my own work as a sliding scale that re-visits the cradles of living landscapes and seeks bridges across chasms of reality. (Harris, "Apprenticeship" A 223-224)

As already stated, Harris's metaphors concerning physics and particular branches of the contemporary Western scientific world are not central to this study, however, it is meaningful to recall them here because the links Harris draws in the introduction to *Jonestown* anticipate a recurring theme which he widely developed in *The Dark Jester*: the image of the void. In building the imaginative relationship between lost Maya cities and Chaos theory, Harris plants one of those intuitive seeds which eventually blossom through his strategical, continuous re-reading of his own work: "the walls of ruined schools and houses and temples and hospitals and theatres are full with presences and voices though apparently void and empty. Such is the mystery of Chaos" (Harris, *Jonestown* 6). Here, the re-generative possibilities Harris hunts among the ruins of the symmetrical image of ancient Maya cities and 1978 Jonestown seem to find a sort of "womb" in the image of the void, "an intact mystery in time" (6), where historical facts and their memory behave in a way similar to a complex chaotic system which only partially reveals a numinous order, defined by Harris as "the weight of Chaos" (6). What is once more striking, besides the surfacing of the seemingly lateral image of the void anticipated in *Jonestown* as a recurring element in a novel published some five years later, is the possible connection that can be drawn between the centrality the image assumes in Harris's most "Mayan" novels and one precise aspect of this pre-Columbian culture, revealed through historical-anthropological observation. According to Schele, Freidel and Parker, a deep discrepancy between Western and Maya culture can be found in astronomical knowledge, where a possible difference in observation could be read as a meaningful reason for their intrinsically distinct metaphysical-cosmologic approaches: "Today that heart of heaven would be the North Star, Polaris, but in Maya times, the north pivot of the sky fell in a dark area. This black void was the heart of heaven" (Freidel, Schele, and Parker 75). The possibility of an objective difference in the reality observed, leading to two distinct ideas, and consequently to different spiritualities and concepts of time, is challenging and could open a fruitful confrontation with Alejo Carpentier's idea of the "real maravilloso" as the proper quality of Meso-South-American imagery as opposed to European realism. This reading will be shortly discussed in relation to "Atahualpan void" as presented by Harris in *The Dark Jester*, while here it is useful to report another intuitive link that may rise from the close confrontation of Harris's texts with non-fictional information about the Maya.

Taken singly, such allusions and feeble references may seem mere coincidence, but in a broader frame they reveal the fundamental, constitutive role of pre-Columbian cultures in the formation of Wilson Harris's imagery and philosophy. Similarly, the next element to be analysed may appear as a detour from the main themes of time, cosmology and history, for its relating more directly to the archetypal themes discussed in chapter 3; on the contrary the image of the cross, or cosmic tree, in ancient and contemporary Maya culture will help to introduce the theme of nature, before it gains centrality in the last chapter. When the extended reading of the symbolism of the Christian Trinity opened the discussion on other possible archetypal interpretations of the cross in sub-section 3.2.3, the fourfold quality of this symbol emerged in relation to Maria Prophetissa's axiom and Jungian images of mandala; yet a cross-cultural analysis could acknowledge the wide scope of Harris's imagination even further. According to many Mayanists, the relatively easy acceptance of the imported Christian symbol of the cross into Meso-American cultures may be explained through the superimposition on the traditional image of the Cosmic Tree or "World Tree" of the new one, re-dressed as the traditional "foliated cross."[71] A similar overlap occurs in Harris's imaginative world in which it is possible to single out "the recurring symbol of the tree":

> the great tree of flesh and blood that appears to the Dreamer in *Palace of the Peacock*, the tree felled by the Macusi woodman in *The Four Banks of the River of Space*, and the "Phallic tree" of "sacrificial sculpture" witnessed by Francisco Bone in *Jonestown*, to give a few examples. Each of these trees appears in a state of metamorphosis, as it shifts into the cross on which Christ was crucified. (Emery, *Modernism* 232)

According once again to Schele, Freidel, and Parker, "the Maya appropriated and reinterpreted this most Christian of all symbols by merging it with the World Tree of the Center" (39). The tree is related to the cosmic imagery of the Maya which, as already mentioned, shares with the Guyanese Amerindian a particular interest in the Milky Way. This group of stars is central in Maya myths of Creation which contemplate, as represented on several stelae and inscriptions, the imagined celestial road as a central element in the etiological myths of "First Father" and the "Maize God."[72] Thanks to Schele's sharp intuition while researching on the relationship of Maya imagery and constellation, the mythic elements of the World Tree, the Milky Way and the centre of the universe can now be recognised in representations such as the inscriptions on Pakal's sarcophagus in Palenque, where the king is shown "at the moment of his death falling down the World Tree," or, in other words, "entering the road" (Freidel, Schele, and Parker 76). Precise correspondences have been found between World Tree representations and cosmic elements, particularly this relation with the Milky Way, revealing a deep complexity in Maya cosmology; however, the main interest here is about the World Tree as a religious symbol and about its ecological implications. From a religious point of view the cosmic element of the World Tree presents similarities with the Christian cross as an image, but it shows a different sym-

---

[71] A kind of foliated cross, a modified Christian cross common among present-day Maya, is presented by Freidel, Schele, and Parker as a contemporary representation of the ancient World Tree hybridised with post-conquest cross images.

[72] Several other constellations around the milky way, such as the Belt of Orion and the Pleiades, play important roles in Maya cosmology, but for the sake of brevity they will not be analysed here.

bolic referent,[73] akin to the Jungian mandala. A closer look reveals the Maya view of the superimposed image of the cross and the tree as often linked to the fourfold quality of their gods:

> We think this complex and powerful image of the cross contains one of the fundamental covenants of Classic Maya belief. It is not merely an icon [...], but a declared relationship between humanity and the gods. Freidel believes that the cross itself is an embodiment of First Father. (Freidel, Schele, and Parker 418)

The First Father, an important god among many, shared the widespread aspect of a fourfold being, reflecting the four cardinal points, with the greater part of Maya divinities: "their divinities already had multiple (commonly fourfold) aspects" (Freidel, Schele, and Parker 49). "In the Classic system, the Chakob, the K'awilob, the Pawahntunob, and many others were also fourfold gods" (130). This interpretation offers a meaningful insight because it supports the hypothesis of the grounding of several aspects of Harris's intuitive imagination in actual pre-Columbian traditions and cultures and enriches the possible meanings of many recurring fictional images which have often been linked to precise European traditions, but generically considered as totally imaginative reconstructions when related to non-Western cultural features. In conclusion, a closer look at the religious function of the tree-cross image among the Classic Maya offers a perfect exemplification of the achievements of Harris's cross-cultural imagination: it is as if his alchemical preoccupations collided with his pre-Columbian background in a new creative interpretation of the extremely widespread symbol of the cross, particularly through the complex fictional "enriched triads" of *Jonestown* analysed in 3.2.3, which once more reveal their indebtness to the Maya tradition at a deep level.

---

73   "[...] the striking resemblance between the World Tree and the modern Christian-Maya cross [...]. The first Europeans who saw the images of the World tree at Palenque called the buildings housing them the Temple of the Cross and the Temple of the Foliated Cross with good reason. These Maya 'crosses' had the same basic shape and were as elaborately decorated, as those gracing the altars of large European churches. The carvings of these ancient trees are outlined with reflective mirrors, and they wear jade necklaces and loincloths as if they were living beings. Modern Christian-Maya crosses both in Yukatan and Chiapas are decorated with mirrors and dressed in clothing, or flowers and pine boughs. They too are considered to be living beings." (Freidel, Schele, and Parker 53)

In addition, this reading offers a further interpretation for the character of Mr. Mageye, who apart from being "the magus-jester of history," plays the role of the fourth in the "enriched triad" of Jones-Bone-Deacon (3.2.3), and helps to interpret the fourth element in the triad of the "Maries," where the character of the animal goddess (under various "masks" such as Kali or "an animal goddess such as Circe") can also be read as a direct pre-Columbian reference in opposition to typically European figures such as Marie Antoinette, "an acceptable face in European eyes for Virgins."[74] It is through Mageye's camera that Bone recognises the Amerindian and Maya legacies in his present and compares them to the other cross-cultural elements characterising his experience of a tragic rehearsal in the "Memory Theatre." Because of Mr. Mageye's conciliatory role contemplating the mentioned pre-Columbian elements besides European Christian-Greek-Alchemical imagery, Elsa Linguanti's possible interpretation based on the assonances of his enigmatic name appears as perfectly grounded: "Mr. Mageye the schoolmaster (Magus, a Maya, one of the magi?)" (Linguanti, "Intersection" 47)

At the same time, the World Tree as presented above can cast a new light over Harris's concerns about nature and living landscapes and offers a strong link to Demarest's interpretation of Maya economics. In fact, both for Harris and for Maya culture, the centrality of the image of the tree is not exclusively determined by its religious and cosmologic function, but it has a symbolic value for the ecological aspect of the relationship between man and nature. As mentioned at the beginning of this sub-section, the rise and fall of the Maya civilisation has posed several interpretative problems. Arthur Demarest, in his *Ancient Maya* puts forward an interesting hypothesis about the economic system which allowed the Maya to subsist in a rainforest environment and proliferate up to the construction of noticeable urban centres, thanks to their particular relationship with nature. This might not solve the riddle of their (presumedly) sudden fall, but it confutes earlier theories which justified the decline of Classic Maya cities on the basis of a despoilment of the fragile rainforest ecosystem, and gives an interesting insight into Harris's concern about nature and living landscapes which he recently stressed in several essays and talks. According to Demarest, "since the beginnings of exploration in the Maya lowlands, the 'mystery of the collapse' of Classic-period civilization has been a driving force in Maya archae-

---

74 The two quotations refer to *Jonestown* (129). However, to fully acknowledge the complex "carnival masquerade" of "broken archetypes" involving the mentioned female figures which takes place in the second part of the novel would require a separate section, while here a short reference is sufficient for the main discussion.

ology" (240); even Harris's curiosity may have been ignited by this romantic view, as appears from the first pages of *Jonestown*, despite the emerged stronger connections at less superficial levels. This has been the case also of several Mayanists, justifying Demarest's urge in proposing a less biased view: "Whatever happened to many of the southern lowland cities, it was *not* a uniform, total collapse of the states, and it was in no way an end or even decline of the enduring Maya tradition" (242). Freidel, Schele, and Parker confirm the enduring of this tradition through their anthropological works among the contemporary Maya, while Demarest stresses the historical inaccuracy of the misleading idea of a complete fall: "the phrase 'the collapse' or 'the fall' of a civilization is a colorful, but misleading term. [...] civilizations never 'die'" (274-275). Despite the closeness of Demarest's interpretation and Harris's view of the evolution of pre-Columbian culture, the main reason for introducing this topic is the widespread explanation given by Mayanists about the causes of the presumed decline: "The decline or collapse of southern Maya cities in the ninth century was seen as the inevitable consequence of the limitations of the rain forest" (Demarest 128). Within this context, the riddle of Maya cities, to which Demarest does not try to give any definitive solution, begins to slide towards an interesting theme: the economic-ecological system underlying Maya urban formation, which appears particularly "exotic" to a classically scientific European mind. To quote Demarest's words once more, it appears that "Western civilization's urban-versus-rural distinction is inapplicable to the Classic Maya world" (119), and the preconception of Maya cities as environment-exploiting machines akin to any Western metropolis reveals its inefficacy. In fact, according to Demarest's analysis of Maya agricultural habits and their system of raised fields, it emerges that "If properly managed, rain forest subsistence systems can support large and complex societies" (121); and from his archaeological investigations "no indications of increasing nutritional stress" (245) resulted. As a consequence, a new approach to Maya history is presented, curiously showing a direct link with Harris's ideas:

> While popular perspectives talk of the 'secret' of the lost civilization of the Maya in terms of hidden treasures or hieroglyphic inscriptions, the true secret of Maya civilization was their successful, sustainable adaptation to the rain forest, a feat we have not been able to duplicate today. In broad terms, the 'secret' of the Maya adaptive strategy was simply to structure their agricultural regimes to imitate the nature of the rain forest itself. (Demarest 128)

The valuable legacies Harris found in Amerindian and Meso-American cultures contemplate, as an important element, besides mythical, cosmologic, and religious issues, the particular relationship with nature, which underlies the non-human centred view of the world of the Maya: "without a sensation of uncharted realms, extra-human dimensions, I am inclined to feel that one is destined to freeze or burn in an absolutely human-centred cosmos inevitably promoting dominion and lust as its hidden agenda" (Harris, *Jonestown* 100).

Harris judges this, in agreement with Demarest, so valuable for the integration of a Western mind, because the "animist" attitude of Meso-South-American cultures not only allows a sustainable perspective of human evolution, but fundamentally affects philosophical approaches to the world, particularly regarding time, history and eclipsed selves.[75] Such considerations similarly affect Demarest's conclusions about the centrality of the ecological system for Maya culture, in a perspective extended to more global concerns:

> In this regard, the study of the ancient Maya is fascinating precisely because their civilization appears to be so different from our own. The structure of ecological adaptations, settlement patterns, and political and economic institutions could not be more unlike the Western, Mesopotamian, Judeo-Christian tradition of our own civilization. For at least 6000 years, the hallmarks of the Western tradition have been linear concepts of time, monocultural agricultural systems, overproduction and exchange of surplus in full market economies, technology-driven development, a long history of attempts to separate religious and political authority, and judgmental gods concerned with individual, personal moral conduct. As we learn from the Maya, none of these traits is universal, none of them was characteristic of Classic Maya civilization, and none of them is critical to the florescence of high civilization. (Demarest 296)

The deriving importance of this distinctive feature of pre-Columbian tradition, suggesting a "profound and unusual treaty of sensibility between human presence on this planet and the animal [vegetal and inanimate] kingdom" (Harris, "Profiles" 202) – "a world alive in all its parts" (Freidel, Schele, and Parker

---

75 According to Demarest, "we can also, at times, simply embrace the essentially subjective and introspective nature of history and archeology and seek from it personal, philosophical insights" (296).

10) – which deeply affects Harris's philosophy and the perspective of human time, will be extensively discussed in the final chapter, while here the analysis is confined to the Inca variant of Harris's pre-Columbian influences and its effect on the writing of *The Dark Jester*.

4.2.2 The Inca and Atahualpan Void

With respect to the Amerindians and to the Maya, the analysis of the influences of the Inca culture on the work of Wilson Harris requires a different approach.[76] It is certainly true that the novel entitled *The Dark Jester* (2001) deals with Inca culture and history, but the way this history represents the precise culture of that population seems very distant from the direct correspondences discussed in relation to the Maya. Harris's tendency to shape historical and cultural elements to his own unifying project has never been denied, but particular attention has been given to those aspects which were supported by interdisciplinary evidence. The case of the Inca is slightly different because, apart from Harris's knowledge of the historical sources about the Inca empire,[77] the main discourse underlying the fictional recreation of the figure of Atahualpa and the Cajamarca massacre seems to relate to a wider conception of pre-Columbian culture, a sort of summary of Harris's ideas, including those discussed above. This reading is also supported by the fact that the time-travelling character of the dreamer attends the Cajamarca execution (1533) and Cortez's entrance into Teotihuacan (1519), while the very same Conquistador is transported many years before at the feet of the Palenque pyramids to stand before Pacal, the Maya king (603-683); that is to say, the narration includes the three main pre-Columbian cultures, Maya, Aztecs, and Inca.

Nevertheless, several historical facts from Inca history are reinterpreted in *The Dark Jester,* and a quick look at the "official" history of the Inca Empire should help one's understanding. One important thing must be made clear at first: the Inca had no such chronological recording system as the Maya calendar and they did not have a proper writing system either, which makes the reconstruction of an absolute chronology difficult, considering that the first chroniclers of the 16th-17th centuries, such as Garcilaso De la Vega, were not able to give a consistent version, and the main source was the indigenous oral tradition

---

[76] This chapter is a re-elaboration of part of a previously published article (Delfino, "Rushdie's Technicolor and Harris's Mist").

[77] Significantly, Harris wrote a review, published in *The Caribbean Quarterly* in 1969, on Felipe Guaman Poma de Ayala's *Nueva corónica y buen gobierno* (1615-1616).

(Rowe 265-284). Only recently has the use of carbon 14 dating offered scientific evidence (which confirms the information gathered by historiographers), and the mainly accepted version of Inca chronology (John Howland Rowe's) did not change (Adamska and Michczynski). What is important for the understanding of *The Dark Jester* is the final period of the Inca Empire, which saw first the opposition of Huáscar and his half-brother Atahualpa in the succession of their father in the 1520s, and then the arrival of the Spaniards led by Francisco Pizarro and the famous violent episodes of the massacre of Cajamarca and the search for the city of Vilcabamba.

The first decades of the 1500s were already a period of turmoil in the Inca state, which had become a vast empire in the course of the previous century. Because of the difficulties arisen in the choice of a successor after the death of Huayna Capac in 1527, the political tension in the Inca state developed into civil war when Ninan Kuyuchi, the first designated heir, died "shortly after the old emperor" (Patterson 120). Huáscar, who lived in Cuzco, was declared the new Inca, but his brother Atahualpa, who was much more considered among the high ranks of the army, reclaimed his right to be the Inca. As a consequence, a civil war developed and the Inca empire witnessed a period of violence and bloodshed, which saw the victory of Atahualpa, who imprisoned Huáscar and slaughtered his whole family. This is the period in which the first news of the Europeans came to Atahualpa's attention. The Cajamarca events took place within a year from the end of the civil war. In November 1532, Pizarro put in practice his plan of kidnapping the Inca by organising a meeting in the city of Cajamarca. There, a sort of ambush was carried out by the Spanish, who managed to disperse Atahualpa's entourage and to hold him as a hostage. According to Patterson, "The Inca leader quickly noticed the Spaniards' obsession with gold and silver and, fearing that the Spaniards were going to kill him, he sought to extricate himself from the situation by offering his captors a large amount of gold and silver as a ransom" (123).

Pizarro, who knew the Inca's wealth to be enormous, agreed on freeing him as soon as the ransom was paid, but he was already planning the betrayal which would remain in history as a symbol of the Conquistadores' baseness. Before that, Pizarro fuelled the turmoil which had just ended by meeting Huáscar and Topa Hualpa, another of the contending brothers, with the intention of further destabilising the kingdom of Peru. However, the danger of a reorganisation by Atahualpa in order to oppose the invaders was quickly eliminated by the execution of the Inca, in spite of the official agreement. The other factions immediately placed themselves under Pizarro's protection and after a brief period in which Topa Hualpa reigned, Manco Inca Yupanqui was put in charge. He cooperated with the Spanish for a period, but later retreated to the mythical city of Vilcabamba, where he attempted a kind of guerrilla resistance. Nevertheless, his son and successor Tupác Amaru was finally captured and executed, determining the end of the Inca rule for good in 1572.

It is important to recall these events to explain the puzzling easiness with which Pizarro's 168 men, with one cannon and 27 horses, managed to take control of a vast empire such as that of the Inca. The state of turmoil and the civil war played a fundamental role in the conquest of Peru, but they also contribute to a less idealised view of this pre-Columbian society, which, as the Aztec did, bore in itself the seeds of violence which Harris has often interpreted as the main cause for the decadence of pre-Columbian cultures. This might be a reason for his choice of portraying the Inca culture in a more idealised way (compared to his depiction of the Maya culture) by consciously limiting the number of references to the actual society as defined by the mediated information available. This should not appear as a peculiar approach, it should rather reinforce the assumption that Harris's reading of pre-Columbian cultures is not biased by over-intellectualisation or excessive idealisation, but characterised by a complex relationship with his own philosophy, which allows him to identify Western "ontic closures" as much as pre-Columbian: "aboriginal people themselves are locked into ontic tautologies: evil is evil is evil" (Harris, "Composition" 16). As Hena Maes-Jelinek correctly points out, "Atahualpa's self-division, his awareness of the 'corruption of empires' [Harris, *Jester* 28], made him lower his defences and prompted him to reverse 'millennia of conquest' by welcoming Pizarro" (Maes-Jelinek, "Unimaginable" 225).

The features consciously idealised by Harris in the figure of Atahualpa may as well be attributed to other pre-Columbian rulers, and this is made clear by the shifts in time and place occurring in *The Dark Jester*. Their discussion is relevant because it may summarise some useful aspects for a final conclusion on Harris's relationship with history: the dreaming dimension, which is once again the ground on which cultures come into contact and their inter-dependance become perceivable; the concept of the void which, as anticipated, is a fundamental element in the differentiation of pre-Columbian philosophies and extensively associated with Atahualpa; and lastly, the episode of the "crying horses," which can be read as a further example of the active role of nature and animals in history.

In *The Dark Jester*, from the prologue on, the reader is introduced to a world of dream, in which the concepts of myth, tradition and history overlap, giving way to the possibility of simultaneity, both in space and in time. The title of the prologue, "Fragment of a Dream," cannot be mistaken, especially when typical Harrisian images are called into play: "I perceive myself [...] as curiously related to live fossil organs invisibly suspended and linked across ages" (*Jester* vii). As usual, Harris allows the protagonists of his novels to confront "areas of tradition that have sunken away and apparently disappeared and vanished and yet that are still active at some level" (Maes-Jelinek, "Numinous" 534-535). The concern about pre-Columbian tradition, as fictionalised in *The Dark Jester*, can be seen in this context: "it is important to remember that in the Americas [...] we have examples of cultures of whose origins we know virtually nothing and of whose demise we know equally little or nothing" (Harris, "Judgement" 18). This is a context in which many of the elements discussed in the previous chapters come into play: the image of the "fossils" buried in the unconscious symbolises the possibility of actualisation in the present of everyday perception, of past events, ancient cultures and lost civilisations: "the necessity there is for Man to 'listen to' his past, to 'exhume the fossils' of history that are buried in his Unconscious, the fossils of his personal history as well as those that are part of the world's collective unconscious" (Dubois, "Wilson Harris" 37). From a different angle, the image of living fossil strata "ties the past to the postcolonial present through a bridge of cross-cultural communication" (S. Murray 53). This image may appear as the integration in space (strata – "condensation") of the two dimensions on which the Freudian concept of dream is constructed. According to Hayden White's reading of Freud's *The Interpretation of Dreams*, the dreaming mind operates along two axes: a horizontal, diachronic one, defined as "displacement," and a vertical, synchronic one, labelled "condensation." The first axis is useful to visualise the stratification in time already mentioned, while the second allows a better understanding of the concept of cross-cultural layering in the present:

> The dream thoughts are packed or layered, creating an effect of depth along a vertical axis. [...] In condensation, as in metaphor, it is the functioning of some third term, usually a shared attribute, which serves as the unspoken justification for the linking of two entities or events. (White, *Figural Realism* 108).

Hence, the metaphorical, allusive language of dream operates a web of "unsuspected [...] linkages within a cross-cultural tradition" (Harris, "Judgement" 20) both in time and space, along which the intuitive imagination discovers "third terms." However, this web of "linkages," as recreated in Wilson Harris's dream-like fiction, can be better explained in relation to the discussed Jungian theory of the collective unconscious: "This kind of fiction therefore takes its ground in a judgement which I would call the world's unconscious" (Harris, "Judgement" 25). As anticipated in 3.3, Harris's terminological differentiation allows possibilities for "complex, intuitive [...] connections" (25), linking, for example, European traditions such as alchemy and Maya imagery, or Atahualpa's destiny with Pacal's, establishing a dialogue with the "historyless" background of the West Indies (in Harris's words "the uncertainties that lay in my background" [25]); while, in addition, it includes fundamental insights such as the active historical role of Tumatumari rocks or, in *The Dark Jester*'s case, the collective conscience surfacing in the Horses' tears: "'there's a stark of photogenic picture for you buried in animal memory. The Horse becomes a god' [...] 'the horses weep'" (Harris, *Jester* 9-11).

In the prologue, another metaphor, recurrent in his writings, is addressed by Harris, who explicitly refers to quantum physics: "Quantum theory remains rich and obscure and open to interpretations beyond the finality of human discourse" (Harris, *Jester* ix). Without discussing this theme in depth, its inclusion here is useful because it may give a further example of the imaginative reading which characterises Harris's approach to the Inca culture. As stated elsewhere, I do not deny any deep knowledge on his side of this scientific subject or of Inca history, which may easily be part of Harris's encyclopaedic erudition, but I stick to his own programmatic enunciation about myth and the possibility of using it without any need for exactness: "One can validate or prove [...] strategies partly through ancient myths. [...] It doesn't mean that such myths exist in an exact form in the work one writes" (Harris, "Judgement" 17). Hence, one can consider such allusions and parallels without particular strictness. Keeping this in mind, the otherwise extremely complex field of quantum theory becomes a fruitful source of interesting concepts:

> creativity possesses within itself proportions that are akin to quantum physics. You know in quantum physics a particle is a wave [...]. That is, whether we are talking about a particle in quantum physics or an image in a literary text, we can only observe its location as it moves away from that location, as it

changes. Such movements occur through space, through geographical space, but also through historical time. So we can begin to see the connections between the most daring theorems in science and also in literature, in the imagination that is in profound dialogue with the past, so that Dante's allegory becomes vivid and alive, though it was written in the thirteenth century. (Harris, "Judgement" 22)

This, in my opinion, makes much clearer the point of introducing quantum theory in the prologue of *The Dark Jester*: the Dreamer's vision of a reality that is the past, Atahualpan world, yet so powerfully present, is the result of such movements through historical time that imagination can perform as does a quantic particle. Thus, Atahualpa's absence becomes questionable:

> in a clarity of dream that is dark and troubled – the maters of unfinished terminations, resurrections, the oddest re-births, arouse at best a notion of myth that is passive and unexplored. The life of myth, the livingness of myth, in the degree that it surfaces, belongs archetypally to another age. (*Jester* ix)

Consequently, time, in *The Dark Jester*, is the time of dream, of "quantum simultaneity," and as long as "Dream is Jest" (*Jester* x), "an attempt to bridge the apparently unbridgeable" (vii), time becomes the possible object of manipulation. Its malleability allows the possibility of a subversive reconstruction of history, "a history of absence, of non-existence" (Dubois, "Wilson Harris" 43), opposed to the "authoritarian realism" of "an account of events set out and approved by a dominant culture" (Harris, *Jester* 1). The bridging quality of Jest enables the narrator to bring to life the "absences" that characterise both Caribbean "historylessness" and pre-Columbian "uncertainties": "non-existences threaded into complex being are the characters of the Play of the arts. They are ignored or treated as invalid by Faustian Ships of civilization" (*Jester* 102-103). In this process the profound interrelationship between conquered and conqueror which a realistic, linear account would have denied becomes visible and throws the basis for a reconciliation: "The constructive reconstruction of history [...] enables the protagonist [as in *The Infinite Rehearsal*] to transcend the painful divisions created by the conquest and the colonial past" (Dubois, "Wilson Harris" 41). Such a possibility, as discussed in section 1.3, is the core of Wilson Harris's Caribbean poeticism, which implies the tragic recognition, in a continuous rehearsal of history, of a way to necessary forgiveness for the regeneration of the post-colonial self "like the halves of a fruit seamed by its own bitter juice" (Walcott, "Muse" 64) through the "power of mythopoetic action" (Henry 94). This emerges in *The Dark Jester* as "the redemptive potential latent within the catastrophic "reverses" of history" (Durrant, "Coming Home" 205), attributed by Harris to certain episodes in the history of pre-Columbian civilisations, specifically to the "encounter" of Pizarro with the Inca emperor Atahualpa and, to a lesser extent, to the fictional confrontation, across time, of Cortes with Pacal, the Maya king of Palenque.

In the complex web of *The Dark Jester,* with a conception that reminds of Walcott's ruins, history becomes the place of a void, the void of Caribbean history that is also the Atahualpan Void: a symbol for the different world views of pre-Columbian and Western cultures.[78] This concept of the void allows the Dreamer to recognise a new possible approach to reality, Atahualpan Form, which is opposed to Western Cartesian Form with its mistrust in linear logic and rationalism:

> What seems unbridgeable is the chasm that separates Atahualpa from Pizarro, pre-Conquest from post-Conquest times, but also the many closures we erect in all spheres in an ordering of life which the Dreamer calls "Cartesian form." Harris has often drawn attention to the limitations of Cartesian logic and its anthropomorphic interpretation of the world, contrasting it with a phenomenal legacy and a tradition, perceivable still in pre-Columbian art, which implies as he says, a "treaty of sensibility between human presence on this planet and the animal kingdom." [...] This is manifest in Inca iconography, the blending of human, animal and cosmic features in myths that inspire in the Dreaming narrator a poetic "Atahualpan" as opposed to the "Cartesian form." (Maes-Jelinek, "Unimaginable" 223)

"[The] Void of Jest in which resonances allow access beyond the Cartesian form of our culture's consciousness to 'Atahualpan form'" (Mitchell, "With Covered Eyes" 116) becomes the kingdom of intuitive imagination, where it is possible to re-stage past events in the present, in a process of "infinite rehearsal" as progressively theorised by Harris, discovering formerly unnoticed aspects, in-

---

[78] The image of the Void is a rich symbol for Harris and defies a stable definition; for a discussion of the void as a central feature in Maya cosmology, see 4.2.1.

troducing new ones, operating transformations in search of clues "as we go through these rehearsals" for a "positive direction" (Harris, "Judgement" 20). According to Dominique Dubois, "In terms of history, Harris [...] suggests that violence is not inevitable, that the course of our world, based on the Conquest and the annihilation of the vanquished can be revised" (Dubois, "Wilson Harris" 45). One of the many possible strategies for revision that Wilson Harris has elaborated is indeed the Dreamer's experience in *The Dark Jester*:

> I had travelled fictionally, it seemed, across centuries to approach a form I called Atahualpa, to know him and it, to know a living / dead form substance that differed in its dying, in its living, from anything by which I had been conditioned in a dominant history, a dominant cultural history. (*Jester* 102)

The answer to the Dreamer's question, "is it the unbearable wings of impossible/possible re-generation blown by art across ages, across centuries?" (*Jester* 90) is implicitly contained in the obscure and misty image of the Void:

> the darkness of the Void subsequent to Atahualpa's fall [and] the precipice in Palenque where the Dreamer penetrates the darkness of oblivion – all are the variable seats of the Dreamer's discovery of the frontiers of regeneration and the possible transmutation of the ruin into origin. (Maes-Jelinek, "Unimaginable" 227)

The ground on which art and imagination can perform such regeneration is clearly identified by Harris in the constitutive interrelationship that he reads in the mysterious behaviour of pre-Columbian rulers (such as Moctezuma or Atahualpa's "self-division") at the time of Conquest. As Hena Maes-Jelinek acutely points out, it is in the shared wound that the two civilisations inherit from their encounter that the possibility of re-generation lies:

> Atahualpa evinces a wound which, in his reconstruction, the Dreamer shares with him, even Pizarro and Cortez cannot entirely conceal the vulnerability they have in common with their victims. [...]
> Such ontological vulnerability opens the way to the sources of creativity [...]. ("Unimaginable" 226)

Actually, the Dreamer recognises that "each wound was a window into a tree of life" (Harris, *Jester* 13), "a complex window through which I looked into possibilities" (91). Harris's possibilities are infinite and they bridge cultures in place and time, linking pre-Columbian Peru with ancient Greece by coupling the fall of Cajamarca with the fall of Troy (*Jester* 35-39), or even alluding to extra-human perspectives, as in the crying horses/gods image.

This last allusion is central because it is based on the concept of extended unconscious ("world's unconscious" – "universal unconscious") which has been discussed in relation to Jung and to the Maya culture. This concept characterises the image of the void by including those levels of reality which Western thought and history tend to deny and which become, in Harris's view, a principal feature of the pre-Columbian world: and they build a "visionary insight into complex overlapping levels of natural and existential being" (Maes-Jelinek, "Unfinished Genesis" 235), leading to a "new understanding of difference in universality" (Harris, *Jester* 28). The episode of the crying horses/gods is one of the numerous manifestations of the close relationship between man and the earth/universe which Harris has been constantly expressing and had already made explicit in the mentioned review of *Nueva corónica y buen gobierno*: "Felipe Guaman Poma lived within the gateway of an Inca/Spanish world [...] he seems to be peering through an unruly cosmos: 'caves, rocks, lakes, mountains and rivers'" (Harris, "Review" 121). This "unruly cosmos" appears to be the Dark Jester's world from which, as unfathomable character, he guides the Dreamer through a travel "across times, across ages," thanks to an extended perspective on reality deriving from the inclusion of extra-human agents, as will be analysed shortly.

5 – Conclusions: The Perspective of Living Landscapes

> What is history?
>
> - Wilson Harris, *The Dark Jester*

> Where are your monuments, your battles, martyrs?
> Where is your tribal memory? Sirs,
> in that gray vault. The sea. The sea
> has locked them up. The sea is History.
>
> - Derek Walcott, "The Sea is History"

In this study a selective approach has been favoured in the discussion of the various influences which contribute to Harris's thought. This has proved necessary because of the extremely wide span of Harris's interests and his tendency to progressively integrate them in the course of the subtle evolution of his work. On the other side, the complex but evident consistency of this evolution requires a constant attention to the overall delineation of a unity of thought which can be considered, with due caution, akin to a proper philosophical system. To support this view, the first chapter of this study has been constructed around the main philosophical readings of Harris's work, which testify its fundamental contribution to "the making of Caribbean philosophy."[79] The consideration of Harris's fiction and essays as a possible answer to Lawrence O. Bamikole's rhetorical question, "but is there Caribbean philosophy?" (70) is subordinated to the broader meaning of the term 'philosophy' adopted in chapter 1,[80] but further confirmation should be provided here with reference to Paget Henry's authoritative opinion: "Caribbean philosophy has been carefully embedded in the practices of non philosophical discourses almost to the point of concealment" (Henry xi).

On the basis of these premises, to perform a complete systematisation of the philosophical issues addressed by Wilson Harris in more than forty years, both in his fiction and essays, would be an impossible task to perform in a single volume. Therefore, a selection has been made in order to analyse one aspect in depth. The theme of history, and consequently of time and historiography, has

---

[79] This expression is borrowed from the work of Leonard Tim Hector, a prominent Antiguan intellectual and political activist, editor of the column "Fire the Flame" in which the articles "The Making of Caribbean Philosophy" (I, II) were published in 1998 (Hector).

[80] For a different opinion on the possible philosophical value of fiction see Margaret G. Holland, "Can Fiction be Philosophy?"

been chosen not solely because of its importance in the Caribbean literary panorama (Walcott; Glissant; Retamar etc.) but also because of the particular approach Harris has directly developed in several of his novels. Besides, the contemporary historiographical debate, as discussed in chapter 2, is already accustomed to fruitful confrontations of fiction and historiography, and it should, therefore, be open to the inclusion of Harris's particular view.

The typical Harrisian character is almost always fragmented into alter egos and is often "spread out" to different and distant historical moments, revealing a puzzling conception of time (or "timelessness") which distinguishes Harris's vision of history and historiography. In the post-colonial world, the concern about the recuperation of particular histories denied by the authoritarian narrative of the empire has been central, as emerged in section 2.2, but in Harris's case the very nature of time, memory and history must be investigated, as partially discussed in this study. To do so, an overview of the contemporary debate about history and historiography has been carried out, deliberately taking into account Western and non-Western positions to show how Harris's approach may prove valuable for both. The contribution of fictional discourse to a crumbling historiography, which feels the effect of its excessive confidence in a questionably scientific nature, has emerged as a primary element in contemporary debates, especially in relation to *metahistory*, (Hayden White's extensive analysis of historiographical discourse). Harris's contribution to this emerging view is evident and extremely valuable, but, as usual, characterised by multiple influences. For this reason the mentioned selective approach has been used to concentrate on two, apparently distant, motifs: psychoanalysis and pre-Columbian traditions.

Harris's fascination with Jungian and alchemical themes has been analysed, as extensively as possible, in chapter 3. It revealed possible connections with his reading of pre-Columbian legacies: a new, extended view of reality based on invisible, cross-cultural threads across time and space which underlie a profound unity, including not only humanity, but the entire cosmos, in a sort of "universal unconscious." This analysis has revealed how Harris's characters are often partial images which refer to a wider archetypal reality whose dimension transcends their immanent representation. In Harris's view, this archetypal reality, which in Jungian terms is unknowable in its entirety, underpins historical manifestations in all cultures and suggests the possibility of a different perspective on time.

In the limited context of pre-Columbian traditions analysed in chapter 4, specific features of this archetypal whole have emerged in relation to a widened conception of consciousness which contemplates the existence of a living cosmos deriving from particular relationships with nature and landscape strictly connected to mythical dimensions and socio-economic approaches to rain-forest environments, such as those discussed in relation to the Guyanese Amerindians, the Maya and the Inca. The direct references made by Harris to these cultures helped to define his idea of "living landscapes" which can contribute to the integration of marginalised realities and "living absences" into a more general historical discourse.

"Historylessnes" has been a quality often referred to the Caribbean historical reality; as a consequence, authoritative interpretations such as Walcott's and Glissant's, resorted to nature to define the "locus" for history in that region; in this context Harris's perspective acquires an even more grounded relevance.

Despite personal issues, which probably informed Walcott's criticism of Harris's difficult style,[81] the ideas about history expressed by the two often point to common elements: "Walcott is no doubt writing from his own perception of the process of artistic creation, but in its appositeness to Harris it is a reminder of how close, in many ways, the two writers are" (Burnett, "Opening" 63). As emerged from the previous chapters, nature as an active element in a mysterious cosmos plays a fundamental role for Harris, informing his approach to several issues and defining his view of historical reality; at the same time, it recurrently characterises Walcott's approach to history and links his famous essay "The Muse of History" to Harris's work: according to Stuart Murray, "There seems little doubt that Harris's thinking [...] influenced Derek Walcott's ideas on history in his 1973 essay 'The Muse of History'" (Murray, Stuart 169). As occasionally emerged, Harris's inclusion in the Caribbean literary panorama reveals several connections with other writers, but his approach to the theme shows a particular originality and has been exceptionally supported by the writer's critical work.

A brief systematisation of the main concepts as expressed by Harris in a number of fundamental essays is here useful for the delineation of a possible confluence of all the issues arising around the theme of living nature and its implications for Harris's view of time and history. First, it should be acknowledged that the theme has surfaced in a large number of essays, since the publication of *Tradition, the Writer and Society* (1967) up to recent works such as *Theatre of the*

---

[81] Harris "is probably the most audacious explorer of our psychic condition so far, but the truth is that he is becoming unreadable. There is a decadence of syntax that results from a poet's fascination with his own brilliance, and this seems to be the cul-de-sac that Harris has reached" (Walcott, "The Explorer" 8; "Tracking" 5).

Arts (2002), but for the sake of conciseness only a selection will be analysed here. For this task, *Explorations: A Selection of Talks* proves once more essentially useful, besides the mentioned *Tradition, the Writer and Society,* and *The Unfinished Genesis of the Imagination*; on the other hand, Harris's application of the theme to his novels will not be systematically considered, due to the numerous analyses already carried out in the course of the four previous chapters. As soon as 1967, Harris mentioned a significant connection between nature and music, which he would develop years later: "Nature operates in series of recurrences which give the effect of rhythms" (Harris, "Question" 18); and he referred this to pre-Columbian views of the world: "to discover what those rhythms were and to follow their complicated but regular beat would, in Aztec philosophy, ensure happy survival of the community"(18). In "Art and Criticism," another essay from the same collection, Harris immediately links his interpretation of nature to the complex archetypal dimension exemplified in chapter 3: "The identity that it [the subject] discovers in the association of life and environment is a deep process immensely altering or breaking the shape of things as [...] in the 'archetype of the collective unconscious' [Jung]" (7-12). Both these concepts are not yet developed to the level discussed in the previous chapters, but it is important to trace their existence in Harris's first critical work. Besides, it should be noticed that his very first publication, the collection of poetry entitled *Eternity to Season* (1954), already bore the seeds of such theorisations, especially in the poem "Charcoal."[82] Only three years after writing "Art

---

82   Bold outlines are drawn to encompass
the history of the world: crude but naked emphasis
rests on each figure of the past
wherein the golden sunlight burns raw and unsophisticated.
Fires of brightness are sheltered
to burn the fallen limbs of men: the green
spirit of leaves like smoke
rises to mark the barrow of earth
and dwindles to perfection. The stars
are sparks
emblems of fire
to blacken the limbs of each god who falls:
spendthrift creation. The stable dew-drop is flame.
The dew burnishes each star in preparation for every deserted lane.
Time lies uneasy between the paintless houses
weather-beaten and dark.
The Negro once leaned upon his spade
breathing the smoke of his labour

and Criticism," Harris addresses these issues in a passage that includes some of the terms which would become typical in later reformulations: "if we are not to succumb to a chasm of proportions – implosion/explosion – the death of numbers through numbers, we must begin, I believe, to visualize the globe within a new corpus of sensibility" ("Interior" 12). There, referring to human progress and population growth, he introduces the phrase "new corpus of sensibility" which would become one stable definition of his view of profound relationship with the world and the environment. In 1970 Harris published "History, Fable and Myth in the Caribbean and Guianas," where he further developed some of the concepts related to the role of nature in the Caribbean historical landscape. Addressing J.J. Thomas's book *Froudacity* (1889), which deals with the 19th-century historian Froude, Harris aimed "to make clear the kind of historical stasis which has affected the Caribbean [...] for many generations" (Harris, "History, Fable and Myth," in Bundy, ed., 152). The historical stasis Harris mentioned is, in his opinion, well exemplified by "Froude's emphasis on the dicey, accidental character of nature and society," revealing a sort of "eclipse of sensibility" which "may well be an omen of an age in which, not long before, the person had been property (slave property)" (153). To Harris, Thomas's arguments in the criticism of Froude (where the first confronts, as a liberal, the conservative ideas about slavery of the second) show their entrapment in the same "historical stasis" in which other traditional historiographical approaches revealed their inadequacy for the description of the Caribbean reality. According to Harris,

> The duel which they fought is nevertheless a very instructive one in pointing up the historical stasis which afflicts the West Indian sensibility and which may only be breached in complex creative perspectives for which the historical convention would appear to possess no criteria. [...] they consolidated an intellectual censorship of significant vestiges of the subconscious imagination which they needed to explore if they were to begin to apprehend a figurative meaning beyond the real or apparently real world. It is my intention [...] to concentrate, in some degree, on those ves-

---

the arch of his body banked to shelter or tame
fury and diamond

or else like charcoal to grain
the world. (Harris, "Charcoal," *Eternity to Season* 23)

tiges as part and parcel of the arts of the imagination. ("History, Fable and Myth," in Bundy, ed., 156)

In this dense passage Harris summarises in the clearest way his motivations for the historical enterprise in which he inscribes his novels and critical production and legitimates his "tools" by noting the inadequacy of "historical convention": the vestiges he mentions represent the many elements which contribute to form the Caribbean subject, including the pre-Columbian elements discussed in chapter 4, and the subconscious imagination which contains and preserves them, reflecting the Jungian image of "collective unconscious" analysed in chapter 3. Moreover, Harris advances the offer of undertaking the task of representing those vestiges through his literary "art of the imagination" which he sees as the fittest solution. The essay continues by addressing elements of the Afro-Caribbean tradition, discussed and reinterpreted with enlightening wit, but, due to the methodological choice informing this study, they will not be analysed here, for the immediate intention is that of discussing the application of this historical enterprise to pre-Columbian and Amerindian elements and the discovery of Harris's idea of "cosmic unity." Some clues can be found in the same essay, such as the reference to the "art of creative coexistence" which represents the capacity of renewal "native to the Caribbean" and particularly to the Amerindian reality. According to Harris, the Caribbean complex situation of apparent "historylessness" should be investigated from a new perspective: "the apparent void of history which haunts the black man may never be compensated until an act of imagination opens gates between civilizations, between technological and spiritual apprehensions" ("History, Fable and Myth," in Bundy, ed., 159). This observation, which may appear to particularly refer to the Afro-Caribbean, "takes on even greater proportions with the Amerindian" (161) and involves, as discussed in chapter 4, pre-Columbian elements, as long as they promote the awareness of "a subconscious perspectival landscape" (161), only perceivable through "a creative philosophy born of immersion in elements of myth that have long been ignored" (163).

It is clear how, in a few years, Harris's conceptualisation evolved in the definition of nature and environment as fundamental elements for Caribbean philosophy and history. At this point, the main foundations of this view have been glimpsed, but Harris's continuous revision of his own work and thought still continues to problematise the issues, offering new and subtle insights. In "The Phenomenal Legacy" (1970), for example, the existence of such cultural elements in a unified context is clearly formulated for the first time, addressing

5 Conclusions: The Perspective of Living Landscapes 177

what Harris calls a "residue of experience we all share" (43), in strong connection with Jung's theories.

It is important to report a methodological explanation which may help to confute the challenges of over-intellectualisation often addressed in the course of this study: Harris takes care to emphasise that his approach to such "residue of experience" is "not intellectual, but rather part of a hard and continuous wrestling within the medium of my own work, a process more akin to something active and unpredictable rather than planned and theoretical" ("Phenomenal" 43). Thanks to this unconventional method, Harris is able to visualise the faults of a traditional historical approach, which are mainly identified in its excessive fixity about facts and documents; they may constitute the foundation of scientific historiography, but do not take into account those facets of historical reality that he is addressing:

> It is possible to consolidate the usual picture of the Amerindian, and by clever narrative constructive gain apparent clarity or coherency, sensational chronicle or even sensitive documentary. Nevertheless the poverty of conception in such enterprise remains enormous. Indeed if history has anything to tell us, it is of the danger which resides in the wilful conscription of primitive character: a uniform consolidation of so called historical features through an account of deeds whose motivation or mind we have not penetrated leads inevitably to vulgarization or tyranny. ("Phenomenal" 44)

As an alternative solution, Harris proposes a different approach, which could account for "the riddling archetypal mystery of life" and finally include the expanded perspective which is central to this discussion: "the man made ruin and the 'faults' of landscape enter into a new, sometimes extreme original unity or wholeness of being" (45). It should be noted once more how Harris's ideas parallel, at least in the choice of words, some of Walcott's statements: for both, the symbolic role of ruins is a significant element in the definition of Caribbean history: "the sigh of history rises over ruins, not over landscapes, and in the Antilles there are few ruins to sigh over" (Walcott, "Antilles" 68). Harris reverses Walcott's ironic view and offers the possibility of a history based both on the (not so few)[83] human ruins, and the landscape, identifying the typical condition of the Caribbean subject.

Finally, the conceptualisation of the natural themes included in Harris's literary production since the early poem "Charcoal" has reached a substantially stable definition; successive re-elaborations will add nuances to it, but the main elements are already present. The structural involvement of landscape in the historical discussion has been theorised and begins to generate new perspectives: "our involvement with the Amerindian past now begins to disclose itself upon a new scale" (Harris, "Phenomenal" 46).

Above all, the reference to a "new scale" needs to be stressed, which in terms of the rhythmic quality of nature discussed above will shortly help the delineation of a musical parallel which will consider the change of perspective as a fundamental operation for the recognition of "the mysterious pace inherent to all appearance, the uncanny cycles of nature which sometimes contradict to fulfil each other" ("Phenomenal" 47), which informs Harris's extended view of history. Before that, the connection with the mythical view of the world of the Amerindians and the Maya, cited by Harris as a fundamental source, will be repeated here, to refresh the connections which emerged in chapter 4. In "The Native Phenomenon" Harris discusses the "immense" bearing on "the nature of creativity [...] of Amerindian vestiges of legend" (49). Here is a reminder of the direct correspondence between "Amerindian vestiges" and nature as expressed in this 1972 essay: According to Harris, pre-Columbian legacies express

> an objective validation of landscape in depth – the shock of great rapids and complex landscapes and forests – playing through memory to confirm perspectives of imperilled community and creativity reaching back into the pre-Columbian mists of time. [...] an invocation of indestructible harmony at the heart of the cosmos. (54)

Nature becomes an active subject in the dimension of environmentalism, which strongly emerges in Harris's most recent lectures, but the following was published as early as in 1973:

> it would seem that nature in the *persona* of science has become a subjective personality and that man in some peculiar way has be-

---

[83] Both Walcott and Harris heavily resort to the cultural legacies of colonialism, such as Greek mythology, which could be considered as a sort of intellectual ruins.

come an object for nature, and nature in some remarkable way is attacking man, attacking his modes of thought, his modes of thinking, referring him back to an artistic and poetic heritage built into which is the depth and mystery of subjective personality. (Harris, "Subjective Imagination 58")

The issue of environmentalism will be discussed in relation to "Theatre of the Arts," while some considerations about the literary implications of the issues raised in the above passage should be pointed out here. In addition to Central and South-American writers such as Carpentier, whose affinity with with Harris's view has often been cited, it will be useful to elaborate here on one of the latest works by Amitav Ghosh, already mentioned in chapter 2 for his constant concern with history. It is striking to notice the similarity of the concepts informing the view of nature and history expressed in *The Hungry Tide* (2004) to what is quoted above. It is interesting how Ghosh treats the Sundarban environment in relation to time and historical events. Though it means summarising a complex novel in a few words, it can be pointed out that the cruel, seemingly indifferent rhythm of the tides not only witnesses the historical events and the social turmoil of the 1970s Sundarbans, but constantly intervenes as an active agent, conditioning the everyday life and the long-term history of the region, despite the blind tendency of the majority of the characters to stick to their exclusively human perspectives. An exception may be seen in Fokir, the traditional fisherman, who engages himself with the rhythms of nature and consequently appears as a timeless character. The rhythms of nature and Fokir's view, Ghosh seems to suggest, should not be excluded from history, but their mythical dimension should integrate scientific knowledge in a project of ecological equilibrium which appears as the only possible way to survive in the Sundarbans.

Similarly, Harris's "new treaty of sensibility" seems to point to the recognition of the authority of the natural perspective inherited from pre-Columbian traditions through the valorisation of the intuitive capacities of the human mind, such as imagination, which seem to Harris to be the fittest to completely recognise the Amerindian, pre-Columbian, alchemical and psychological legacies of the past. The intuitive dimension of imagination and living nature requires what Jung labelled "a new conceptual language" (Jung, *Synchronicity, Collected Works*, Vol. 8, 512), the need of which Harris first experienced when trying to describe his formative journeys as a surveyor in the interior of Guyana: "One was aware of one's incapacity to describe it, as though the tools of language one possessed were inadequate" ("Subjective Imagination 58"). This is also one of the reasons for Harris's literary choice of his particular style which refuses linear realism and promotes a profound dialogue among different disciplines also on the basis of these considerations: according to Ashcroft, Griffiths and Tiffin, "Harris sees language as the key to these transformations. Language must be altered, its power to lock in fixed beliefs and attitudes must be exposed, and words and concepts 'freed' to associate in new ways" (*Emipre* 149). Harris's particular view seems to promote a sort of mutuality with the past and with neglected aspects of reality which can be perceived through the recourse to an active imagination:

> The mystery of the subjective imagination lies, I believe, in an intuitive [...] grasp of a play of values as the flux of authentic change through and beyond what is given to us and what we accept, without further thought, as objective appearances. It is not a question of rootlessness but of the miracle of roots, the miracle of a dialogue with eclipsed selves which appearances may deny us or into which they may lead us. ("Subjective Imagination" 65-66)

As regards the main theme of time and history as related to the extended reality of living nature, Harris clarifies the role of the imagination as presented above: "The arts of the subjective imagination arching back across the centuries may help us, I think, to relate ourselves to time as the mystery of manifold distortion and distinctions between similar and yet dissimilar spaces/ appearances." ("Fossil and Psyche" 68).

How does this arch across the centuries relate to the livingness of nature? I suggest that Harris's view of living landscapes deeply affects many aspects of his philosophy. First, as he often emphasises, his fictional language is shaped by his experience of the interior of Guyana: "when I travelled in the rain forests it seemed to me that rivers, the sounds of the rivers, were part of the language of my blood" ("Originality" 126). Then, as emerged in chapter 3, the archetypal reality underlying his fictional imagery is characterised by the extension of consciousness to animals, trees, rivers and rocks, in a sort of "universal unconscious." Lastly, as discussed in chapter 4, his relationship with pre-Columbian cultural legacies determines a view based on mythologies and social systems which contemplate the active role of the forest as a fundamental element of everyday reality:

> according to their cosmologies, the forest is conceptualised and experienced by Amerindian peoples as a social-ecological landscape that is holistic, interconnected, adaptive, diverse, unpredictable, dynamic and complex – connecting temporal and spatial notions of history, identity, cultures. (Chung Tiam Fook 6)

All these and several other elements which were not discussed for methodological reasons can be viewed as comprised in the musical metaphor which Harris creates in his radio typescript "The Music of Living Landscapes," in which he brings together the numerous issues dealt with in the course of this chapter in an elaborate answer to a self-addressed question: "Is there a language akin to music threaded into space and time which is prior to human discourse?" ("Music" 40). For Harris, an affirmative answer should be based on the interpretation of Amerindian and pre-Columbian cultures and their myths, which still represent his main source of inspiration: "there are Amerindian legends which tell of sleeping yet, on occasion, singing rocks that witness to the traffic of history" (41), building an ideal link with the rhythmic element emerging in *Tradition, the Writer and Society*. Harris, here, explicitly links the question to music: "Nature is not passive. Nature erupts into orchestras of Nemesis" ("Music" 43). The parallel between Harris's art of fiction and music aims at the relativisation of human language, which he tries to liberate from "hubris" by subordinating it to a musicality which transcends its exclusivity as an essentially human medium. This is inscribed in the project of foregrounding the "life of the planet" as a fundamental agency with which humanity should recover a kind of mutuality such as recognised by the Amerindians and the Maya. Harris's fictional work is therefore informed by the need of representing a reality in which "consciousness attunes itself to living landscapes" ("Music" 46). This is developed by Hena Maes-Jelinek in "Ut Musica Poesis," where she explains: "Harris believes in the interrelatedness of all elements in life. Nature, humanity, fauna and flora partake of the same essence, are partial materializations of an 'unfathomable' wholeness" (495). In relation to the musical metaphor, she defines the ground on which Harris's work reveals its musical quality:

> Clearly, then, music is a major element in Harris's fiction and the cross-culturalism he detects in both life and art. It informs his conception of nature, of the human existential process, of the universe, and of the relation between all three. (504)

On other occasions musical approaches have been used to discuss Harris's work, such as in Russell McDougall's "'Corporeal Music': The Scale of Myth and Adjectival Insistence in *Palace of the Peacock*," but no reference has been made to the category of time, central to both Harris's art of fiction and music.

In this study, the quotations referring to musical aspects of Harris's work have been essentially centred on rhythm to build a possible connection with music which can take into account time and its variable nature determined by perceptual perspectives. In his novel *Midnight's Children* (1981) Salman Rushdie addressed the problem of history with a curious approach which can be usefully adapted for the interpretation of Harris's "timelessness":

> Reality is a question of perspective; the further you get from the past, the more concrete and plausible it seems – but as you approach the present, it inevitably seems more and more incredible. Suppose yourself in a large cinema, sitting at first in the back row, and gradually moving up, row by row, until your nose is almost pressed against the screen. Gradually the stars' faces dissolve into dancing grain; tiny details assume grotesque proportions; the illusion dissolves. (189)

As Rushdie suggests, the perception of time may be conditioned by the same perspectival process: the apparent "timelessness" which informs Harris's view may not ultimately be a negation of history as it may appear at a superficial analysis, it may just raise a question of perspective. This aspect, in my opinion, could be finally clarified with a musical concept: Stockhausen's view of the unity of musical time, which may offer an interesting insight.

Between 1958 and 1962, the late German composer Karlheinz Stockhausen wrote a piece entitled *Kontakte* and published, in the same time period, the seminal article ."..How Time Passes..." (1957) and the essay "The Concept of Unity in Electronic Music" (1962). With these papers he changed forever the way musicians heard and catalogued sound. The difference between pitch and rhythm collapsed under his intuition supported by the psycho-acoustic quality of sound: whether it is considered noise or pitched sound, it obeys a set of rules determined by human perception revealing a surprisingly uniform reality which may mirror, in its unity, the effective outcome of an alchemical *coniunctio*, like Harris's idea of "wholeness of being." According to Stockhausen, not only do pitch and rhythm pertain to the same scale, but complex musical forms and structures share the same nature of a single pulse. In other words:

> the most important insight of '…How Time Passes…' is a unified view of the relationship between the various time scales of musical structure. Stockhausen begins by noting the generality of the concept of a period, an interval between two cycles. Period appears in both rhythm [...] and pitch. The key here is that pitch and rhythm can be considered as one and the same phenomenon, differing only in their respective time scales. Taking this argument deeper into the microtemporal domain, the tone color or steady-state spectrum of a note can also be seen as a manifestation of microrhythm over a fundamental frequency. This point of view can also be applied in the macrotemporal domain. Thus, an entire composition can be viewed as one time spectrum of a fundamental duration. (Roads 73).

To explain the technical aspect of this insight in simpler terms in order to tie it up with Harris's thought: Below 16-20 repetitions per second, a single, short sound referred to as "pulse" is perceived by the human ear as a rhythmic sequence; above that frequency, the repetition of the very same material begins to be perceived as a continuous pitch; even more strikingly, the most structured piece of music could be seen as a sequence of pulses, generating the seemingly paradoxical possibility of the compression of a whole symphony by Beethoven into a single, continuous pitch. On the other hand, every moment of the symphony could be slowed down until a completely different rhythmic sequence would be heard; in Stockhausen's words: "the concentration on 'now' – on every 'now' – makes vertical incisions as it were, incisions which break through a horizontal concept of time, leading to timelessness" (interview).

Apart from the striking similarity between Stockhausen's words and some of Harris's expressions, the image of water "falling motionlessly" (Harris, *Guyana* 128) used by the latter to define the waterfall in the final chapter of *Palace of the Peacock* can, in my opinion, be perfectly matched. Whether we perceive movement or not is a question of perspective, but the falling water is, *per se*, both moving and still, as a pulse is at the same time rhythm and pitch. This observation leads to complex and interesting parallels with the philosophical insights derived from quantum physics, such as the particle/wave nature of light often quoted by Harris, but this aspect has been deliberately left out here. The main point here is the concept expressed by the "falling motionlessly" oxymoron, also expressed as the "open-ended *stillness* of flying time" (Harris, *Beggar* 48), which recalls Rushdie's cinematographic metaphor. Harris pushes this even farther to include the rhythms and pitches of "the music of living landscapes." This broader perspective may derive from his idea of archetypal world and from his reading of pre-Columbian cultures. As opposed to a Western world whose specificity of knowledge has investigated reality to the point of knowing the details of every "pulse," Harris saw in the legacy of neglected traditions, alchemy, Amerindian and pre-Columbian archetypal psychology the integrating perspective that could enable humanity to acknowledge the unity and organicity of a structured symphony, the symphony of the cosmos. This perspective, in which linear human time collapses in simultaneous presents and futures, may help to integrate the biases and the partialities of the "orthodox" historical discourse, as in Harris's mythical fiction, with a broader, complex concept of history, truer to the reality of the world as a whole.

The function nature performs in Harris's philosophy has several manifestations, and the relativisation of human time is just one aspect. This is, nevertheless, very important as it conditions his whole approach to history: "timelessness" and "historylessness" are notions that acquire new meanings in the context of living nature. As often remarked, historiography, as the narration of past events, relies on a concept of history which is essentially human, and therefore has a limited perspective. Whether the span of a historical narration includes the everyday life of the people in a particular age, or the rise and fall of an empire over several centuries, there are realities in nature and the cosmos which exceed it. As the voice over in the opening section of a 1996 famous documentary[84] on the life of the insects affirms, there is a completely different world which has its own concept of time in every yard of a country field. At the same time, there is a universe above, whose first instants of life (matter is believed to have formed in the first 10-11 seconds as particle physics experiments could not reach beyond) appear meaningless if compared to the presumed date of the Big Bang (about $13{,}7 \pm 0{,}2$ billions of years ago), yet one of the main task of contemporary research in physics is aimed to describe those first moments (LHC at Geneva's CERN). Harris's approach to history aims to imaginatively take into account all those unmeasurable aspects which exceed historiographical representation such as the intellectual legacies discussed in chapters 3 and 4. Their existence is undeniable and their effect on "knowable" realities is actually perceivable, yet they

---

[84] "Dans ce monde, le sablier du temps s'accélère: une heure pour un jour, un jour pour une saison, une saison pour une vie..." (Nuridsany, *Microcosmos*).

are often neglected, as Harris thinks, because of persistent traditions of blind realism.[85]

The "life of the earth," among those neglected aspects of reality which Harris's fiction testimonies, does not only shape his own approach to time and history, it may also be considered as a fundamental characteristic of Caribbean philosophy, and it is recognised by several authoritative intellectuals. Walcott may be listed among them, and the epigraph to this chapter can be taken as an example; the same could be said of Edouard Glissant, whose marxist approach is complicated by the function he attributes to nature and Caribbean landscape: "landscape is its own monument: its meaning can only be traced on the underside. It is all History" (*Caribbean Discourse* 11).[86]

The work of several other Caribbean writers collected in *Caribbean Literature and the Environment* (2005) shows some affinity with Harris's writing about nature and the landscape; this includes Antonio Benítez-Rojo, whose postmodern approach to Caribbean Literary criticism, *The Repeating Island*, is informed by his intuition that the modification of the natural environment by the colonial economy has conditioned not only the life of the workers but also the intellectual development in the Caribbean. This derives from the fact that "there is probably no other region in the world that has been more radically altered in terms of human and botanic migration, transplantation, and settlement than the Caribbean" (DeLoughrey, Gosson and Handley 1). Besides the excerpts and essays by these and other Caribbean intellectuals, *Caribbean Literature and the Environment* includes a contribution by Harris and a critical essay about him. Harris's "Theatre of the Arts" is one of his most recent critical contributions, and, although it had already appeared in a different volume by Harris (*Theatre of the Arts: Wilson Harris and the Caribbean*), it perfectly fits the context of the collection. This is due to the fact that the evolution of Harris's thought has reached in recent years a more openly ecocritical dimension. The importance that the theme of nature has in Harris's philosophy needs no further exemplification, but his involvement in environmental criticism has often been lateral, except for isolated episodes such as the reference to the threats of pollution in the opening of "A Talk on the Subjective Imagination" (1973) or in *Jonestown*. In "Theatre of the Arts" the subject of landscapes finally acquires a dimension

---

[85] For a different view of realism in post-colonial contexts, see Laura Moss, "'The Plague of Normality.'"

[86] "Notre paysage est son propre monument: la trace qu'il signifie est repérable par-dessous. C'est tout histoire" (Glissant, *Le discours antillais* 21).

which expands the intellectual implications analysed in the course of this study, bringing the question to a more overtly political level, a theme that could function as a starting point for another research project. Nevertheless, it deserves a concise discussion in order to integrate the issues analysed in this study: landscape and the environment as subjects not only participate as fundamental elements in the constitution of a Caribbean post-colonial identity, they can also be included in a global discourse in order to relativise the role of human-centred history and technology at a political level. The concept of a "living earth" should be acknowledged as an important agent in history. The recognition of the concept's fundamental role for the survival of the complex ecosystem which includes humanity and is seriously threatened by man's technological hubris and self-centred approach should also lead to its inclusion in the current political debate.[87] According to Harris, "we have blocked the flow of measureless cross-culturalities" ("Theatre" 1) which include, as constantly reminded, the animal world and broadly speaking, "the life of the earth" (2). In other words,

> There is a *measureless* nature to the life of the earth in the midst of catastrophes, drought and famine and flood that we blindly invite, a *precarious* freedom we need to understand if our cultures are to awaken from their "sleep" or "obliviousness." (2)

Such themes, whose urgency becomes more evident as climate changes progressively manifest, have been neglected by official history and realist fiction because of their "measureless nature" and therefore, according to Harris, they need to be envisioned in a new medium within fiction, a new form which could grant them the necessary testimony:

> cross-culturality between living nature and humanity [is] the timeless instrument of art. (Harris, *Beggar* 50)

> The life of the earth needs to be seen *in fiction* as sensitively woven into the characters that move upon it, whose history, may I say, reflects a profound relationship to the earth. [...] This is the mystery of fiction if not of science. (Harris, "Theatre" 4; emphasis in the original)

---

[87] In an exclamatory sentence Harris speaks of "Not only nature's catastrophes but catastrophes administered by a blind and deaf civilization" (Harris, *Beggar* 57).

To return to the main theme, it must be acknowledged that the lack of consideration of these issues is determined, according to Harris, not only by the marginalisation of "unmeasurable" phenomena in nature, but has originated in a context of cultural totalitarianism which has seen the West promoting a rigid, scientistic approach to reality through colonial domination and subsequent cultural imperialism. This approach has determined the marginalisation of alternative traditions, such as the pre-Columbian or the pre-modern ones, which could contribute to a deeper and probably, in the long-term run, more lasting rapport with the earth and the cosmos. Harris writes: "we have brushed aside ancient legends of gods of the wind and the sea and the earth and the air without a thought of their *intuitive* depth," even though, "we are ourselves sculptures awaiting a *dream* of life" ("Theatre" 4; emphasis in the original).

As a final consideration on this subject, the extended perspective proposed by Harris, and perceivable, in his view, through "wounds" in history, such as colonialism, can help in the making of a new philosophy. The dramatic event of conquest has revealed the existence of a much wider reality, a sort of "mutual awakening" (Harris, *Beggar* 11), beyond the fixity of the Western mind, which had already begun to marginalise alchemical and gnostic traditions, and the closure of pre-Columbian empires such as the Inca and the Aztec ones, in which power had already corrupted the mythical legacies of the Amerindians and the Maya.[88] This dimension, timeless to the human mind, is revealed through the "Wound"[89] as a mythical, archetypal, and spiritual reality; in Harris's words:

> The multifarious life of the earth [...] teaches us to pay the closest care and attention to variations and movements on the stage on which we live: and not to invest absolutely or fixedly on such a stage. We are told of parallel universes by scientific speculations, parallel universes of which we know nothing except perhaps that there is a *Wound* – akin to the Wound of being and non-being we carry in ourselves – that may take us into the *spirit* of timelessness. ("Theatre" 7-8; emphasis in the original)

---

88 "They fell back on religious ritual and dogma" (Harris, *Beggar* 142).
89 This term, like the "Void" mentioned above, has, for Harris, extended meanings however, unlike with the "Void," it is possible to find a fairly stable definition: "*The Wound is a curious, creative possibility of bringing together cultures that are separate into an unseizable wholeness*" (*Beggar* 77; emphasis in the original).

This quotation may suggest a mystical image of Harris's thought, supporting, in a way, the criticisms of over-intellectualisation and excessive abstractness, however, as a natural result of this study, a different picture should emerge. Gnostic (section 1.3), Jungian (chapter 3) and pre-Columbian (chapter 4) interpretations of reality help us to understand Harris's image of a "living earth" and to concretely visualise "the sentience of the earth and the threshold such sentience provides into parallel universes of the imagination through a tree of life existing long before we arrived in our present shape and form" (Harris, "Theatre" 8).

At this point, Hena Maes-Jelinek's assumption about the concrete grounding of Harris's philosophy in actual, multifarious traditions should not require further argumentation, especially regarding the specific connection she stresses:

> Although Harris is often said to be an 'abstract' writer, his fictional language is obviously inspired by concrete reality. [...] His metaphysical perception of a world in the making has grown out of the landscape and the specific history of the Americas. ("From Living Nature" 258-259)

This has been shown here through a detailed analysis of Harris's philosophical approach to time and history as applied to pre-Columbian traditions and to the typically Western field of Jungian psychoanalysis, in order to demonstrate the effectiveness of Harris's cross-cultural imagination, its grounding in reality, and its useful integration of historical discourse into the making of a truly Caribbean philosophy.

Bibliography
Wilson Harris: Fiction and Poetry

Harris, Wilson. *The Age of the Rainmakers*. London: Faber & Faber, 1971. Print.
___. *The Angel at the Gate*. London: Faber & Faber, 1982. Print.
___. *Ascent to Omai*. London: Faber & Faber, 1970. Print.
___. *Black Marsden*. London: Faber & Faber, 1972. Print.
___. *Carnival*. London: Faber & Faber, 1985. Print. Rpt. in *The Carnival Trilogy*.1993. Print.
___. *The Carnival Trilogy*. Introd. by Harris. London: Faber & Faber, 1993. Print.
___. *Companions of the Day and Night*. London: Faber & Faber, 1975. Print.
___. *Da Silva da Silva's Cultivated Wilderness and Genesis of the Clowns*. London: Faber & Faber, 1977. Print.
___. *The Dark Jester*. London: Faber & Faber, 2001. Print.
___. *Eternity to Season*. Georgetown: published privately, 1954. Print Rpt. London: New Beacon, 1978. Print.
___. *The Eye of the Scarecrow*. London: Faber & Faber, 1965. Print.
___. *The Far Journey of Oudin*. London: Faber & Faber, 1961. Print. Rpt. in *The Guyana Quartet*. 1985. Print.
___. *The Four Banks of the River of Space*. London: Faber & Faber, 1990. Print. Rpt. in *The Carnival Trilogy*.1993. Print.
___. *The Ghost of Memory*. London: Faber & Faber, 2006. Print.
___. *The Guyana Quartet*. With a Note on the Genesis of *The Guyana Quartet*. London: Faber & Faber, 1985. Print.
___. *Heartland*. London: Faber & Faber, 1964. Print.
___. *The Infinite Rehearsal*. London: Faber & Faber, 1987. Print. Rpt. in *The Carnival Trilogy*.1993. Print.
___. *Jonestown*. London: Faber & Faber, 1996. Print.
___. "Kanaima." *Black Orpheus: Anthology*. Ed. Ulli Beier. Ibadan: Longmans, 1964. Print. Rpt. in *Racconti Dai Caraibi*. Ed. Paolo Bertinetti. Trans. Paolo Bertinetti, Maria Clara Pasetti, and Irene Pologruto. Milano: Arnoldo Mondadori Editore, 1997. 197-206. Print.
___. *The Mask of the Beggar*. London: Faber & Faber, 2003. Print.
___. *The Palace of the Peacock*. London: Faber & Faber, 1960. Print. Rpt. in *The Guyana Quartet*. 1985. Print.
___. *Resurrection at Sorrow Hill*. London: Faber & Faber, 1993. Print.
___. *The Secret Ladder*. London: Faber & Faber, 1963. Print. Rpt. in *The Guyana Quartet*. 1985. Print.
___. *The Sleepers of Roraima: A Carib Trilogy*. London: Faber & Faber, 1970. Print.
___. *The Tree of the Sun*. London: Faber & Faber, 1978. Print.
___. *Tumatumari*. London: Faber & Faber, 1968. Print.

____. *The Waiting Room.* London: Faber & Faber, 1967. Print.
____. *The Whole Armour.* London: Faber & Faber, 1962. Print. Rpt. in *The Guyana Quartet*. 1985. Print.

Wilson Harris: Non-Fiction

____. "The Absent Presence: The Caribbean, Central and South America." In Riach and Williams, eds., *Radical Imagination* 81-92. Print. Rpt. *Hambone* 10 (Spring 1992): 212-223. Print.
____. "The Age of the Imagination." *Journal of Caribbean Literatures* 2.1-3 (Spring 2000):17-25. Print.
____. "The Amerindian Legacy." *History, Fable and Myth in the Caribbean and Guyanas* 33-34. Print . Rpt. in Bundy, ed. *Selected Essays* 167-175. Print.
____. "Apprenticeship to the Furies." *River City: A Journal of Contemporary Culture* 16.2 (Summer 1996): 104-115. Print. Rpt. in Bundy, ed. *Selected Essays* 226-236. Print. [Cited in the text as "Apprenticeship" A. This is a different text from the one listed below under the same title.]
____. "Apprenticeship to the Furies." *Post-Colonial Theory and the Emergence of a Global Society*. Ed. Gordon Collier, Dieter Riemenschneider, and Frank Schulze-Engler. ACOLIT, Special Issue 3. Frankfurt am Main: ASNEL, 1998. [This is a different text from the one listed above under the same title.]
____. "An Approach to Couvade." *Couvade: A Dream-Play of Guyana*. Ed. Michael Gilkes. Mundelstrup: Dangaroo Press, 1990. xi-xiv. Print.
____. "Art and Criticism." 1967. *Tradition, the Writer and Society*. London: New Beacon, 1973. 7-12. Print.
____. "Aubrey Willliams." *Third Text* 34 (Spring 1996): 79-82. Print Rpt. in Bundy, ed., *Selected Essays* 222-225. Print. [Cited in the text as "Aubrey" A. This is a different text from the one listed below under the same title.]
____. "Aubrey Williams." *Journal of Caribbean Literatures* 2.1-2-3 (Spring 2000): 26-30. Print. [This is a different text from the one listed above under the same title.]
____. "'Benito Cereno'." In Bundy, ed., *Selected Essays* 123-134. Print.
____. "Carnival of Psyche: Jean Rhys's *Wide Sargasso Sea*." *Kunapipi* 11.2 (1980): 142-150. Print. Rpt. in Maes-Jelinek, *Explorations* 125-134. Print.
____. "Comedy and Modern Allegory: A Personal View." *A Shaping of Connections: Commonwealth Literature Studies – Then and Now*. Ed. Hena Maes-Jelinek, Kirsten Holst Petersen, and Anna Rutherford. Mundelstrup: Dangaroo Press, 1989. 127-140. Print.
____. "The Complexity of Freedom." Maes-Jelinek, *Explorations* 113-124. Print. Rpt. in Adewale Maja-Pearce, ed. *Wole Soyinka: An Appraisal*. Oxford: Heinemann, 1994. 22-35. Print.

———. "The Composition of Reality: A Talk with Wilson Harris." Interview by Vera Kutzinski. *Callaloo* 18.1 (Winter 1995): 15-32. Print.
———. "Concentric Horizons." In Bundy, ed., *Selected Essays* 109-117. Print.
———. "Continuity and Discontinuity." In Bundy, ed., *Selected Essays* 176-183. Print.
———. "Creative and Re-Creative Balance Between Cultures." In Riach and Williams, eds., *Radical Imagination* 103-115. Print.
———. "Creoleness: The Crossroads of a Civilization?" In Bundy, ed., *Selected Essays* 237-247. Print.
———. "The Enigma of Values." *New Letters* 40 (Oct. 1973): 141-149. Print.
———. "Fossil and Psyche." 1974. Print. Rpt. in Maes-Jelinek. *Explorations* 68-82. Print.
———. "The Frontier on which *Heart of Darkness* Stands." *Research in African Literatures* 12.1 (Spring 1981): 86-93. Print. Rpt. in Childs, ed., *Post-Colonial Theory* 227-233. Print.
———. "The Fabric of the Imagination." In Riach and Williams, eds., *Radical Imagination* 69-79. Print. [Cited in the text as "Fabric" A. This is a different text from the one listed below under the same title.]
———. "The Fabric of the Imagination." *Third World Quarterly* 12.1 (January 1990):175-186. Print. Rpt. in Anna Rutherford, ed., *From Commonwealth to Post-Colonial*. Dangaroo Press, Mundelstrup 1992. 18-25. Print. [This is a different text from the one listed above under the same title.]
———. "History, Fable and Myth in the Caribbean and Guianas." 1970. Print. Rpt. in In Bundy, ed., *Selected Essays* 152-166. Print.
———. "Imagination Dead Imagine: Bridging a Chasm." *Yale Journal of Criticism* 7.1 (1994): 185-195. Print.
———. "In the Name of Liberty." In Bundy, ed., *Selected Essays* 212-221. Print.
———. "Interior of the Novel: Amerindian/European/African Relations." *National Identity: Papers Delivered at the Commonwealth Literature Conference. University of Queenlsand, Brisbane, 9-15 August 1968*. Ed. K.L. Goodwin. London/Melbourne: Heinemann, 1970. Print. Rpt. in Maes-Jelinek, *Explorations* 10-19. Print.
———. Interview by Ian Munro and Reinhard Sander. *Kas-Kas: Interviews with Three Caribbean Writers in Texas*. Austin: University of Texas, 1972. 43-55. Print.
———. Interview by Alan Riach. In Riach and Williams, eds., *Radical Imagination* 33-65. Print.
———. Interview by Jane Wilkinson. *Kunapipi* 8.2 (1986): 30-45. Print.
———. "Jean Rhys's 'Tree of Life.'" *Review of Contemporary Fiction* 5.2 (Summer 1985): 114-117. Print. Rpt. in Bundy, ed., *Selected Essays* 118-122. Print.
———. "Judgement and Dream" In Riach and Williams, eds., *Radical Imagination* 17-31. Print. Rpt. in Cribb, ed., *Imagined Commonwealth* 51-67. Print.

___. "Letter from Francisco Bone to W.H." In Bundy, ed., *Selected Essays* 47-52. Print.

___. "The Limbo Gateway." Extract from "History, Fable and Myth in the Caribbean and the Guianas." In Ashcroft, Griffiths, and Tiffin, eds., *Post-Colonial Studies Reader*. 378-382.

___. "Literacy and the Imagination." *The Literate Imagination: Essays on the Novels of Wilson Harris*. Ed. Michael Gilkes. London: Macmillan, 1989. 13-30. Print. Rpt. in Bundy, ed., *Selected Essays* 75-89. Print.

___. "The Making of Tradition." *The Commonwealth Writer Overseas: Themes of Exile and Expatriation*. Ed. Alastair Niven. Brussels: Didier, 1976. 33-39. Print. Rpt. in Maes-Jelinek, *Explorations* 88-96. Print.

___. "Merlin and Parsifal, Adversarial Twins." *Temenos Aacademy Papers* 9. London, 1997. Print. Rpt. in Bundy, ed., *Selected Essays* 58-66. Print.

___. "Metaphor and Myth." *Myth and Metaphor*. Ed. Robert Sellick. Adelaide: Centre for Research in the New Literatures in English, 1982. 1-14. Print.

___. "The Music of Living Landscapes." *Hambone* 14 (Fall 1998): 169-176. Print. Rpt. in Bundy, ed., *Selected Essays* 40-46. Print.

___. "The Native Phenomenon." *Common Wealth*. Ed. Anna Rutherford. Aarhus: Akademisk Boghandel, 1971. 144-150. Print. Rpt. in Maes-Jelinek, *Explorations* 49-56. Print.

___. "New Preface to *Palace of the Peacock*." In Bundy, ed., *Selected Essays* 53-57. Print.

___. "Oedipus and the Middle Passage." *Landfall* 170, 43.2 (June 1989): 198-208. Print. Rpt. in Davis and Maes-Jelinek, eds., *Crisis and Creativity* 9-21. Print.

___. "Originality and Tradition." 1991. In Riach and Williams, eds., *Radical Imagination* 117-134. Print.

___. "The Phenomenal Legacy." *Literary Half-Yearly* 11 (July 1970): 1-6. Print. Rpt. in Maes-Jelinek, *Explorations* 43-48. Print.

___. "Profiles of Myth and the New World." In Bundy, ed., *Selected Essays* 201-211. Print.

___. "The Quest for Form." *Kunapipi* 5.1 (1983): 21-27. Print.

___. "The Question of Form and Realism in the West Indian Artist." 1967. *Tradition, the Writer and Society*, London: New Beacon, 1973. 13-20. Print.

___. "Quetzalcoatl and the Smoking Mirror." *Wasafiri* 20 (Autumn 1994): 38-43. Print. Rpt. in Bundy, ed., *Selected Essays* 184-196. Print.

___. *The Radical Imagination: Lectures and Talks*. Ed. Alan Riach and Mark Williams. Liège: L3 - Liège Language and Literature, English Department, University of Liège, 1992.

___. "Reflection and Vision." *Commonwealth Literature and the Modern World*. Ed. Hena Maes-Jelinek. Brussels: Didier, 1975. 15-19. Print. Rpt. in Maes-Jelinek, *Explorations* 83-87. Print.

___. "Reflections on *Intruder in the Dust* in a Cross-cultural Complex." In Bundy, ed., *Selected Essays* 90-98. Print.

___. "Resistances to Alterities." *Resisting Alterities: Wilson Harris and Other Avatars of Otherness*. Ed. Marco Fazzini. Amsterdam/New York: Rodopi, 2004.

___. Review of *New Chronicle and Good Government: An Indian Account of the pre-Incas and Incas of Peru*, by Felipe Guaman Poma de Ayala. *Caribbean Quarterly* 15.1-2 (June-September 1969): 121-122. Print.

___. "Scented Gardens for the Blind." *Bird, Hawk, Bogie*. Ed. Jeanne Delbaere. Mundelstrup: Dangaroo Press, 1978. 63-67. Print. Rpt. in Maes-Jelinek, *Explorations* 107-112. Print.

___. "The Schizophrenic Sea." *The Womb of Space* 15-26. Print. Rpt. in Bundy, ed., *Selected Essays* 99-108. Print.

___. *Selected Essays of Wilson Harris: The Unfinished Genesis of the Imagination*. Ed. Andrew Bundy. London/New York: Routledge, 1999. Print.

___. "Some Aspects of Myth and the Intuitive Imagination." Lecture given at the University of Guyana in March 1978. In Maes-Jelinek, *Explorations* 97-106. Print.

___. "A Talk on the Subjective Imagination." *New Letters* 40 (Oct. 1973): 37-48. Print. Rpt. in Maes-Jelinek, *Explorations* 58-60. Print.

___. "Theatre of the Arts." In Maes-Jelinek and Ledent, eds., *Theatre of the Arts* 1-10. Print.

___. *Tradition, the Writer and Society*. 1967. London: New Beacon, 1973. Print.

___. "Tradition and the West Indian Novel." In Bundy, ed., *Selected Essays* 140-151. Print.

___. "Unfinished Genesis: A Personal View of Cross-Cultural Tradition." (University of Cambridge 1990). In Riach and Williams, eds., *Radical Imagination* 93-102. Print.

___. *"The Unfinished Genesis of the Imagination."* In Bundy, ed., *Selected Essays* 248-260. Print.

___. "Validation of Fiction: A Personal View of Imaginative Truth." 1989. Print. Rpt. in *Kyk-Over-Al* 38 (June 1988): 27-34. Print.

___. "Ways to Enjoy Literature." *Union in Partition: Essays in Honour of Jeanne Delbaere*. Ed. Gilbert Debusscher and Marc Maufort. Liège: L3 Liège Language and Literature, English Department, University of Liège, 1997. 201-208. Print.

___. "The Whirling Stone." *The Womb of Space: The Cross-Cultural Imagination*. Westport, Connecticut: Greenwood Press, 1983. 55-83. Print.

___. "Wilson Harris: An Autobiographical Essay." 1992. Print. Rpt. in *Exploring the Palace of the Peacock: Essays on Wilson Harris*. Ed. Irving Adler. Mona, Jamaica: University of West Indies Press, 2003. vii-xxxiv. Print.

___. *The Womb of Space: The Cross-Cultural Imagination*. Westport, Connecticut: Greenwood Press, 1983. Print.

___. "The Writer and Society." 1967. Tradition, the Writer and Society. London: New Beacon, 1973. 48-64. Print.

Other Sources

Achebe, Chinua. "An Image of Africa: Racism in Conrad's *Heart of Darkness*." *Massachusetts Review*. 18 (1977). Print. Rpt. in *Heart of Darkness: An Authoritative Text, Background and Sources*. 1961. Ed. Robert Kimbrough. London: W. W. Norton and Co., 1988, 251-261. Print

___. *Things Fall Apart*. 1958. Oxford: Heinemann, 1986. Print.

Adamska, Anna, and Adam Michczynski. *Towards Radiocarbon Chronology of the Inca State*. Centre for Precolombian Studies of the University of Warsaw (2005). Web . 28 Nov. 2011. <http://www.maa.uw.edu.pl/obp/MICH_ADA.HTM>.

Adelaide-Merlande, Jacques. *Histoire générale des Antilles et des Guyanes*. Paris: Ed. Caribéennes, 1994.

Adler, Joyce Sparer, ed. *Exploring the Palace of the Peacock: Essays on Wilson Harris*. The Mona, Jamaica: University of the West Indies Press, 2003. Print.

___. "Tumatumari and the Imagination of Wilson Harris." *Journal of Commonwealth Literature* (July 1969): 20-31. Print.

Ahmad, Aijaz. "Jameson's Rhetoric of Otherness and the 'National Allegory'." Ashcroft, Griffiths, and Tiffin, eds., *Post-Colonial Studies Reader* 77-84. Print.

Alexis, Stephen. *Black Liberator: The Story of Toussaint L'Ouverture*. London: Ernest Benn Limited, 1949. Print.

Alternative Considerations of Jonestown and Peoples Temple. Department of Religious Studies at San Diego State University (1998-1999). Web. 25 Nov. 2011. <http://jonestown.sdsu.edu>.

Arens, William E. *The Man-Eating Myth: Anthropology and Anthropophagy*. Oxford: Oxford UP, 1979. Print.

Armstrong, Andrew. "Bloody History! Exploring a Capacity for Revision: Restaging History in Wilson Harris's *Jonestown* and Caryl Phillips' [sic] *The Nature of Blood*." *Jouvert* 6.3 (Spring 2002). Web. 28 Nov. 2011. <http://english.chass.ncsu.edu/jouvert/v613/armstr.htm>.

Ashcroft, Bill, Gareth Griffiths, and Helen Tiffin, eds. *The Empire Writes Back: Theory and Practice in Post-Colonial Literatures*. London: Routledge,1989. Print.

___. *The Post-Colonial Studies Reader*. London: Routledge, 1995. Print.

Bachtin (Bakhtin), Michail M. *Estetica e romanzo: Un contributo fondamentale alla "scienza della letteratura."* Trad. Clara Strada Janovič. Torino: Einaudi, 1979. Print.

Bamikole, Lawrence O. "Creolization and the Search for Identity in Caribbean Philosophy." *Caribbean Quarterly* 53.3 (2007): 70-82. Print.

Barnaby, Karin, and Pellegrino D'Acierno, eds. *C.G. Jung and the Humanities: Toward a Hermeneutics of Culture.* London: Routledge, 1990. Print.

Beckett, Samuel. "Imagination Dead Imagine." *The Complete Short Prose 1929-1989.* New York: 1996. 182-185. Print.

Benítez-Rojo, Antonio. *La isla que se repite: El Caribe y la perspectiva posmoderna.* 1989. *The Repeating Island: The Caribbean and the Postmodern Perspective.* Trans. James E. Maraniss. Durham: Duke UP, 1996.

Benjamin, Walter. "Angelus Novus." *Literature in the Modern World.* Trans. H. Zohn. 1968. Ed. Dennis Walder. Oxford: Oxford UP/Open University, 1990. 364. Print.

___. "Über den Begriff der Geschichte, Kapitel IX." 1940. Gesammelte Schriften I. Frankfurt am Main: Suhrkamp, 1974. 691-704. Print.

Berthelsen, K. "Surveying the Psyche: A Jungian Reading of Wilson Harris' *The Guyana Quartet.*" *Jung: The e-Journal of the Jungian Society for Scholarly Studies* 1.3. 10 Apr. 2005. Web. 24 Nov. 2011. <http://www.thejungiansociety.org/Jung%20Society/e-journal/Volume-1/Berthelsen-2005.html>

Bhabha, Homi. *The Location of Culture.* London: Routledge, 1994. Print.

___. *Nation and Narration.* London: Routledge, 1990. Print.

Blake, William. *The Marriage of Heaven and Hell.* Introd. and commentary by Sir Geoffrey Keynes. London & New York: Oxford UP, 1975. Print.

___. *Songs of Innocence and of Experience.* 1789-1794. Ed., introd. and notes by Andrew Lincoln. London: The William Blake Trust; The Tate Gallery, 1991. Print.

___. "To Thomas Butts." *The Oxford Book of English Mystical Verse.* Ed. Nicholson & Lee. Oxford: Clarendon Press, 1917. Print. New York: Bartleby.com (2000). Web. 28 Nov. 2011. <http://www.bartleby.com/236/61.html>.

Bolland, Nigel, ed. *The Birth of Caribbean Civilization: A Century of Ideas About Culture and Identity, Nation and Society.* Kingston, Jamaica: Ian Randle, 2004. Print.

Brathwaite, E. K. "Timehri." J. Michael Dash. *The Other America.* Charlottesville: University of Virginia Press, 1998. 71-72. Print.

Brett, William Henry. *Legends and Myths of the Aboriginal Indians of British Guiana.* London: William Wells Gardner, 1880. HTML by Christopher Weimer, *Sacred Texts Online - Caribbean Amerindian Centrelink* (March 2003). Web. 28 Nov. 2011. <http://www.centrelink.org/Brett.txt>.

Brink, André. *A Dry White Season.* 1979. London: Vintage, 1998. Print.

Brown, John, M.D. *The History and Present Condition of St. Domingo*. Vol. II. Philadelphia: William Marshall and Co., 1837. *Google Books Library Project*. 24 Nov. 2011. Web. <http://books.google.com/books?vid= ISBN9781154091571>.

Brusasco, Paola. *Writing Within/Without/About Sri Lanka: Discourses of Cartography, History and Translation in Selected Works by Michael Ondaatje and Carl Muller*. Stuttgart: Ibidem, 2010. Print.

Bundy, Andrew, ed. *Selected Essays of Wilson Harris: The Unfinished Genesis of the Imagination*. London/New York: Routledge, 1999. Print.

Burnett, Paula. "Memory Theatre and the Maya: Othering Eschatology in Wilson Harris's *Jonestown*." *Journal of Caribbean Literatures* 2.1,2,3 (Spring 2000): 215-232. Print.

___. "Opening New Doors: Harris and Walcott." Maes-Jelinek and Ledent, eds., *Theatre of the Arts* 61-82. Print.

Canary, Robert H., and Henry Kozicki, eds. *The Writing of History: Literary Form and Historical Understanding*. Madison WI: University of Wisconsin Press, 1978. Print.

Carpentier, Alejo. "De lo real maravilloso americano." *Tientos y diferencias*. Montevideo: Arca, 1967. 96-112. Print.

___. *The Kingdom of This World*. 1959. Trans. Harriet de Onís. New York: Farrar, Straus and Giroux, 1989. Print.

___. "On the Marvelous Real in America." Trans. L.P. Zamora and T. Huntington. *Magical Realism: Theory, History, Community*. 1995. Ed. L.P. Zamora and W.B. Faris. Durham: Duke UP. 75- 88. Print.

___. *Los pasos perdidos*. 1953. Madrid: Alianza Editorial, 2000. Print.

___. *El reino de este mundo*. 1949. Barcelona: Seix Barral, 2002. Print.

___. *El siglo de las luces*. 1962. Barcelona: Seix Barral, 1990. Print.

Carr, David. "History, Fiction, and Human Time." *History and the Limits of Interpretation: A Smposium*. 15-17 March 1996. *Humanities Research Center*. Web. 24 Nov. 2011. <http://cohesion.rice.edu/humanities/csc/conferences.cfm?doc_id=350>.

Césaire, Aimé. "Discourse on Colonialism." *The Birth of Caribbean Civilization: A Century of Ideas About Culture and Identity, Nation and Society*. Ed. Nigel Bolland. Kingston, Jamaica: Ian Randle, 2004. 212-220. Print.

___. Interview by René Depestre. Bolland, ed., 220-227. Print.

Chakrabarty, Dipesh. "Postcoloniality and the Artifice of History: Who Speaks for 'Indian' Pasts." Ashcroft, Griffiths, and Tiffin, eds., *Post-Colonial Studies Reader* 383-390. Print.

Childs, Peter, ed. *Post-Colonial Theory and English Literature*. Edinburgh: UP, 2000. Print.

Chung Tiam Fook, Tanya. "Constructing Shared Meaning and Practice: An Amerindian Knowledge-Based Approach to Collaborative Wildlife Conservation in Guyana." The Society for Caribbean Studies (UK). Ed. Sandra Courtman. *Annual Conference Papers* 7 (2006). Web. 28 Nov. 2011. <http://www.caribbeanstudies.org.uk/papers/2006/olvol7p7.PDF>.

Coetzee, J.M. *Waiting for the Barbarians*. 1980. London: Vintage, 2000. Print.

Coetzee, P.H., and A.P. Roux, eds. *The African Philosophy Reader*. London/NY: Routledge, 1998. Print.

Collingwood, R.G. *The Idea of History*. 1946. Oxford: Clarendon Press, 1993. Print.

Concilio, Carmen. "Cryptic Chaosmos in Wilson Harris's *Jonestown*." *Journal of Caribbean Literatures* 2.1,2,3 (Spring 2000): 242-252. Print.

___. "Wilson Harris, Cross-Culturalism *Contra* Hybridity." A. Monti, J. Douthwaite, eds. *Migrating the Texts: Hybridity as a Postcolonial Literary Construct*. Torino: L'Harmattan, 2003. 137-156. Print.

Creighton, Al. "The Human Comedy Carnival and *The Infinite Rehearsal*." *Wilson Harris: The Uncompromising Imagination*. Ed. Hena Maes-Jelinek. Sydney-Mundelstrup: Dangaroo Press, 1991. 192-199. Print.

Crew, Gary. "The Eternal Present in Wilson Harris' *The Sleepers of Roraima* and *The Age of the Rainmakers*." *WLWE* 19.2 (1980): 218-227. Print.

Cribb, T.J. "T.W. Harris: Sworn Surveyor." *Journal of Commonwealth Literature* 28.1 (1993): 33-46. Print.

___, ed. *Imagined Commonwealth: Cambridge Essays on Commonwealth and International Literature in English*. Basingstoke: Macmillan, 1998. Print.

Davis, Geoffrey, and Hena Maes-Jelinek, eds. *Crisis and Creativity in the New Literatures in English*. Amsterdam/ Atlanta: Rodopi, 1990. Print.

de Andrade, Mario. *Macunaíma, O Herói sem Nenhum Caráter*. 1926. *Macunaíma, L'eroe senza nessun carattere*. Trans. Giuliana Segre Giorgi. Milano: Adelphi, 2002. Print.

de Certeau, Michel. *Heterologies: Discourse on the Other*. 1986. Trans. Brian Massumi. Minneapolis: University of Minnesota Press, 2000. Print.

de Landa, Diego. *Relación de las cosas de Yucatán*. 1566. *European Association of Mayanists* (2003). Web. 28 Nov. 2011. <http://www.wayeb.org/download/resources/landa.pdf>.

Delfino, Gianluca. "Rushdie's Technicolor and Harris's Mist: Two Strategies for Restoring the Past." *English Studies 2006*. Torino: Trauben, Università di Torino, 2007. 79-102. Print.

DeLoughrey, Elizabeth M., Renée K. Gosson, and George B. Handley, eds. *Caribbean Literature and the Environment: Between Nature and Culture*. Charlottesville: University of Virginia Press, 2005. Print.

de Man, Paul. "Sign and Symbol in Hegel's Aesthetics." *Critical Inquiry* 8.4 (Summer 1982): 761-75. Print.
de Mandeville, John. *Mandeville's Travels*. Project Gutenberg (2002). Web. 28 Nov. 2011. <http://www.gutenberg.org/etext/782>.
Demarest, Arthur. *Ancient Maya: The Rise and Fall of a Rainforest Civilization*. Cambridge: Cambridge UP, 2004. Print.
Dente, Carla, et al., eds. *Proteus: The Language Of Metamorphosis*. Aldershot: Ashgate Publishing, 2004. Print.
Derrida, Jacques. *De la Grammatologie*. Paris: Les éditions de minuit, 1967. *Of Grammatology*. Trans. Gayatri Chakravorty Spivak. Baltimore: Johns Hopkins, 1984. Print.
Descourtilz, Michel Étienne. *Histoire des désastres de Saint-Domingue*. Paris: Chez Garnery, 1795. Print. *The Louverture Project* (Sept. 2009). Web. 18 Nov. 2011. <http://thelouvertureproject.org/index.php?title=History_of_the_Disasters_in_Saint-Domingue>.
Diop, Cheikh Anta "5. La Falsification de l'Histoire." *Cheikh Anta Diop.net* (2007). Web. 24 Nov. 2011. <http://www.cheikhantadiop.net/cad_interview4_son_mp3.MP3>.
Dobson, D. "Archetypal Literary Theory in the Postmodern Era." *Jung: The e-Journal of the Jungian Society for Scholarly Studies* 1.1 (2005, April 10). Web. 24 Nov. 2011. <http://www.thejungiansociety.org/Jung%20Society/e-journal/Volume-1/Dobson-2005.html>.
Doyle, Arthur Conan. *The Lost World*. 1912. New York: Berkley, 1965. Print.
Dubois, Dominique. "The Creative Mind and the Rewriting of History in Wilson Harris's *The Tree of the Sun*."*Journal of Caribbean Literatures* 2.1-2-3 (Spring 2000): 134-146. Print.
___. "The Redemptive Powe of Bone's Revisionary Fiction." Maes-Jelinek and Ledent, eds., *Theatre of the Arts* 195-204. Print.
___. "Wilson Harris's *Infinite Rehearsal* or the Imaginative Reconstruction of History." *Commonwealth* 21.1 (Autumn 1998): 37-46. Print.
Durix, Jean-Pierre. *Mimesis, Genres and Post-Colonial Discourse: Deconstructing Magic Realism*. Basingstoke: Macmillan, 1998. Print.
___. "Origins in *Palace of the Peacock*." Maes-Jelinek and Ledent, eds., *Theatre of the Arts* 83-101. Print.
___. "The Palimpsest of Fiction: *The Infinite Rehearsal*." Maes-Jelinek, ed., *The Uncompromising Imagination* 210-220. Print.
___, ed. *Theory and Literary Creation / Théorie et Création Littéraire*. Dijon: Éditions Universitaires de Dijon, 1999. Print.
___. "The Visionary Art of Wilson Harris." *World Literature Today* (Winter 1984): 19-23. Print.

———. "Weaving the Tapestry of Memory: Wilson Harris's *The Four Banks of the River of Space*." *Callaloo* 18.1 (Winter 1995): 60-69. Print.

———. "Wilson Harris: From the Void into the Unknown." *Essays on Post-Colonial Fiction*. Ed. Albert Wertheim and Hedwig Bock. Munich: Max Hueber, 1986. 275-294. Print.

———. "Wilson Harris and *Palace of the Peacock*." *Mimesis, Genres and Post-Colonial Discourse: Deconstructing Magic Realism* 171-185. Print.

Durrant, Samuel. "Coming Home 'Upon Threads of Desolation': The Reversal of Prophecy in Wilson Harris's *The Dark Jester*." Maes-Jelinek and Ledent. eds., *Theatre of the Arts* 205-215. Print.

———. "Hosting History: Wilson Harris's Sacramental Narratives." *Jouvert* 5.1 (Autumn 2000). Web. 28 Nov. 2011. <http://social.chass.ncsu.edu/jouvert/v5i1/samdur.htm>.

Edlund, Rebekka. "Carnival and Quantum Theory Metaphors of Identity in Wilson Harris's *The Carnival* Trilogy." The Society for Caribbean Studies (UK). *Annual Conference Papers* 7 (2006). Ed. Sandra Courtman. Web. 28 Nov. 2011. <http://www.caribbeanstudies.org.uk/papers/2006/olvol7p1.PDF>.

Edwards, W., and K. Gibson. "An Ethnohistory of Amerindians in Guyana." *Ethnohistory* 26.2 (Spring 1979): 161-175. Print.

Emery, Mary Lou. "Limbo Rock, Wilson Harris and the Arts of Memory." *Callaloo* 18.1 (Winter 1995): 110-124. Print.

———. *Modernism, the Visual, and Caribbean Literature*. Cambridge: Cambridge UP, 2007. Print.

Evans-Pritchard, Edward Evan. *Witchcraft, Oracles and Magic Among the Azande*. 1937. Oxford: Oxford UP, 1976. Print.

Eze, Emmanuel Chukwudi, ed. *Postcolonial African Philosophy: A Critical Reader*. Oxford: Blackwell, 1997. Print.

Fanon, Frantz. *Les damnés de la terre*.1961. Paris: La Découverte&Syros, 2002. Print.

———. *Peau noire, masques blancs*. Editions du Seuil, Paris 1952.

———. *The Wretched of the Earth*. Trans. C. Farrington. New York: Grove Press, 1963. Print.

Feard, Rev. John R. *Toussaint L'Ouverture: A Biography and Autobiography*. 1863. Boston: James Redpath Publisher, 2001. *Documenting the American South*. The University of North Carolina at Chapel Hill (2004). Web. 24 Nov. 2011. <http://docsouth.unc.edu/neh/beard63/beard63.html>.

Fordham, Frieda. *Introduction to Jung's Psychology*. 1953-1966. The Jung Page (2002). Web. 28 Nov. 2011. <http://www.cgjungpage.org/index.php?option=com_content&task=view&id=852&Itemid=41>.

Freidel, David, Linda Schele, and Joy Parker. *Maya Cosmos: Three Thousand Years on the Shaman's Path*. 1993. New York: Perennial, Harper Collins, 2001. Print.

Foucault, Michel. *L'archéologie du savoir*. Paris: Gallimard, 1969. Print.
___. *Histoire de la folie à l'âge classique: Folie et déraison*. 1961. Paris: Gallimard, 1998.
___. *Histoire de la sexualité*. 1976-1984. Paris: Gallimard, 1984. Print.
___. *Les mots et les choses: Une archeologie des sciences humaines*. 1966. Paris: Gallimard, 1993. Print.
___. "Truth and Power." *Power/Knowledge: Selected Interviews and Other Writings, 1972-1977*. Ed. Colin Gordon. NY: Pantheon, 1980. 293-307. Print.
Franco, José L. *Historia de la revolución de Haití*. La Habana: Academia de Ciencias, 1966. Print.
Frye, Northrop. *Anatomy of Criticism: Four Essays*. New York: Atheneum, 1965.
___. "Forming Fours." *Hudson Review* 4.4 (1958): 611-619. Print.
Fuchs, Eckhardt, and Benedikt Stutchey. "Introduction: Problems of Writing World History: Western and Non-Western Experiences, 1800-2000." Fuchs and Stutchey, eds., *Writing World History* 1-44. Print.
___, and Benedikt Stutchey, eds. *Writing World History: 1800-2000. Studies of the German Historical Institute*. Oxford/New York: Oxford UP, 2003. Print.
Ghose, Zulfikar. "Reading Wilson Harris's The Mask of the Beggar." *Context* 14. Dalkey Archive Press. Web. 28 Nov. 2011. <http://www.dalkeyarchive.com/article/show/226>.
Ghosh, Amitav. *In an Antique Land*. London: MacMillan, 1992. Print.
___. *The Calcutta Chromosome*. 1996. London: Picador, MacMillan, 1997. Print.
___. *The Hungry Tide*. London: Harper Collins, 2004. Print.
___. "The Slave of Ms. H.6." *Subaltern Studies* 7: "Writings on South Asian History and Society." New Delhi: Oxford UP, 1993.159-220. Print.
___. "A Talk with Amitav Ghosh." Interview by Paolo Bertinetti et al. *Il Tolomeo* 10 (2007): 78-83. Print.
Gil, Juan. *Miti e utopie della scoperta: L'Eldorado, alla ricerca della città dell'oro*. Trans. of *Mytos y utopías del descubrimiento*, 1989, by M. Finassi Parolo. Milano: Garzanti, 1993. Print.
Gilkes, Michael. *Couvade*. 1974. Mundelstrup: Dangaroo Press, 1998. Print.
___, ed. *The Literate Imagination: Essays on the Novels of Wilson Harris*. London: Macmillan, 1989. Print.
___. *Wilson Harris and the Caribbean Novel*. London, Trinidad and Jamaica: Longman Caribbean, 1975. Print.
Glissant, Édouard. *Caribbean Discourse*. Trans. J. Michael Dash. Charlottesville: UP of Virginia, 1989. Print.
___. *Le discours antillais*. Paris: Seuil, 1981. Print.

von Goethe, Johann Wolfgang. *Faust*. Cleveland, Ohio New York, N.Y.: The World Publishing Company. Trans. Bayard Taylor. *Project Gutenberg* (Jan 2005). Web. 28 Nov. 2011. <http://www.gutenberg.org/etext/14591>.

Gossman, Lionel. "History and Literature: Reproduction or Signification." *The Writing of History: Literary Form and Historical Understanding*. Ed. Robert H. Canary and Henry Kozicki. Madison WI: University of Wisconsin Press, 1978. 3-39. Print.

Grass, Vernon W. "Myth and the Reconciliation of Opposites: Jung and Levi-Strauss." *Journal of the History of Ideas* 42.3 (1981): 471-487. Print.

Graves, Benjamin. "Can the Subaltern Speak?" *Political Discourse: Theories of Colonialism and Postcolonialism*. *Postcolonialweb* (2006). Web. 24 Nov. 2011 <http://postcolonialweb.org/poldiscourse/spivak/spivak2.ht ml>.

Hakluyt, Richard. *The Principal Navigation, Voyages, Traffics, and Discoveries of the English Nation*. London: G. Bishop, R. Newberie & R. Barker, 1598-1600. *Project Gutenberg* (Dec 2004). Web. 28 Nov. 2011. <http://www.gutenberg.org/etext/7182>.

Hamner, Robert D., ed. *Joseph Conrad: Third World Perspectives*. Washington D.C.: Three Continents Press, 1990. Print.

Harris, Marvin. *Cannibal and Kings: The Origins of Culture*. New York: Random House, 1977. Print.

Hector, Leonard Tim. "The Making of Caribbean Philosophy" (I, II). *Fan the Flame* (May 1998). Web. December 2011. <http://www.candw.ag/~jardinea/ffhtm/ff980 529.htm>

Hegel, Georg Wilhelm Friedrich. "The Embodiment Spirit Assumes: The State." § 49.1837. *Reason in History: A General Introduction to the Philosophy of History*. Trans. R. S. Hartman. Indianapolis: Bobbs-Merril, 1953. Print. *Hegel by HyperText*. *Marxist Internet Archive*. Web. 24 Nov. 2011. <http://www.marxists.org/reference/archive/hegel/works/hi/history4.htm#049>.

___. *Phenomenology of Mind*. 1807. *Hegel by HyperText*. *Marxist Internet Archive*. Web. 24 Nov. 2011. <http://www.marxists.org/reference/archive/hegel/works/ph/phconten.htm>.

___. *The Philosophy of History*.1837. *Hegel by HyperText*. *Marxist Internet Archive*. Web. 24 Nov. 2011. <http://www.marxists.org/reference/archive/hegel/works/hi/index.htm>.

Heidegger, Martin. *Basic Writings from 'Being and Time' (1927) to 'The Task of Thinking' (1964)*. Ed. and introd. by David Farrell Krell. London: Routledge and Kegan Paul, 1978. Print.

Hemming, John. *The Search for El Dorado*. London: Phoenix Press, 1978. Print.

Henry, Paget. *Caliban's Reason: Introducing Afro-Caribbean Philosophy*. New York/London: Routledge, 2000. Print.

Holland, Margaret G. "Can Fiction be Philosophy?" Boston, Massachusetts: University of Northern Iowa, Proceedings of the Twentieth World Congress of Philosophy, (August 10-15, 1998). Web. 22 Dec. 201. <http://www.bu.edu/wcp/Papers/Lite/LiteHoll.htm>

Hudson, William Henry. *Green Mansions: A Romance of the Tropical Forest*. 1904. London/Glasgow: Collins New Classic Series, 1957. Print.

Hulme, Peter; Whitehead, Neil. *Wilde Majesty: Encounters with the Caribs from Columbus to the Present Day: An Anthology*. New York: Oxford UP, 1992. Print.

von Humboldt, Alexander. *Le voyage aux régions equinoxiales du nouveau continent, fait en 1799-1804, par Alexandre de Humboldt et Aimé Bonpland*. Paris, 1807. *Personal Narrative of Travels to the Equinoctial Regions of America During the Years 1799-1804*. Vols. I, II, III. Trans. Thomasina Ross. *Project Gutenberg* (Aug. 2004). Web. 28 Nov. 2011. <http://www.gutenberg.org/etext/ 6322>.

Im Thurn, Sir Everard. *Among the Indians of Guiana*. 1883. New York: Dover Publications, Inc., 1967. Print.

Jaggi, Maya. "New Worlds." *The Guardian* (24 March 2001). Web. 24 Nov. 2011. <http://www.guardian.co.uk/books/2001/mar/24/fiction.reviews1>.

James, C.L.R. *The Black Jacobins: Toussaint L'Ouverture and the San Domingo Revolution*. 1938. New York: Vintage, 1989. Print.

___. *Wilson Harris: A Philosophical Approach*. St Augustine / Port of Spain: Extra-Mural Department, University of the West Indies, General Public Lecture Series: West Indian Literature 1, 1965. Print.

James, Louis. *Caribbean Literature in English*. New York: Longman, 1999. Print.

___. "'The Closeness of Profound Curiosity': The Parallel Visions of Wilson Harris and Denis Williams." *Journal of Caribbean Literatures* 2.1-2-3 (Spring 2000): 46-53. Print.

___. "Schrodinger's Cat versus Melville's Jaguar: Science and the Imagination in the Work of Three Guyanese Writers." In Jean-Pierre Durix, ed. *Theory and Literary Creation / Théorie et Création Littéraire*. Dijon: Editions Universitaires de Dijon 1999. 121-127. Print.

Jameson, Frederick. *The Political Unconscious: Narrative as Socially Symbolic Act*. London: Methuen, 1981. Print.

Johnson, Kerry L. "From Muse to Majesty: Rape, Landscape and Agency in the Early Novels of Wilson Harris." *WLWE* 35.2 (1996): 71-89. Print.

___. "Translation of Gender, Pain, and Space: Wilson Harris's *The Carnival Trilogy*." *Modern Fiction Studies* 44.1 (Spring 1998): 123-143. Print.

Jung, Carl Gustav. *Alchemical Studies*. 1967. *The Collected Works of C.G. Jung* Vol. 13. Ed. and trans. Gerhard Adler and R.F.C. Hull. Princeton, NJ: Princeton UP, 1967. Print.

___. "The Archetypes of the Collective Unconscious." 1954. *The Collected Works of C.G. Jung* Vol. 9i. Ed. and trans. Gerhard Adler and R.F.C. Hull. Princeton, NJ: Princeton UP, 1968. 3-41. Print.

___. "Concerning the Archetypes, with Special Reference to the Anima Concept." 1936. *The Collected Works of C.G. Jung* Vol. 9i. Ed. and trans. Gerhard Adler and R.F.C. Hull. Princeton, NJ: Princeton UP, 1968. 54-72 Print.

___. "Concerning Mandala Symbolism." *Collected Works of C.G. Jung* Vol. 9i. Ed. and trans. Gerhard Adler and R.F.C. Hull. Princeton, NJ: Princeton UP, 1968. 355-384. Print.

___. *Memories, Dreams, Reflections*. 1973. Trans. Richard and Clara Winston. New York: Vintage, 1989. Print.

___. "Mind and Earth." 1927. *The Collected Works of C.G. Jung* Vol. 10. Ed. and trans. Gerhard Adler and R.F.C. Hull. Princeton, NJ: Princeton UP, 1970. 29-49. Print.

___. *Mysterium Coniunctionis*. 1955-56. *The Collected Works of C.G. Jung* Vol. 14. Ed. and trans. Gerhard Adler and R.F.C. Hull. Princeton, NJ: Princeton UP, 1970. Print.

___. "On the Nature of the Psyche." 1947. *The Collected Works of C.G. Jung* Vol. 8. Ed. and trans. Gerhard Adler and R.F.C. Hull. Princeton: Princeton UP, 1972. 159-234. Print.

___. "The Phenomenology of the Spirit in Fairytales." 1948. *The Collected Works of C.G. Jung* Vol. 9i. Ed. and trans. Gerhard Adler and R.F.C. Hull. Princeton, NJ: Princeton UP, 1968. 207-254. Print.

___. "The Problem of the Fourth." 1948. *The Collected Works of C.G. Jung* Vol. 11. Ed. and trans. Gerhard Adler and R.F.C. Hull. Princeton, NJ: Princeton UP, 1969. 164-192. Print.

___. *Psychology and Alchemy*. 1944. *The Collected Works of C.G. Jung* Vol. 12. Ed. and trans. Gerhard Adler and R.F.C. Hull. Princeton, NJ: Princeton UP, 1968. Print.

___. "A Psychological Approach to the Dogma of the Trinity." 1942. *The Collected Works of C.G. Jung* Vol. 11. Ed. and trans. Gerhard Adler and R.F.C. Hull. Princeton, NJ: Princeton UP, 1969. 107-200. Print.

___. "The Psychology of the Child Archetype." 1941. *The Collected Works of C.G. Jung* Vol. 9i. Ed. and trans. Gerhard Adler and R.F.C. Hull. Princeton, NJ: Princeton UP, 1968. 151-181. Print.

___. *La simbolica dello spirito: Studi sulla fenomenologia psichica*. Con un contributo di Riwkah Scharf. [Trans. Olga Bovero Caporali.] Torino: G. Einaudi, 1975. Print.

___. "The Structure of the Psyche." 1960. *The Collected Works of C.G. Jung* Vol. 8. Ed. and trans. Gerhard Adler and R.F.C. Hull. Princeton: Princeton UP, 1972. 139-158. Print.

___. "Synchronizität als ein Prinzip akausaler Zusammenhänge." C.G. Jung and W. Pauli. *Naturerklärung und Psyche*. Zürich: Rascher Verlag, 1952. Print.

___. "Synchronicity: An Acausal Connecting Principle." 1952. Ed. and trans. Gerhard Adler and R.F.C. Hull. *The Collected Works of C.G. Jung* Vol. 8. Princeton: Princeton UP, 1972. 417-519. Print.

___. "The Unity and Trinity of Mercurius." 1948. *The Collected Works of C.G. Jung* Vol. 13. Ed. and trans. Gerhard Adler and R.F.C. Hull. Princeton, NJ: Princeton UP, 1967. 221-224. Print.

Kant, Immanuel. "Idea for a Universal History from a Cosmopolitan Point of View." *On History*. 1784. Trans. Lewis White Beck. Indianapolis: The Bobbs-Merrill Co., 1963. Transcribed by Rob Lucas for *Marxist Internet Archive*. Web. 24 Nov. 2011. <http://www.marxists.org/reference/subject/ethics/kant/universal-history.htm>.

Kaphagawani, D. "What is African Philosophy?" *The African Philosophy Reader*. Ed. P.H. Coetzee and A.P. Roux. London/New York: Routledge, 1998. Print. 86-98.

Kellman, Anthony. "Towards a National Caribbean Epic." The Society for Caribbean Studies (UK). Ed. Sandra Courtman. *Annual Conference Papers* 6 (2005). Web. 30 Nov. 2011 <http://www.caribbeanstudies.org.uk/papers/2005/olvol6p2.PDF>.

Kimbrough, Robert, ed. *Joseph Conrad, Heart of Darkness: An Authoritative Text, Background and Sources Criticism*. A Norton Critical Edition. New York/ London: Norton & Company, 1988. Print.

Kirke, Henry. *Twenty Five Years in British Guiana*. 1898. Connecticut: Negro UP, 1970.

Koch-Grünberg, Theodor. *Indianermärchen aus Südamerika*. 1920. In *Favole e Miti dell'Amazzonia*. Trans. Lydia Magliano and Italo Sordi. Milano: Xenia, 1992. Print.

L'Ouverture, Toussaint. *The Louverture Project* (2006). Web. 30 Nov. 2011. <http://thelouvertureproject.org/>.

Lawlor, Leonard. "Jacques Derrida." *The Stanford Encyclopedia of Philosophy*. Ed. Edward N. Zalta. (Fall 2011). Web. 26 Sept. 2011. <http://plato.stanford.edu/archives/fall2011/entries/derrida/>.

Lévi-Strauss, Claude. *Le cru et le cuit*. Paris: Plon, 1964. Print.

___. *La pensée sauvage*. Paris: Plon, 1962. Print.

___. *Tristes tropiques*. 1955. Paris: Plon, 1973. Print.

Lévy-Bruhl, Lucien. *How Natives Think: Les Fonctions Mentales dans les Sociétés Inferieures*. 1910. Trans. Lilian A. Clare. Princeton: Princeton UP, 1985. Print.

Lewis, Krishna Ray. "The Infinite Rehearsal and Pastoral Revision." *Callaloo* 18.1 (Winter 1995): 83-92. Print.

Lichtenstein, David P. "Experimental Vision: Harris's Use of Combination to Propose A New Form of Postcolonial Unity." *Caribbean Literature. Postcolonialweb*

(1999). Web. 30 Nov. 2011. <http://www.usp.nus.edu .sg/post/caribbean/harris/theme.html>.

Linguanti, Elsa. "At the Intersection of Physics and Literature." In *Proteus: The Language Of Metamorphosis*. Ed. Carla Dente, George Ferzoco, Miriam Gill, Marina Spunta. Aldershot: Ashgate Publishing, 2004. 35-49. Print.

___, Francesco Casotti, and Carmen Concilio, eds. *Co-terminous Worlds*. Amsterdam: Rodopi, 1999. Print.

Lovera, José Rafael. *Antonio de Berrío: La obsesión por El Dorado*. Caracas: PDVSA, 1991. Print.

Macaulay, Thomas Babington. *The History of England: From the Accession of James the Second*. London: Longmans, Green and co., 1849. *Street Corner Society* (1997). Web. 30 Nov. 2011. <http://www.strecorsoc.org/macaulay/title.html>.

Maes-Jelinek, Hena. "Another Future for Post-Colonial Studies? Wilson Harris's Post-Colonial Philosophy and the 'Savage Mind.'" *Wasafiri* 24 (1996): 3-8. Print.

___. "*Carnival, The Infinite Rehearsal,* and *The Four Banks of the River of Space*: Ulyssean Carnival of Epic Metamorphoses." In Maes-Jelinek, *The Labyrinth of Universality* 377-394. Print.

___ and Geoffrey Davis, eds. *Crisis and Creativity in the New Literatures in English*, Amsterdam/ Atlanta: Rodopi, 1990.

___, ed. and introd. *Explorations: A Selection of Talks and Articles 1966-1981*. Mundelstrup: Dangaroo Press, 1981. Print.

___. "Fictional Breakthrough and the Unveiling of 'Unspeakable Rites' in Patrick White's *A Fringe of Leaves* and Wilson Harris's *Yurokon*." *Kunapipi* 2.2 (1980): 33-43. Print.

___. "From Living Nature to Borderless Culture in Wilson Harris's Work." In DeLoughrey, Gosson, and Handley, eds., *Caribbean Literature and the Environment* 258-259. Print.

___. "From *The Sleepers of Roraima* to *The Angel at the Gate*: The Novel as a Painting." In Maes-Jelinek, *The Labyrinth of Universality* 229-235. Print.

___. "Immanent Substance. Reflections on the Creative Process." In Maes-Jelinek, *The Labyrinth of Universality* 325-342. Print.

___. *The Labyrinth of Universality*. Amsterdam – New York: Rodopi, 2006. Print.

___. "Latent Cross-Culturalities in Wilson Harris's and Wole Soyinka's Creative Alternative to Theory." *European Journal of English Studies* 2.1 (April 1998): 37-48. Print.

___. "*The Mask of the Beggar:* Transfigurative Art." In Maes-Jelinek, *The Labyrinth of Universality* 451-468. Print.

___. *The Naked Design: A Reading of* 'Palace of the Peacock.' Mundelstrup: Dangaroo Press, 1976. Print.

___. "'Numinous Proportions': Wilson Harris's Alternative to All Posts." 1993. In Tiffin and Adam, eds. *Past the Last Post* 47-64. Print. Rpt. in Maes-Jelinek, *The Labyrinth of Universality* 527-547. Print.

___. "Ouverture." *Journal of Caribbean Literatures* 2.1-2-3 (Spring 2000): 6-16. Print.

___. "Re-visionary Strategies. The Wisdom of Uncertainty." In Maes-Jelinek, *The Labyrinth of Universality* 343-356. Print.

___, Petersen, Kirsten Holst, and Anna Rutherford, eds. *A Shaping of Connections: Commonwealth Literature Studies – Then and Now.* Mundelstrup: Dangaroo Press, 1989. Print.

___, and Bénédicte Ledent, eds. *Theatre of the Arts: Wilson Harris and the Caribbean.* Amsterdam/New York: Rodopi, 2002. Print.

___. "Tricksters of Heaven, Visions of Holocaust in *Jonestown* and Fred D'Aguiar's *Bill of Rights*." In Maes-Jelinek, *The Labyrinth of Universality* 419-438. Print.

___. "'Unfinished Genesis': *The Four Banks of the River of Space*." In Maes-Jelinek, ed., *The Uncompromising Imagination* 230-238. Print.

___. "'Unimaginable Imaginer': The Dark Jester." In Maes-Jelinek and Ledent, eds., *Theatre of the Arts* 217-230. Print.

___. "Ut Musica Poesis." In Maes-Jelinek, *The Labyrinth of Universality* 495-504. Print.

___, Bénédicte Ledent and Daria Tunca, eds. *The Wilson Harris Bibliography* (1999). Web. 22 Nov. 2011. <http://www.l3.ulg.ac.be/harris/whprim.html>.

___, ed. *Wilson Harris: The Uncompromising Imagination.* Sydney/Mundelstrup: Dangaroo Press, 1991. Print.

Manzu Islam, Syed. "Postcolonial Shamanism: Wilson Harris's Quantum Poetics and Ethics." *Journal of West Indian Literature* 16.1 (Nov. 2007): 59-82. Print.

Marlowe, Christopher. *The Tragical History of Doctor Faustus.* 1604. Project Gutenberg (Jan 1997). Web. 30 Nov. 2011. <http://www.gutenberg.org/etext/779>.

Marx, Karl. *A Critique of the German Ideology.* 1845-1846. Marx and Engels Internet Archive (2000). Web. 16 Sept. 2011. <http://www.marxists.org/archive/marx/works/1845/german-ideology/ch01b.htm#5a7>.

McDougall, Russell. "'Corporeal Music': The Scale of Myth and Adjectival Insistence in *Palace of the Peacock*." In Maes-Jelinek, ed., *Wilson Harris* 9-105. Print.

___. "Walter Roth, Wilson Harris and a Caribbean/Postcolonial Theory of Modernism." *University of Toronto Quarterly* 67.2 (Spring 1998): 567-591. Print.

___. "Wilson Harris and the Frontiers of Myth-Criticism 1978-1983." *The Journal of Caribbean Literatures* 2.1,2,3 (Spring 2000): 109-121. Print.

Melville, Pauline. *The Ventriloquist's Tale.* London: Bloomsbury, 1997.

___. "Wilson Harris, 'In the Forests of the Night.'" *The Review of Contemporary Fiction* 17.2 (1997): 50-52. Print.

Menezes, Mary Noel. *The Amerindians in Guyana 1803-1873: A Documentary History*. London: Frank Cass, 1979. Print.
Mink, Louis O. "Narrative Form as a Cognitive Instrument." *The Writing of History: Literary Form and Historical Understanding*. Ed. Robert H. Canary and Henry Kozicki. Madison WI: University of Wisconsin Press, 1978. 129-149. Print.
Mitchell, Michael. *Hidden Mutualities: Faustian Themes from Gnostic Origins to the Postcolonial*. Amsterdam/New York: Rodopi, 2006. Print.
___. "The Magus at Angel Inn." In Maes-Jelinek and Ledent, eds., *Theatre of the Arts* 153-163. Print.
___. "The Seigniory of Faust: Gnostic Scenery in *The Infinite Rehearsal*." *Journal of Caribbean Literatures* 2.1-3 (Spring 2000): 168-178. Print.
___. "With Covered Eyes: Amerindians and the Art of Seeing in Wilson Harris and Steve McQueen." *The Journal of Commonwealth Literature* 39.3 (2004): 107-118. Print.
Mittelholzer, Edgar. *Children of Kaywana*. 1952. London: Peter Neville Limited, 1952. Print.
___. *Corentyne Thunder*. 1941. London: Heinemann, 1970. Print.
___. *My Bones and My Flute*. 1955. New York: Longman Caribbean, 1982. Print.
___. *Kaywana Blood*. 1958. London: Corgi, 1976. Print.
___. *Shadows Move Among Them*. 1951. Philadephia/New York: J.B. Lippincott Company, 1951. Print.
Moss, Laura. "'The Plague of Normality': Reconfiguring Realism in Postcolonial Theory." *Jouvert* 5.1 (Autumn 2000). Web. 01 Dec. 2011. <http://english.chass.ncsu.edu/jouvert/v5i1/moss.htm>.
Munro, Arlene. "Writers of History in the Nineteenth Century." *Kyk-Over-Al: History This Week* 25 (22 Jun. 2006). Web. 01 Dec. 2011. <http://kykoveral.blogspot.com/2006/06/writers-of-history-in-nineteenth.html>.
Murray, Christopher John; ed. *Encyclopedia of Modern French Thought*. London: Routledge, 2004. Print.
Murray, Stuart. "Wilson Harris in His Essays at the End of the Millenium: Time, Countertime, Writing." In Maes-Jelinek and Ledent, eds., *Theatre of the Arts* 165-175. Print.
Naipaul, Shiva. *Black and White*. London: Hamish Hamilton, 1980. Print.
Naipaul, V.S. *The Middle Passage*. 1962. Harmondsworth: Penguin, 1985. Print.
Nelson, Cary; and Lawrence Grossberg; eds. *Marxism and the Interpretation of Culture*. Urbana: University of Illinois Press, 1988. Print.
Nelson, Stanley. *Jonestown: The Life and Death of Peoples Temple*. PBS American Experience. Firelight Media, 2006. DVD.

Nicholson, D. H. S., and A. H. E. Lee, eds. *The Oxford Book of English Mystical Verse*. Oxford: The Clarendon Press, 1917. *Bartleby.com* (2000). Web. 28 Nov. 2011. <www.bartleby.com/236/>.

Nietzsche, Friedrich Wilhelm. *The Birth of Tragedy & The Genealogy of Morals*. Trans. F. Golffing. New York: Doubleday & Co., 1956. Print.

___. *Die Geburt der Tragödie*. 1872-1886. *Project Gutenberg*. (2005). Web. 18 Nov. 2011. <http://www.gutenberg.org/ebooks/ 7206>.

___. *Zur Genealogie der Moral*. 1887. *Spiegel Online Kultur*. Projekt Gutenberg – De. Web. 18 Nov. 2011. <http://gutenberg.spiegel.de/buch/3249/1>.

___. "Vom Nutzen und Nachteil der Historie für das Leben." 1874. *Zeno.org Philosophie*. Web. 18 Nov. 2011. <http://www.zeno.org/nid/2000 9229817>.

___. "The Use and Abuse of History." 1874. Trans. A. Collins. Indianapolis and New York: Library of Liberal Arts, Bobbs-Merril Co., 1957. Print.

Niranjana, Tejaswini. *Siting Translation: History, Poststructuralism, and the Colonial Context*. Berkeley, Los Angeles, Oxford: University of California Press, 1992. Print.

Nuridsany, Claude and Marie Perennou. *Microcosmos*. Ed. Yoyotte, Marie-Josephe Marie Florence Ricard. France/Switzerland/Italy: Galatée Films, 1996. DVD.

O'Brien, Patrick Karl. "The Deconstruction of Myths and Reconstruction of Metanarratives in Global Histories of Material Progress." *Writing World History: 1800-2000*. Studies of the German Historical Institute London. Ed. Benedikt Stutchtey and Eckhardt Fuchs. Oxford/New York: Oxford UP, 2003. 67-90. Print.

Ondaatje, Michael. *Anil's Ghost*. London: Picador/MacMillan, 2000. Print.

___. *In the Skin of a Lion*. 1987. London: Picador/MacMillan, 1988. Print.

Orama, Luís. *En pos del Dorado*. Caracas: Tip. Garrido, 1947. Print.

Outlaw, Lucius. "African, African American, Africana Philosophy." *Postcolonial African Philosophy*. Ed. Emmanuel Eze. Oxford: Blackwell, 1997. Print. 29.

Patterson, Thomas C. *The Inca Empire*. Oxford: Berg, 1997. Print.

Pauli, Wolfgang. "Der Einfluss archetypischer Vorstellungen auf die Bildung naturwissenschaftlicher Theorien bei Kepler." *Naturerklärung und Psyche*. By C.G. Jung and W. Pauli. Zürich: Rascher, 1952. 109-194. Print.

___. "The Influence of Archetypal Ideas on the Formation of Scientific Theories in Kepler." *The Interpretation of Nature and Psyche*. By C.G. Jung and W. Pauli. Trans. R.F.C. Hull. New York: Bollingen Series LI, Pantheon, 1955. 147-240. Print.

Paz, Octavio. *El laberinto de la soledad*. 1950. *Postdata*. 1970. *Vuelta a El laberinto de la soledad*. 1979. México: Fondo de Cultura Económica, 1994. Print.

Petersen, Kirsten Holst, and Anna Rutherford. *Enigma of Values: An Introduction*. Mundelstrup: Dangaroo Press, 1975. Print.

___. "Fossil and Psyche." Ashcroft, Griffiths, and Tiffin, eds., *Post-Colonial Studies Reader* 185-189. Extract from Petersen and Rutherford, *Enigma of Values*.
Pieri, Paolo Francesco. *Dizionario Junghiano*. Torino: Bollati Boringhieri, 1998. Print.
Polia, Mario. *Gli Incas*. Milano: Xenia, 1999. Print.
Poma de Ayala, Felipe Guaman. *El primer nueva corónica y buen gobierno*. 1615-1616. *El sitio de Guaman Poma*. Det Kongelige Bibliotek (Sept. 2004). Web. 01 Dec. 2011. <http://www.kb.dk/permalink/2006/poma/info/es/frontpage.htm>.
Population & Housing Census 2002 – Guyana National Report (2002). Web. 25 Nov. 2011. <http://www.statisticsguyana.gov.gy/pubs/Chapter2_Population_Compositi on.pdf>.
Rainsford, Marcus. *An Historical Account of the Black Empire of Hayti: Comprehending a View of the Principal Transactions in the Revolution of Saint-Domingo; with its Ancient and Modern State*. London, 1805. Excerpt. *The Louverture Project* (Sept. 2009). Web. 18 Nov. 2011. <http://thelouverture project.org/index.php?title=Historical_Account_of_the_Black_Empire_of_Hayti_-_Toussaint>.
Raleigh, Walter. *The Discovery of the Large, Rich, and Beautiful Empire of Guiana, with a Relation of the Great and Golden City of Manoa (Which the Spaniards call El Dorado)*. 1596. *Project Gutenberg* (March 2006). Web. 28 Nov. 2011. <http://www.gutenberg.org/ebooks/2272>.
Retamar, Roberto Férnandez. "Calibán." *Casa de las Américas* Sept.-Oct. 1971. 68. Print. Rpt. in *Órbita*. By Roberto Férnandez Retamar. La Habana: Ediciones Unión, 2001. Print.
___. *Caliban and Other Essays*. Trans. Edward Baker. Minneapolis: UMP, 1989. Print.
Ricoeur, Paul. "Narrative Time." *Critical Inquiry* 7.1 (Autumn 1980): 169-190. Print.
Rivière, Peter. *Individual and Society in Guiana*. Cambridge: Cambridge UP, 1984. Print.
Roads, Curtis. *Microsound* . Cambridge/London: MIT Press, 2004. Print.
Robinson, Jeffrey. "The Aboriginal Enigma: *Heart of Darkness*, *Voss*, and *Palace of the Peacock*." *Journal of Commonwealth Literature* 20.1 (1985): 148-155. Print.
Ross, Jack. "Wilson Harris, Joseph Conrad, and the South American 'Quest' Novel." *Landfall* 184 (1992): 455-468. Print.
Roth, Walter E. *An Inquiry into the Animism and Folk-Lore of the Guiana Indians*. Thirtieth Annual Report of the Bureau of American Ethnology, 1908-1909. Washington D.C. 1915. 103-386. Print. *Caribbean Amerindian Centrelink*. HTML by Christopher M. Weimer (2004). Web. 01 Dec. 2011. <http://www. centrelink.org/Roth.txt>.
Rowe, John Howland. "Absolute Chronology in the Andean Area." *American Antiquity* 10.3 (Jan 1945): 265-284. Print.
Rulfo, Juan. *Pedro Paramo*. 1955. Madrid: Catedra, 1993. Print.

Rushdie, Salman. *Imaginary Homelands, Essays and Criticism 1981-1991*. New York: Granta – Penguin, 1992. Print.

___. *Midnight's Children*. 1981. New York: Penguin, 1991. Print.

Said, Edward W. *Culture and Imperialism*. 1993. New York: Vintage, 1994. Print.

___. *Orientalism*. 1978. London: Penguin, 2003. Print.

Samuels, Andrew, Bani Shorter, and Fred Plaut, eds. *A Critical Dictionary of Jungian Analysis*. London: Routledge & Kegan Paul, 2000. Print.

Sánchez, Domingo P. "Glosario de astronomía de los Caribes de Venezuela." *KACIKE: Journal of Caribbean Amerindian History and Anthropology* (2002). Web. 01 Dec. 2008 <http://web.archive.org/web/20081017104431/ http://www.kacike.org/DomingoSanchez.htm>.

Sartori, Agnese. *Gli Aztechi*. Milano: Xenia, 1997. Print.

Sartre, Jean-Paul. *Critique de la raison dialectique*. 1960-1985. Paris: Gallimard, 1985. Print.

Scarano, Tommaso. "Spanish American Magical Realism." *Co-terminous Worlds*. Ed. Elsa Linguanti, Francesco Casotti, and Carmen Concilio. Amsterdam: Rodopi, 1999. 9-28. Print.

Schomburgk, R.H. *A Description of British Guiana, Geographical and Statistical, Exhibiting its Resources and Capabilities Together with the Present and Future Condition and Prospects of the Colony*. London: Simpkin Marshall & co., 1840. Print.

Seeley, John Robert. *The Expansion of England*. London: Macmillan, 1899. Print.

___. *The Growth of British Policy: an Historical Essay*. Cambridge Cambridge: UP, Cambridge 1895. Print.

Selvon, Samuel. *The Lonely Londoners*. 1956. New York: Longman Caribbean, 1979. Print.

Serper, Alon. "Lévy-Bruhl's Major Contribution to the Field of Psychology; Another Reason for Studying Lévy-Bruhl in 1996." *Alon Serper's Web Pages*. University of Bath (2004). Web. 02 Dec. 201. <http://people.bath.ac.uk/pspas/Levy-bruhl.htm>.

Seymour, A..J. Introduction. *Eternity to Season*. By Wilson Harris. Georgetown, published privately, 1954. Print. Rpt. London: New Beacon, 1978. 53-54. Print.

___, ed. *New Writing in the Caribbean*. Georgetown: Caribbean Festival of the Arts, 1972. Print.

Shakespeare, William. *Othello*. 1603-1604. Ed. M. R. Ridley. London/New York: Routledge, 1992. Print.

___. *The Tempest*. 1611-1612. Ed. Virginia Mason Vaughan and Alden T. Vaughan. London: Arden Shakespeare, 2005. Print.

Sharp, Daryl. *Jung Lexicon: A Primer of Terms & Concepts*. 1991. *The Jung Page* (July 2007). Web. 28 Nov. 2011. <http://www.cgjungpage.org/index.php?option =com_content&task=view&id=869&Itemid=4>.

Sharrad, Paul. "The Art of Memory and the Liberation of History: Wilson Harris's Witnessing of Time." *Callaloo* 18.1 (Winter 1995): 94-108. Print.

Shaw, Gregory. "The Novelist as a Shaman: Art and Dialectic in the Work of Wilson Harris." *The Literate Imagination: Essays on the Novels of Wilson Harris*. Ed. Michael Gilkes. London: Macmillan, 1989. 141-151. Print.

___. "Wilson Harris's Metamorphoses: Animal and Vegetable Masks in *Palace of the Peacock*." *Callaloo* 18.1 (Winter 1995): 158-170. Print.

Simon, Louis. "Writing, Reading and Altered Consciousness in *Jonestown*." *Journal of Caribbean Literatures* 2.1-2-3 (Spring 2000): 207-214. Print.

Soyinka, Wole. *Aké: The Years of Childhood*. 1981. London: Methuen, 2000. Print.

Spivak, Gayatri Chakravorty. "Can the Subaltern Speak?" *Marxism and the Interpretation of Culture*. Ed. Cary Nelson and Lawrence Grossberg. Urbana: University of Illinois Press, 1988. Print.

___. *The Spivak Reader: Selected Works of Gayatri Chakravorty Spivak*. Ed. Donna Landry and Gerald MacLean. New York: Routledge, 1996. Print.

Stockhausen, Karlheinz. "The Concept of Unity in Electronic Music." Trans. Elaine Barkin. *Perspectives of New Music* 1.1 (Autumn 1962): 39–48. Print.

___. ."..How Time Passes..." 1957. Trans. Cornelius Cardew. *Die Reihe* 3 ("Musical Craftsmanship" 1959): 10–40. Print.

___. Interview at the West German Radio in Cologne on January 12th 1961. CD booklet. Kontakte. 1960. Wergo, 1992. CD.

___. "...wie die Zeit vergeht..." *Die Reihe* 3 ("Musikalisches Handwerk" 1956). 13-42. Print.

Stutchey, Benedikt, and Eckhardt Fuchs. "Introduction: Problems of Writing World History – Western and Non-Western Experiences, 1800-2000." In Stutchey and Fuchs, eds., *Writing World History* 1-44. Print.

___. "World Power and World History: Writing the British Empire 1885-1945." In Stutchey and Fuchs, eds., *Writing World History* 213-253.

___, and Eckhardt Fuchs, eds. *Writing World History: 1800-2000. Studies of the German Historical Institute*. Oxford/New York: Oxford UP, 2003. Print.

Swan, Michael. *British Guiana: The Land of Six Peoples*. London: H.M. Stationery Off., 1957. Print.

___. *The Marches of El-Dorado*. Harmondsworth: Penguin, 1961. Print.

Thieme, John. *Postcolonial Con-texts: Writing Back to the Canon*. London: Continuum, 2001. Print.

Thomas, J.J. *Froudacity: West Indian Fables by James Anthony Froude*. London and Port of Spain: New Beacon, 1969. Print.

Thompson, J. Eric S. *Maya History and Religion*. 1970. Norman: University of Oklahoma Press, 1976. Print.
___. *The Rise and Fall of Maya Civilization*. 1954-1966. London: Gollancz; Norman: University of Oklahoma Press, 1956. Print.
Tiffin, Helen, and Ian Adam, eds. *Past the Last Post*. Hemel Hempstead: Prentice-Hall,1993. Print.
Toews, John E. "Foucault and the Freudian Subject: Archaeology, Genealogy, and the Historicization of Psychoanalysis."*Foucault and the Writing of History*. Ed. Jan Goldstein. Oxford/Cambridge: Blackwell, 1994. 116-134. Print.
Todorov, Tzvetan. *La conquête de l'Amérique: La question de l'autre*. Paris: Seuil, 1982. Print.
Trollope, Anthony. *The West Indies and the Spanish Main*. 1860. Leipzig: B. Tauchnitz, 1860. Print.
Vankin, Jonathan, and John Whalen. *50 Great Conspiracies of All Time: History's Biggest Mysteries, Coverups, and Cabals*. Secaucus NJ: Citadel Press, 1995. Print.
Vargas Llosa, Mario. *El hablador*. Barcelona: Seix Barral, 1987. Print.
Vico, Giambattista. *La scienza nuova*. 1725-1744. La Spezia. Fratelli Melita, 1987. Print.
Voltaire. *Encyclopédie, ou Dictionnaire raisonné des sciences, des arts et des métiers, par une société de gens de lettres*. Tome 8 (H-IT). Neufchastel: Chez Samuel Faulche & Compagnie, Libraires & Imprimeurs, 1765. *Eliohs Electronic Library of Historiography*. Ed. Guido Abbattista and Rolando Minuti. Firenze: Università degli Studi di Firenze (March 1996). Web. 1 Aug. 2011. <http://www.eliohs.unifi.it/testi/700/voltaire/histoire.html>.
Walcott, Derek. "The Antilles: Fragments of Epic Memory." 1992. *What the Twilight Says* 65-86. Print.
___. *Collected Poems, 1948-1984*. 1986. London: Faber & Faber, 1992. Print.
___. "The Explorer is in Danger of Disappearing: New Books in Brief." *Sunday Guardian*, 27 Feb. 1966: 8. Print.
___. "A Far Cry from Africa." in *Collected Poems* 17-18. Print.
___. "The Muse of History." 1974. *What the Twilight Says* 36-64. Print.
___. *Omeros*. London: Faber & Faber, 1990. Print.
___. "Tracking Mr Wilson Harris." *Sunday Guardian*, 24 April 1966: 5. Print.
___. "The Sea Is History." *Collected Poems* 364-367. Print.
___. *What the Twilight Says: Essays*. London: Faber & Faber, 1998. Print.
Walder, Dennis, ed. *Literature in the Modern World: Critical Essays and Documents*. Oxford: Oxford UP/Open University, 1990. Print.
Waugh, Evelyn. *A Handful of Dust*. 1934. Harmondsworth: Penguin, 1976. Print.
___. *Ninety-Two Days*. 1934. Harmondsworth: Penguin, 1985. Print.

White, Hayden. *The Content of the Form: Narrative Discourse and Historical Representation*. Baltimore/London: Johns Hopkins UP, 1987. Print.

___. *Figural Realism: Studies in the Mimesis Effect*. Baltimore; London: Johns Hopkins UP, 1999. Print.

___. "The Historical Text as a Literary Artifact." *The Writing of History: Literary Form and Historical Understanding*. Ed. Robert H. Canary and Henry Kozicki. Madison WI: University of Wisconsin Press, 1978. Print.

___. *Metahistory: The Historical Imagination in Nineteenth-Century Europe*. Baltimore, London: The Johns Hopkins UP, 1973. Print.

White, Patrick. *Voss*. 1957. London: Vintage, 1994. Print.

Wiener, Philip P., ed. in chief. *Dictionary of the History of Ideas*. 1968. Uva Text Collection, University of Virginia Library (2011). Web. 25 Nov. 2011. <http://etext.virginia.edu/cgi-local/DHI/dhi.cgi?id=dv1-04>.

Williams, Denis. *Image and Idea in the Arts of Guyana*. Georgetown: The Edgar Mittelholzer Memorial Lectures, 2nd series, National History and Arts Council, 1969. Print.

___. *Prehistoric Guiana*. Kingston, Jamaica: Ian Randle, 2003. Print.

___. *Other Leopards*. 1963. London: Heinemann, 1983. Print.

___. "The Sperm of God." Exctract in *New Writing in the Caribbean*. Ed. A. J. Seymour. Caribbean Festival of the Arts, Georgetown, 1972. 301- 316. Print.

Wiseman, H. D. *A Short History of the West Indies*. London: University of London Press, 1950. Print.

Wynter, Sylvia. "1492: A 'New World' View." *The New World* 2 (Spring/Summer 1991): 4-5. Print.

Yates, Frances. *The Art of Memory*. 1966. London: Pimlico, 1992. Print.

Yeats, William Butler. *Rosa Alchemica*. 1913. Project Gutenberg (2004). Web. 02 Dec. 2011. <http://www.gutenberg.org/ebooks/5794>.

Young, Robert. *White Mythologies: Writing History and the West*. London/New York: Routledge, 1990. Print.

Zabriskie, Philip T. "Introduction." *C.G. Jung and the Humanities: Toward a Hermeneutics of Culture*. Ed. Karin Barnaby and Pellegrino D'Acierno. London: Routledge, 1990. Print.

Zamora, Lois Parkinson, and Wendy B. Faris, eds. *Magical Realism: Theory, History, Community*. Durham: Duke UP, 1995. Print.

STUDIES IN ENGLISH LITERATURES

Edited by Koray Melikoğlu

ISSN 1614-4651

1   Özden Sözalan
    The Staged Encounter
    Contemporary Feminism and Women's Drama
    2nd, revised editon
    ISBN 3-89821-367-6

2   Paul Fox (ed.)
    Decadences
    Morality and Aesthetics in British Literature
    ISBN 3-89821-573-3

3   Daniel M. Shea
    James Joyce and the Mythology of Modernism
    ISBN 3-89821-574-1

4   Paul Fox and Koray Melikoğlu (eds.)
    Formal Investigations
    Aesthetic Style in Late-Victorian and Edwardian Detective Fiction
    ISBN 978-3-89821-593-0

5   David Ellis
    Writing Home
    Black Writing in Britain Since the War
    ISBN 978-3-89821-591-6

6   Wei H. Kao
    The Formation of an Irish Literary Canon in the Mid-Twentieth Century
    ISBN 978-3-89821-545-9

7   Bianca Del Villano
    Ghostly Alterities
    Spectrality and Contemporary Literatures in English
    2nd, revised editon
    ISBN 978-3-89821-714-9

8   Melanie Ann Hanson
    Decapitation and Disgorgement
    The Female Body's Text in Early Modern English Drama and Poetry
    ISBN 978-3-89821-605-5

9   Shafquat Towheed (ed.)
    New Readings in the Literature of British India, c.1780-1947
    ISBN 978-3-89821-673-9

10 Paola Baseotto
    "Disdeining life, desiring leaue to die"
    Spenser and the Psychology of Despair
    ISBN 978-3-89821-567-1

11 *Annie Gagiano*
    Dealing with Evils
    Essays on Writing from Africa
    ISBN 978-3-89821-867-2

12 *Thomas F. Halloran*
    James Joyce: Developing Irish Identity
    A Study of the Development of Postcolonial Irish Identity in the Novels of James Joyce
    ISBN 978-3-89821-571-8

13 *Pablo Armellino*
    Ob-scene Spaces in Australian Narrative
    An Account of the Socio-topographic Construction of Space in Australian Literature
    ISBN 978-3-89821-873-3

14 *Lance Weldy*
    Seeking a Felicitous Space on the Frontier
    The Progression of the Modern American Woman in O. E. Rölvaag, Laura Ingalls Wilder, and Willa Cather
    ISBN 978-3-89821-535-0

15 *Rana Tekcan*
    The Biographer and the Subject
    A Study on Biographical Distance
    ISBN 978-3-89821-995-2

16 *Paola Brusasco*
    Writing Within/Without/About Sri Lanka
    Discourses of Cartography, History and Translation in Selected Works by Michael Ondaatje and Carl Muller
    ISBN 978-3-8382-0075-0

17 *Zeynep Z. Atayurt*
    Excess and Embodiment in Contemporary Women's Writing
    ISBN 978-3-89821-978-5

18 *Gianluca Delfino*
    Time, History, and Philosophy in the Works of Wilson Harris
    ISBN 978-3-8382-0265-5

FORTHCOMING (MANUSCRIPT WORKING TITLES)

Kevin Cole
Levity's Rainbow
Menippean Poetics in Swift, Fielding, and Sterne
ISBN 3-89821-654-3

Fatma Tuba Terci
Postmodern Goddesses in Contemporary Chicana Feminist Novel
Peel my Love Like an Onion, Caramelo, or, Puro Cuento: A Novel and Face of an Angel
ISBN 978-3-8382-0023-1

Geetha Ganga
Historicizing Somalia through Literary Narrative
The Fiction of Nuruddin Farah
ISBN 978-3-8382-0083-5

Busuyi Mekusi
Negotiating Memory and Nation Building in New South African Drama
ISBN 978-3-8382-0232-7

Series Subscription

Please enter my subscription to the series **Studies in English Literatures**, ISSN 1614-4651, as follows:

- ❏ complete series   OR   ❏ English-language titles
- ❏ German-language titles

starting with
- ❏ volume # 1
- ❏ volume # ___
  - ❏ please also include the following volumes: #___, ___, ___, ___, ___, ___
- ❏ the next volume being published
  - ❏ please also include the following volumes: #___, ___, ___, ___, ___, ___

- ❏ 1 copy per volume   OR   ❏ ___ copies per volume

Subscription within Germany:

You will receive every title on 1st publication at the regular bookseller's price incl. s & h and VAT.

Payment:
- ❏ Please bill me for every volume.
- ❏ Lastschriftverfahren: Ich/wir ermächtige(n) Sie hiermit widerruflich, den Rechnungsbetrag je Band von meinem/unserem folgendem Konto einzuziehen.

Kontoinhaber: _____ Kreditinstitut: _____
Kontonummer: _____ Bankleitzahl: _____

International Subscription:

Payment (incl. s & h and VAT) in advance for
- ❏ 10 volumes/copies (€ 319.80)   ❏ 20 volumes/copies (€ 599.80)
- ❏ 40 volumes/copies (€ 1,099.80)

Please send my books to:

NAME_____DEPARTMENT_____
ADDRESS _____
POST/ZIP CODE_____COUNTRY _____
TELEPHONE _____EMAIL_____

date/signature_____

Please fax to: **0511 / 262 2201 (+49 511 262 2201)**
or mail to: *ibidem*-Verlag, Julius-Leber-Weg 11, D-30457 Hannover, Germany
or send an e-mail: ibidem@ibidem-verlag.de

***ibidem*-**Verlag

Melchiorstr. 15

D-70439 Stuttgart

info@ibidem-verlag.de

www.ibidem-verlag.de
www.ibidem.eu
www.edition-noema.de
www.autorenbetreuung.de